SHENANDOAH COLLEGE
LIBRARY
WINCHESTER, VA.

WITHDRAWN

THE COMPOSITION OF
TENDER IS THE NIGHT

THE COMPOSITION OF
TENDER IS THE NIGHT

A Study of the Manuscripts

by
MATTHEW J. BRUCCOLI

UNIVERSITY OF PITTSBURGH PRESS

Copyright 1963 by Matthew J. Bruccoli
Library of Congress Catalog Number: 62-14379

```
PS      Bruccoli, Matthew Joseph
3511
.I9     The composition of Tender
T45       is the night
1963
813 F576brc
```

FOR *Arlyn* AND *Mary Bruccoli*

Table of Contents

INTRODUCTION . . . . *xiii*
    Editorial Method   xvii
    The "Author's Final Version"   xx
    The Drafts   xxii
    Diagram of the Development of *Tender is the Night*   xxv

CHAPTER I *1*
    The Reception of *Tender is the Night*   2
    The Reputation of *Tender is the Night*   9

CHAPTER II *17*
    Background   17
    First Draft. The holograph third-person draft of the Francis Melarky-matricide version   24
    Second Draft. The typescript third-person draft of the Francis Melarky-matricide version   32
    Third Draft. The holograph narrator draft of the Francis Melarky-matricide version   38
    Fourth Draft. The typescript narrator draft of the Francis Melarky-matricide version   47

CHAPTER III *59*
    Fifth Draft. The Kelly-shipboard version   59

CHAPTER IV *67*
    Sixth Draft. The second typescript third-person draft of the Francis Melarky-matricide version   67

CHAPTER V *74*
    General Notes for the Dick Diver version—*The Drunkard's Holiday*   74

CHAPTER VI 89
   Seventh Draft—*The Drunkard's Holiday*. First holograph draft of the Dick Diver version   89
      Book I   94
      Book II   103
      Book III   128

CHAPTER VII 161
   Eighth Draft—*Doctor Diver's Holiday*. First typescript of the Dick Diver version   161
   Ninth Draft. Revised second typescript of *Doctor Diver's Holiday*   169
   Tenth Draft. Carbon-copy for serial   175
   Eleventh Draft. Typescript printer's copy for serial   178

CHAPTER VIII 184
   Twelfth Draft. Galleys for serial and typescript revisions   184
   Thirteen. Page proof for *Scribner's Magazine*   190
   Fourteen. *Scribner's Magazine*   190
   Fifteen. Tearsheets from *Scribner's Magazine*   192
   Sixteen. Book galleys   193
   Seventeen. Book page-proof   197

CHAPTER IX 198
   The Book   198
   The Text   206

APPENDICES 219
   Appendix 1: Unlisted Sections of Manuscript   219
   Appendix 2: Textual Collation of Serial and First Six Chapters of the Book   221
   Appendix 3: Structural Comparison of the First Edition with the "Author's Final Version"   234

REFERENCES 237

LIST OF WORKS CONSULTED 245

INDEX 249

List of Illustrations

Diagram of the development of *Tender is the Night* *xxv*

Holograph manuscript pages *44-45*
53
62-63
113-117
141-158

Fitzgerald's summary of Part III, first half . . . *131*

But, my God! it was my material, and it was all I had to deal with.

F. Scott Fitzgerald

When Scott was writing "Tender Is the Night"—he didn't think he ought to talk about the books he was doing, and so put it this way—he said that the whole motif was taken from Ludendorf's memoirs. They were moving up the guns for the great Spring offensive in 1918, and Ludendorf said, "The song of the frogs on the river drowned the rumble of our artillery." When he told me this, it puzzled me, but when I read the book I realized that there was all this beautiful veneer, and rottenness and horror underneath.

Maxwell Perkins

If she has a success coming, she must associate it with work done in a workmanlike manner for its own sake, and part of it done fatigued and uninspired, and part of it done when even to remember the original inspiration and impetus is a psychological trick.

F. Scott Fitzgerald

Introduction

No PART of the glamorous legend that surrounds F. Scott Fitzgerald is more spectacular or more appropriate than the Fitzgerald revival of 1945-1950, which elevated him from relative obscurity to the first rank of American letters. That this revival was more than a freak run of misplaced nostalgia is attested to by the fact that after fifteen years a counterreaction has not yet occurred. All his books—except his play, *The Vegetable*—are currently in print; two of his novels and a collection of stories are in student editions; his first editions command high prices; scores of articles on Fitzgerald, popular and scholarly, are published each year.

Yet despite all this solid popular and critical interest, it is apparent that Fitzgerald scholarship has in some cases failed to establish well-defined principles for assessing his work. Although there is considerable appreciation of *Tender is the Night*, there is also considerable disagreement about its rank in the Fitzgerald canon. In a sense, Fitzgerald continues to be victimized by the color of his life, which hampered serious criticism of his work when he was still writing.

Responsible and intelligent commentators are often lured into discussing Fitzgerald's work purely in terms of his personal history. To be sure, there is justification for this approach to a writer who declared, "Whether it's something that happened twenty years ago or only yesterday, I must start out with an emotion—one that's close to me and that I can understand." [1] There is no denying that all of Fitzgerald's best work is intensely personal, but this does not mean that it must be approached through biographical or historical methods. There is a necessity for objective study of his craftsmanship, and this has been largely neglected. The Fitzgerald Papers at the

Princeton University Library offer an incredibly rich archive, but this material has merely been picked over. Scholars have examined Fitzgerald's manuscripts, exclaimed in print over the fact that there are various versions of his novels, but have failed to do any detailed work on this basic material. *Tender is the Night* is known to have had the most intricate history of all of Fitzgerald's novels, but few American novels have generated so much sentimental nonsense or solemn guesswork.

Although some critics have picked *Tender is the Night* as Fitzgerald's best book, most critics have categorized it as a noble failure, a work in which—because of a faulty structure—the parts are more brilliant than the whole. These critics often take their lead from the author's own rejection of the original structure, but this rejection does not constitute a warrant to ignore the evidence to be found in Fitzgerald's plans and working drafts about the composition of the novel.

To be sure, the book—or, rather, the history of the book—encourages guesswork scholarship. The author struggled with it for nearly a decade, and what he expected would be his greatest popular and critical success was a qualified failure. A few snatches of information have been published about the development and composition of the story, and this little has engendered a quantity of theorizing. The most common notions are that Fitzgerald worked on *Tender is the Night* so long that he rewrote it to death; that he changed his plot without really changing his characters and thereby introduced a basic confusion into the book; that after years of fumbling with a subject that was too profound for him, he hastily and carelessly assembled the book; that (and this is inevitable) he wrote *Tender is the Night* drunk; or that it suffers from having been drastically cut down from a much larger work. All this is clearly contradicted by the manuscripts, but no one has troubled to investigate them thoroughly—not even Fitzgerald's first biographer, who gives a very sketchy account of the composition of *Tender is the Night,* or Malcolm Cowley, whose appendix on the manuscripts in his edition of the "author's final version" of *Tender is the Night* is the sole study of the material. In fairness to Mr. Cowley it must be said that a detailed study of the manuscripts was outside the scope of his project, and it is doubtful if his publishers would have granted him the space the job requires.

It is not really surprising that the very abundance of the material has discouraged analysis of it; moreover, it is in such a disorganized state that it took me seven months to catalogue it. There are some 3,500 pages of holograph manuscript and typescript, plus proof, representing seventeen drafts and three versions of the novel.

This study is an attempt to inventory the manuscripts of *Tender is the Night* and to interpret the material. I have reconstructed in detail the composition of the novel, chiefly from the manuscripts, although I have used other sources—such as Fitzgerald's letters and short stories. I have tried to show what the manuscripts reveal about Fitzgerald's intentions, and I have essayed an interpretation of the purpose and meaning of the novel. Throughout I have attempted to present a picture of a deliberate and serious literary artist at work. It is my hope that this analysis of the composition of *Tender is the Night* presents Fitzgerald as a craftsman, and that it shows how his natural talent was refined by firm standards of self-criticism. Where the intuitive artist left off, the professional took over.

I would be disingenuous were I not to admit that I have been especially keen to destroy a few of the popular stories that surround *Tender is the Night*. Although the stories may be better than the facts, it is time for us to apply the same standards to Fitzgerald criticism that we insist on for other authors. Either Fitzgerald was the playboy of American literature who squandered a remarkable talent while accidentally producing a superb novel or two—or he was a serious writer whose private life was irregular. We cannot have it both ways.

During the course of this project I have incurred obligations, which I cheerfully acknowledge. I would acknowledge them fulsomely were not untempered gratitude in bad form. To Alexander Clark, Curator of Manuscripts at the Princeton University Library, I am obliged for many courtesies during my trips to the Library. Had he not encouraged my plans for working on this material, this study would not have been possible. For friendly professional services I am indebted to the entire staff of the Alderman Library of The University of Virginia—and in particular to John Cook Wyllie, Francis L. Berkeley, Jr., and Miss Louise Savage. I am indebted, too, to C. Waller Barrett for granting me the freedom of his monumental American literature collection. The Yale University Library and the Enoch Pratt Free Library, Baltimore, also supplied material. Malcolm Cowley, Matthew Josephson, Edmund Wilson, and the late Theodore Chanler patiently searched their memories for me. Charles Scribner, Jr., Burroughs Mitchell, and Josiah Q. Bennett—all of Charles Scribner's Sons—helped me to work with that firm's records. Ivan von Auw, Jr. of Harold Ober Associates, was of great help in arranging for permissions to quote from unpublished Fitzgerald material and from the letters of Harold Ober. I am grateful to Frederick A. Hetzel, of the University of Pittsburgh Press, for his loyalty and labor in connection with this book. Mrs. Robert A. Stocking, my typist, slaved over my working drafts. Professor Robert M. Estrich, Chairman of the Department of English, Ohio State University, arranged for secretarial help in the preparation of printer's copy for this book.

Permission to quote from the published work of F. Scott Fitzgerald and from the letters of Maxwell Perkins has been generously granted by Charles Scribner's Sons. Part of Chapter I of this book originally appeared in *Modern Fiction Studies*.

Professor Fredson Bowers served as adviser when this study was prepared as a University of Virginia dissertation, and to him I am deeply indebted for many things—but especially for his patience. To my second reader, Professor Floyd Stovall, I am equally indebted.

My greatest obligations are to Mrs. Samuel J. Lanahan and to the late Harold Ober, who granted me the extraordinary privilege of working with this material and who always acceded to my pleas for additional privileges.

Editorial Method

One reason why a detailed study of the composition of *Tender is the Night* has not been prepared before is that the sheer bulk and confusion of the material are intimidating. There are roughly 3,500 pages of holograph manuscript and typescript—plus galley proof, page proof, and tearsheets. The *Tender is the Night* archive has been likened to a barrel into which many buckets of water have been poured, so that the problem of cataloguing the manuscripts is like separating out of the barrel the contents of each bucket. This figure may seem less hyperbolic—and less self-congratulatory on my part— when its creator is identified as the Curator of Manuscripts at the Princeton University Library.

Seven manuscript cartons of *Tender is the Night* material are at Princeton. Each of these cartons is little more than a storage container; there is little intramural or intermural organization. A given box includes parts of several drafts; and the parts range from notes on scraps of paper to fragmentary scenes to complete chapters. For reasons that will be detailed later, Fitzgerald sometimes changed his pagination system in the middle of a scene. Some sequences of writing were used in various spots and consequently bear multiple sets of paginations. But the individual pages are surprisingly easy to work with. Fitzgerald wrote his holograph drafts in soft pencil on pulp paper that has yellowed; nevertheless, his handwriting is quite legible, and it is even possible to read almost all the crossed-out words.

The first practical problem in preparing this study was to select a method for identifying the various pieces of material and organizing them for discussion. Since I could not discover a real precedent for this problem, I decided on a method that would reveal the nature of the unsorted material and at the same time allow the reader to check my reconstruction of Fitzgerald's work. Accordingly, each differentiable unit of work within the archive—that is, each section of material that can be isolated from the material around it—has been provided with a chronological key number from #1 to #199. It did not matter whether the section consisted of one page or 100 pages. Thus, section #1 is a fifty-one page holograph chapter which I believe to be the earliest surviving piece of work Fitzgerald did on the first chapter of the first draft of the first version of *Tender is the Night*; it was found in manuscript box 2. Section #44 consists of a single page of typed notes for the third version; it was the first piece in box 1.

Each of these 199 sections has been catalogued in a way that should make it readily identifiable. Although most of my work was done with microfilm, the catalogue has been checked against the actual material at Princeton. My intention has been to trace the composition of *Tender is the Night* by a method that would permit the reader to check me at every point. I have made no attempt to reorganize the Princeton archive into the drafts I have reconstructed: the manuscripts have been left as I found them.

At the beginning of each division of this study there is a textual headnote which catalogues the sections of material to be discussed. This headnote is divided into five columns: (1) the physical description and pagination of the section; (2) the part of the first edition of *Tender is the Night* to which it corresponds, with roman numerals representing the books of the novel and arabic numerals representing the chapters; (3) brief notes on any special identifying features of the section; (4) the number of the manuscript carton at the Princeton University Library in which the section was found; and (5) the key number.

In noting the pagination in the headnotes I have used square brackets to indicate unnumbered pages and angle brackets for cancelled paginations. The entry 2-3, [4], 5-7, 9-10 would mean that pages 1, 4, and 8 are wanting, but that there is an unnumbered page between 3 and 5 that is obviously to be reckoned as page 4. The entry 10-20 <20-30> would mean that pages 10-20 were at some time numbered 20-30. Paginations in parentheses indicate a single page so numbered by Fitzgerald. Thus section #2 is described: 48, (49-50), 51, 51½, 52, [ ], 53, 53½, 54-55, 44½, 56-60, 62-66, 68-69, 71-74, 77-78, 78½, 79-84, 84½, 85-86, (87-91), 92-98, 98½, 99-123, insert A-B, 124-131. 92-96 also numbered <31-32, (33-34), 35-36>. This is the pagination that appears on the pages of the section. Number 48 appears on the first page; then comes one page headed 49-50 which Fitzgerald inserted in place of two cancelled pages; then come pages numbered 51, 51½, and 52; then comes an unnumbered page; then come pages 53 and 53½; then come pages 54 and 55; then comes a page headed 44½; and so on.

Fitzgerald was not a methodical worker, and the *Tender is the Night* material, written during a particularly disturbed and disorganized period of his life, does not have a simple pattern. I have reconstructed twelve drafts before page proof, and in most of these drafts he salvaged material from earlier drafts. That a particular section was used in an earlier draft presents a problem in organizing the material for discussion. Since the chief purpose of this study is to reconstruct the composition of *Tender is the Night,* I discuss the material in a draft-by-draft order to show how the novel developed during the decade Fitzgerald worked on it. A given section is included with each draft it appeared in. The 200 sections have been sorted into drafts by several means. The changing of characters' names—both within and between drafts—proved to be the most useful kind of evidence. A chapter in which Abe is surnamed Herkimer is earlier than one in which he is surnamed Grant, and Grant is earlier than North.[2] A chapter in which the name Francis is crossed out and replaced by the name Rosemary was obviously written as part of the first version and then incorporated into the third version. The use of paginations to differentiate drafts proved reliable, too. Multiple paginations in a section indicate that the section was moved from an earlier draft and/or had occupied a different position in its present draft. Since Fitzgerald was a tireless polisher of his style, some sections—and indeed whole drafts—were readily differentiated by stylistic tests.

The following symbols are used in the catalogues of manuscripts:

    H Holograph
    T Original typescript
    CC Carbon copy of typescript
    X Crossed-out
    R Revised
    [Changed to, as VI[VII

Combinations of these symbols are used, so that RT would signify a revised typescript.

Throughout this study page references to *Tender is the Night* supplied in parentheses refer to the first edition—New York: Charles Scribner's Sons, 1934.

The "Author's Final Version"

Although Malcolm Cowley's introduction and appendix to the "author's final version" of *Tender is the Night* are generally helpful—they are, in fact, the only published analysis of the material—some of his comments on details are wrong or misleading. Cowley gives the impression that the first draft of the Dick Diver version was considerably longer than the published form and that what we read is in some ways a condensation of the novel Fitzgerald projected: "He had watched it grow from a short dramatic novel like *The Great Gatsby* to a long psychological or philosophical novel on the model of

Vanity Fair, and then, as he omitted scene after scene, he had watched it diminish again to a medium-length novel, but one in which he was sure that the overtones of the longer book remained."[3] The first part of this statement—that the novel grew and expanded while Fitzgerald worked on it—is misleading unless qualified by the information that the short form was the early matricide version. The Dick Diver version did not develop in scope while it was in progress. Fitzgerald's preliminary plan indicates that he had fixed his design and scope when he began the Dick Diver version; and the drafts themselves clearly reveal that the Dick Diver version was composed straight through on this plan—without any narrative growth. The second part of Cowley's statement—that Fitzgerald cut "scene after scene"—is misleading because the scenes Fitzgerald omitted from the published book would total perhaps thirty printed pages, hardly enough to change the bulk of the work from a long to a medium-length book. Moreover, some of these scenes exist only as rough sketches and were never part of a finished draft. The impression that *Tender is the Night* was originally much longer is supported by Fitzgerald's claim that he had "thrown away three-fourths of it"; but that was certainly an exaggeration.[4] The assertion is not supported by the surviving manuscripts, and it is extremely unlikely that Fitzgerald destroyed that much manuscript. He did reject material written for the early versions, but he also salvaged much of it too.

On the evidence of the manuscripts, Cowley is also wrong in saying that Fitzgerald could have written separate novels about Abe and Rosemary.[5] This comment implies that Fitzgerald cancelled great sections of material about these two characters; but in fact there is little information about Abe and Rosemary in the manuscripts that was not used in the novel. Comments like these have led people to assume that *Tender is the Night* was originally double its published length or that there were sub-versions within the Dick Diver version. This is not the case. The development of *Tender is the Night* is a sufficiently complex story; and these embellishments only obscure the real problem—which is to discover not what Fitzgerald left out, but rather what he salvaged and transformed.

As will be seen later, Cowley is open to challenge on other points. The purpose of these objections is not to attack Malcolm Cowley, who has served Fitzgerald well, but to correct an influential account of the manuscripts.

The Drafts

The following summary account of the composition of *Tender is the Night* is offered by way of a briefing for the detailed study of the manuscripts which forms the body of this study.

In the summer of 1925 Fitzgerald began work on his fourth novel. It was to be a compact, rather sensational novel of American expatriate life on the French Riviera; and it was to deal with matricide. The central figure was Francis Melarky, a young motion picture technician. Fitzgerald wrote parts of three long chapters—perhaps one-quarter of the book—in holograph. In this earliest stage the prototypes of the Norths and the Divers appear. The holograph draft was followed by a typescript, with many holograph revisions and inserts. In these first two drafts the story is told in straight third-person narrative.

In 1926 Fitzgerald recast the story so that it is told by a narrator who is passively involved in most of the action. The holograph draft of this form of the story, which includes salvaged typescript from the third-person form of the story, advances the plot by one chapter. The typescript of the narrator form—with holograph material—advances the plot still further. A good deal of the Paris material in these narrator-drafts found its way into the published novel. At various times this version was entitled *Our Type, The Boy Who Killed His Mother, The Melarky Case,* and *The World's Fair.*

In the summer of 1929 Fitzgerald discarded the matricide plot for a new plot, the Kelly version, which survives in only two long holograph chapters set on an ocean liner; but this false start introduces a young actress named Rosemary who ultimately became the Rosemary of *Tender is the Night*. The Kelly version of the plot was apparently never given a title.

In 1930 Fitzgerald returned to the matricide idea and patched together from typescript and holograph a new draft in straight third-person narrative—with the narrator character dropped. This was the sixth draft.

Early in 1932 Fitzgerald drafted a plan for the third version of the novel. This was the Dick Diver story. He prepared a complete holograph draft, which was first revised in typescript and then in the carbon copy of that typescript. The first draft of the third version was entitled *The Drunkard's Holiday*, which was changed to *Doctor Diver's Holiday* and then *Tender is the Night*. A second typescript was prepared from the revised carbon, and this new typescript was revised in the original and carbon. The original of the second typescript was used as printer's copy for the *Scribner's Magazine* serial galleys, which were extensively rewritten and then reset for final serial galley proof. Fitzgerald then partly revised the serial page proof. Some of the author's tearsheets—pages ripped from the magazine—survive, but they were not revised.

The galley proof for the book was set from the serial version; and the book galleys were then revised in great detail. It is possible that Fitzgerald also made some revisions in the page proof for the book.

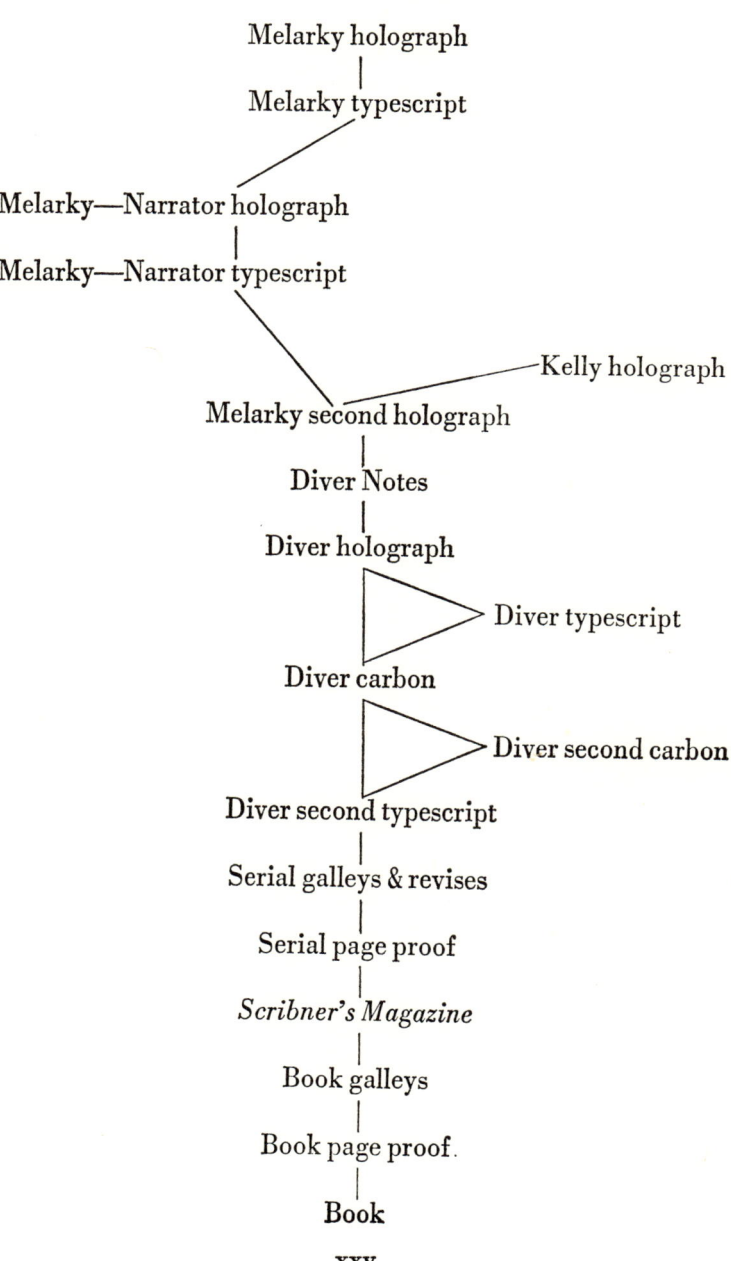

THE COMPOSITION OF
TENDER IS THE NIGHT

Chapter I

WHAT follows seems to be a representative sampling of critical opinions of *Tender is the Night:*

... some of his admirers have reserved this title [Fitzgerald's masterpiece] for the long and complicated *Tender is the Night* (1934).... Whatever merits the novel may have, few deny that it is confusing and faulty in its development. [Edward Wagenknecht] [1]

... his conception of his subject in *Tender is the Night* had shifted in the course of his writing it so that the parts of that fascinating novel do not always quite hang together.... [Edmund Wilson] [2]

Tender is the Night, on which he laboured for years, is far less satisfactory as a whole [than *The Great Gatsby*], not only because in both versions the construction is unsound but also because Dick Diver and his story refuse to carry the load; but it contains some magnificent scenes and passages, some flashes of insight into the richly decaying society it represents: it is indeed more fascinating than many novels far less open to hostile criticism. [J. B. Priestly] [3]

... huge and sprawling.... It shows, on the one hand, the consequences of a too hasty composition; on the other, the results of a prolonged but fumbling concern over form. [Frederick J. Hoffman] [4]

The reviews were not only uncomplimentary but brutal; readers had tired of the depiction of a frivolous and sterile society.... The depressed readers of the Threadbare Thirties were looking toward comfortable utopias, rather than the arid earth which Fitzgerald still insisted on exploring. [Louis Untermeyer] [5]

Some of the statements are plainly controvertible. It is impossible for a 400-page novel to be "huge"; and extremely difficult for a novel with few characters, one central action, and a four-year time span to be "sprawling." By the same token, *Tender is the Night* is scarcely "complicated." *The Sound and the Fury* is a complicated novel; even *The Great Gatsby* has a more difficult narrative scheme.

Though it is possible to challenge each of these comments, it is more important to recognize that all—except Untermeyer's, which offers the standard explanation of the novel's failure—center on the structure of *Tender is the Night*. There is a shared conviction that the many excellences of *Tender is the Night* merely indicate that it would have been a greater achievement had Fitzgerald invented a better structure. Reading *Tender is the Night* criticism, one develops the feeling that Fitzgerald's commentators set special standards for him. Fitzgerald's achievements are hastily admitted and then are used to bemoan the fact that his work is not still better. This is not really unfair, and it is, of course, highly complimentary to Fitzgerald. But it is demonstrable that some, at least, of the charges aimed at the structure of *Tender is the Night* are baseless. The manuscripts clearly show that Fitzgerald neither composed *Tender is the Night* hastily nor fumbled with its form; and they show that Fitzgerald had a firm control over his material.

The Reception of *Tender is the Night*

It dealt with fashionable life in the 1920s at a time when most readers wanted to forget that they had ever been concerned with frivolities; the new fashion was for novels about destitution and revolt. . . . most reviewers implied that it belonged to the bad old days before the crash. . . . [Malcolm Cowley] [6]

Tender is the Night was published on April 12, 1934; considering the expectation that had been aroused by F. Scott Fitzgerald's nine-year pause after *The Great Gatsby*, the reviews of the new novel were unemotional. In the June number of the *North American Review,* Herschel Brickell mentioned "the kind of violent argument that has been going on about it"; [7] since there was no real controversy in print—only disagreement—this argument must have raged among readers. It has continued ever since, and the publication in 1951 of Malcolm Cowley's edition of the "author's final version" stimulated the debate. Inevitably, the discussions of *Tender is the Night* return to the critical reception of the novel, a topic which includes some folklore.

One of the commonplaces of Fitzgerald criticism is that *Tender is the Night* failed in 1934 because the reviewers ganged up on it and ridiculed the book as an anachronistic hang-over from the twenties. These reviewers, so the story goes, compounded their socio-political prejudice with obtuseness by pretending to find extraordinary difficulty in the elementary flashback structure. The reviewers were allegedly abetted by the reading public, which rejected Fitzgerald and turned its attention to escapism or social tracts. Depending upon whether one is listening to an antirevisionist or a revisionist, this conspiracy between the critics and the public is supposed to have either so befuddled Fitzgerald's critical abilities that he impetuously reorganized the novel in straight chronological order—or to have revealed to him what was wrong with *Tender is the Night* so that he could correct its structural flaws. The winds of favor are currently blowing in the direction of the original version.

Like most of the biographical-critical stories about Fitzgerald, this one is an intriguing pattern of fact and lugubrious balderdash. It is true that Fitzgerald's most ambitious novel was a failure in its own time; and it is true that its reception hurt and puzzled Fitzgerald, and doubtlessly contributed to his crack-up. But it is not demonstrable that Fitzgerald was the victim of a hostile, New-Deal oriented press. In all fairness, the assassination of *Tender is the Night* cannot be added to the catalogue of iniquities perpetrated by the Democratic Party. The majority of the notices were favorable, and there was little outcry against the jazz-age material and the flashback. That some of the favorable reviews tended to patronize Fitzgerald is certainly true, but the critics had patronized him when stocks were high.

A glance at the ten best-selling novels of 1934 provides nothing to suggest that the readers of the Depression rejected Fitzgerald because they preferred socially significant novels about slums: *Anthony Adverse; Lamb in his Bosom; So Red the Rose; Good-Bye, Mr. Chips; Within This Present; Work of Art; Private Worlds; Mary Peters; Oil for the Lamps of China;* and *Seven Gothic Tales.* This is a typical mixture, and there is not one proletarian novel in the lot. Indeed, *Within This Present* is a nostalgic look back at the twenties. That the three top sellers of the year were historical novels, and that the number four book was *Good-Bye, Mr. Chips* may indicate a streak of escapism in the reading public; but historical novels and sentimental books about schoolmasters sell well, boom or bust.

People who lament the failure of *Tender is the Night* generally ignore the fact that Fitzgerald had not had a best seller since *This Side of Paradise,* and even it was not one of the top ten in 1920. Fitzgerald was a popular figure, but he was never really a popular novelist in his lifetime. *The Great Gatsby,* surely one of the great novels written in this country, was a comparative flop in 1925, selling only about 25,000 copies. Yet one never hears laments about the popular failure of this novel. Between the serialization in *Scribner's Magazine* and the 13,000 copies of *Tender is the Night* sold in 1934-35, it probably reached as many readers as did *The Great Gatsby.*

I have located twenty-four reviews of *Tender is the Night.*[8] Although this is not a complete list, it is a good working sample and probably includes all the influential reviews. Ten of the reviewers reacted favorably—including John Chamberlain, C. Hartley Grattan, and Herschel Brickell. Six were more favorable than not—including Horace Gregory, Clifton Fadiman, and the *Times Literary Supplement.* Eight were clearly unfavorable—including William Troy, Lewis Gannett, and Peter Quennell. Only six specifically discuss the flashback, and those split evenly on it. Four reviews take exception to the expatriate material from the twenties. The most interesting fact is that eight reviews criticize the credibility of Dick Diver or the convincingness of his crack-up. In the week following publication of *Tender is the Night,* John Chamberlain commented in the *New York Times* on the mixed reactions of his colleagues: "The critical reception of F. Scott Fitzgerald's *Tender is the Night* might serve as the basis for one of those cartoons on 'Why Men Go Mad.' No two reviews were alike; no two had the same tone. Some seemed to think that Mr. Fitzgerald was writing about his usual jazz age boys and girls; others that he had a 'timeless' problem on his hands. And some seemed to think that Doctor Diver's collapse was insufficiently documented."

The nastiest attack on the jazz-age material was made by *News-Week*, which headlined its review with "A Sinful, Ginful Tale" and noted that "It is a long time since the decay of American expatriates on the Riviera was hot news." But the socially conscious *New Republic* did not harass Fitzgerald about his choice of material. Reviewer Malcolm Cowley developed a sober analysis of Fitzgerald's apparent indecision between writing a psychological or a social novel—Fitzgerald thought of it as a dramatic novel—and then Cowley proposed a theory that has since gained critical favor, the theory that as the novel developed through several versions, the early sections crystallized so that the author was not able to make them harmonize with the later sections. Bluntly stated, this is the view that the novel was rewritten to death.

The *New York Times* reviewed *Tender is the Night* three times. First, Chamberlain covered it in his daily book column on April 13, in an extremely favorable notice which makes only the criticism that the reader is puzzled by the abrupt dismissal of Rosemary at the end of Book I. This criticism is immediately qualified by the statement, "At this point one could almost guarantee that *Tender is the Night* is going to be a failure. But, as a matter of fact, the novel does not really begin until Rosemary is more or less out of the way." This review was followed by a lukewarm one in the Sunday *New York Times Book Review* by J. Donald Adams, who felt that Nicole and Rosemary were unconvincing characters and that Dick's crack-up was contrived. On the following day Chamberlain interrupted a review of Faulkner's *Doctor Martino* to defend the integrity of Dick's characterization. It is difficult to avoid the conclusion that this comment was a rejoinder to Adams. After explaining how Fitzgerald had carefully documented Dick's collapse, Chamberlain concluded with a wry observation: "This seems to us to be a sufficient exercise in cause-and-effect. Compared to the motivation in Faulkner, it is logic personified." However, a third of the reviews I have checked echo Adams' opinion; Henry Seidel Canby, Clifton Fadiman, and William Troy, among others, concurred.

What begins as a study of a subtle relationship ends as the accelerating decline into nothingness of Dr. Driver [sic]—not for no reason, but for too many reasons, no one of which is dominant. This book may be life with its veil over causality, but it is not art which should pierce that veil. [Canby]

The actual decay of these super-civilized people . . . is traced with masterly narrative skill, but the primary causes of the decay are not made clear. (Nicole's mental instability and Dick's infatuation for Rosemary are only the detonators). Dick's rapid acceptance of his failure, for instance, is not convincing; there must have been some fundamental weakness in his early youth to account for his defeatism. . . . The events of the narrative, tragic as they are, are insufficient to motivate his downfall. It is the failure to reach far, far back into his characters' lives that helps to prevent this novel from being the first-rate work of fiction that we have been expecting from F. Scott Fitzgerald. [Fadiman] [9]

. . . our confusion as to the precise reason for the hero's disintegration. Is it that once Nicole is cured of her disease she no longer has need of his kind of love? . . . Is it that her money has acted like a virus to destroy his personality and with it his lifework? Or is it simply that he is a man of weak character, unable to resist temptation and concealing the fact from himself through immersion in alcohol? All these causes are indicated, and any one of them might be made sufficient, but the author's own unwillingness to choose between them, his own uncertainty communicated to the reader, continues to the last. And the result is depressing in the way that confusion in a work of literature is always depressing. [Troy]

D. W. Harding went even further and asserted that Fitzgerald had not supplied any cause for Dick's crack-up. His review is extremely puzzling, for he protests that he had been moved against his will by Dick's decline, and concludes by unconsciously echoing Fitzgerald's style: ". . . I am prepared to be told that this attempt at analysis is itself childish—an attempt to assure myself that the magician didn't really cut the lady's head off, did he? I still believe there was a trick in it." The most comprehensive defense of Dick's decline and of the novel's structure was made by C. Hartley Grattan in the *Modern Monthly*. That Grattan was defending Fitzgerald against other critics is clear from a comment on Dick's final pilgrimage into obscurity: "This fate is so close to that of unstable personalities in any place and time that it has been perversely misread by those critics anxious to avoid the implications of the whole book."

The attacks on the verisimilitude of Dick's decline appear to have troubled Fitzgerald more than anything else the critics wrote. He resented the implication that he had been clumsy and that he had lost control of his material. On April 23, eleven days after date of publication, Fitzgerald wrote to H. L. Mencken to break an engagement and then added an impassioned defense of Book III of *Tender is the Night* (see p. 129 below). It suggests that Fitzgerald's later decision to revise the structure of the novel was not prompted by the desire to circumvent the possible confusion caused by the flashback. The removal of the flashback was the result of Fitzgerald's desire to emphasize the documentation of Dick's decline by putting together all the information about him. This, Fitzgerald hoped, would make apparent that Dick's decline was the result of certain long-standing tensions in his personality. The new structure would also make Dick's final collapse seem less abrupt. The problem was on Fitzgerald's mind in 1938 when he was trying to persuade Maxwell Perkins to bring out an omnibus volume of his novels. Fitzgerald was particularly anxious to give *Tender is the Night* another chance, and remarked that: "Its great fault is that the *true* beginning—the young psychiatrist in Switzerland—is tucked away in the middle of the book." [10] This view of the novel seems to have resulted from a straw vote Fitzgerald took. An inscribed copy he gave to Joseph Hergesheimer reveals Fitzgerald's particular concern about the reactions of fellow writers.[11]

Dear Joe:
    You talked to someone who didn't like this book—I don't know who, or why they didn't. But I could tell in the Stafford Bar that afternoon when you said it was "almost impossible to write a book about an actress" that you hadn't read it thru because the actress fades out of it in the first third & is only a catalytic agent.
    Sometime will you open it at the middle, perhaps at page 155 & read on for five or ten minutes—? If it were not for my sincere admiration for your judgement I would forgo this plea. You were not the only one repelled by the apparent triviality of the opening—I would like this favorite among my books to have another chance in the chrystal light of your taste

Ever yrs
F Scott Fitzgerald

Page 155—*et sq.*

Publicly, at least, Fitzgerald tried to show that he was not greatly disturbed by the reviews. When later in the year he was asked to prepare an introduction to the Modern Library edition of *The Great Gatsby*, he used it as an opportunity to discuss his critics. Though the essay ostensibly deals with *The Great Gatsby*, it is immediately clear that Fitzgerald is referring obliquely to the reception of *Tender is the Night*. Pretending to be indifferent to critical onslaughts, Fitzgerald at first adopts a tough tone: "Your pride is all you have, and if you let it be tampered with by a man who has a dozen prides to tamper with before lunch, you are promising yourself a lot of disappointments that a hard-boiled professional has learned to spare himself." But this shifts to bitter indignation in which Fitzgerald makes a profound comment on his career. "But, my God! it was my material, and it was all I had to deal with." [12]

The Reputation of *Tender is the Night*

Although next to nothing was written about *Tender is the Night* during the thirties, the book was not wholly forgotten. There was a feeling of uneasiness about it, a suspicion that perhaps it had not been fairly treated. "A strange thing is that in retrospect his *Tender is the Night* gets better and better," Ernest Hemingway commented to Maxwell Perkins.[13] This feeling was shared by Peter Monro Jack, who wrote in 1937, "*Tender is the Night* is a ghost wandering by its former triumphs. But instead of crying Revenge! it is still wondering why it was so foully murdered. . . . As one reads *Tender is the Night*, with its charming and evocative writing, one feels how badly Fitzgerald was served by his contemporaries."[14] The friendly articles occasioned by Fitzgerald's death in 1940 concentrated on *The Great Gatsby*, but the publication of *The Crack-Up* in 1945 resulted in a number of reassessments of Fitzgerald's career. In these articles *Tender is the Night* was generally treated with uneasy respect: it was recognized as having brilliance, though these critics followed the lead of the 1934 reviews in citing the novel's structural difficulties or the lack of verisimilitude in the characterization of Dick Diver. In general, the 1945 estimates of *Tender is the Night* indicate that a re-evaluation of the novel was developing; there is a hesitancy to be detected in some of these articles, which indicates that the writers are unwilling to commit themselves just yet. An example is this remark by Alfred Kazin: "But Fitzgerald is one of those novelists whom it is easier to appreciate than to explain, and whom it is possible, even fascinating to read over and over—it has often been remarked that *Tender is the Night* grows better on each re-reading—without always being able to account for the sources of your pleasure." [15]

The publication in 1951 of Cowley's edition of "the author's final version" naturally focused attention on the structural problem. Cowley argued that "the author's final version" is a decided improvement over the 1934 version because the novel now concentrates the reader's attention on Dick Diver and his tragedy:

> One fault of the earlier version was its uncertainty of focus. We weren't quite sure in reading it whether the author had intended to write about a whole group of Americans on the Riviera—that is, to make the book a social study with a collective hero—or whether he had intended to write a psychological novel about the glory and decline of Richard Diver as a person.[16]

This comment is not a rationalization that Cowley invented in 1951 to defend his edition, for it echoes his 1934 review of *Tender is the Night*. Nonetheless, Cowley's feeling that the novel wants focus is puzzling because the 1934 version is clearly Dick's book. His friends are important only as reflector characters. The revisionist and antirevisionist receptions of Cowley's version were about equally strong. But rather than maintaining interest in the structural problem, this edition seems to have ultimately killed interest in the problem. The explanation for this reaction would seem to be that readers recognized that the revised structure did not really have a significant effect on the essential qualities of *Tender is the Night*.

Interest in the revisions gradually diminished until in 1960 Scribners selected the original version for its paperback series. The diminution of interest in the structural problems of *Tender is the Night* has caused interest to shift to other aspects of the novel—mainly in the areas of psychology and sociology. More and more attention has been given to the novel's arraignment of American civilization, and these comments have been predominantly laudatory. In a thoughtful article on Fitzgerald's insights into American life, Edwin S. Fussell states: "The social structure of *Tender is the Night* is epic in scope and intention, though it has the grace and concentration of lyric. . . ." He goes on to explain that Fitzgerald's analysis of society operates on four levels in *Tender is the Night:*

The man of imagination, fed on the emotions of romantic wonder, is tempted and seduced and (in this case, nearly) destroyed by the American dream which customarily takes two forms: the escape from time and the materialistic pursuit of a purely hedonistic happiness. On the historical level, the critique is of the error of American romanticism in attempting to transcend and escape historical responsibility. On the economic level, the critique is of the fatal beauty of American capitalism, its destructive charm and irresponsibility. And on the level of myth, one need only mention the names of Benjamin Franklin and Ponce de Leon to recall the motivations for the quest that Fitzgerald recurrently explores.[17]

Another critic who sees *Tender is the Night* as a continuation of *The Great Gatsby's* arraignment of the American success ethos is Otto Friedrich, who comments, "Yet in spite of its faults, *Tender is the Night* is unquestionably a great novel. While *The Great Gatsby* represents Fitzgerald's most perfectly expressed insight into the fraud of his own dream of success, *Tender is the Night* combines that new insight with a new understanding of how and why the dream disintegrates." [18]

Less happy are the studies inspired by the psychological aspects of *Tender is the Night.* Although it is not specifically a novel about a psychologist or even a psychological novel, this subject matter has inevitably generated considerable interest. Comments range from Robert Stanton's comparatively conservative attempt to demonstrate that *Tender is the Night* is unified by "incest-motifs" (the term is used loosely enough to cover love between a mature man and a younger woman) which symbolize both "Dick's loss of allegiance to the moral code of his father" and "a social situation existing throughout

Europe and America during the Twenties"—to D. S. Savage's statement that "The incest motive is in fact central to all of Fitzgerald's novels" and Maxwell Geismar's view that "Fitzgerald's work, like Poe's, is colored by the imagery of incest."[19] Leslie Fiedler views the novel as presenting sexual ambiguities in which the male and female characters exchange roles.[20]

Interesting as the comments on the social and incestuous aspects of *Tender is the Night* are—and the former is indubitably a valid approach to the novel—the book is principally concerned with Dick Diver's tragedy; and there continues to be a strong body of opinion that he is not a credible figure and that his collapse seems unconvincing or insufficiently documented. This criticism almost always argues that Fitzgerald confused his own tragedy with Dick's and consequently, in Friedrich's words, "fell into the old trap of ascribing his own experiences to largely unrelated causes that he provided for the sake of plot."[21] A representative, if elementary, attack on the characterization of Dick—and it is so typical that it is worth quoting at some length—was included in Albert Lubell's 1955 protest against the Fitzgerald revival.

The point is that even in the new version, while Fitzgerald's intention is made clearer, the novel still suffers from an all but fatal diffuseness, which can be explained only by the author's lack of control over his material. Whatever unity the novel possesses is one of tone and mood, resulting largely from Fitzgerald's style, which in this book is at its richest and best.

Fitzgerald's lack of control over his material can best be seen in his treatment of his central character; hence it may be said that Dick Diver represents for the author a step backward from Gatsby rather than one forward. After presenting Dick Diver as a successful psychiatrist and husband, as a brilliant social luminary around whom certain lesser ones revolved as about a sun, Fitzgerald does not prepare us sufficiently to witness the disintegration of his personality. Malcolm Cowley, on the other hand, thinks that, at the point when his hero's deterioration began, Fitzgerald was right when he "stopped telling the story from Dick's point of view and allowed us merely to guess at the hero's thoughts, so that we are never quite certain of the reason for his decline." But here, it is reasonable to argue, lies the fatal weakness of the novel, namely, the inability on the part of the author to understand his own creation. The reason—or reasons—for the disintegration of a fictional character should grow clearly out of his nature as we learn to know it and out of the circumstances of his life, or, better, out of the interaction between these two forces. If the writer of fiction fails to show us how this has come about, he fails in his basic job, which is to create characters that convince us of their fundamental reality.

The reason for Fitzgerald's failure to understand Dick Diver is not far to seek. Dick Diver is a projection of Fitzgerald himself after, say, 1932. About this time he first became conscious of a failing of his powers, of a general depletion of energy, of an emotional exhaustion, which he later likened to the situation of a person who has been spending money recklessly and suddenly finds himself overdrawn at the bank. Beyond that he could not go in giving a reason for his failing powers. Fitzgerald understood Dick Diver no better than he understood himself. From this point of view, it may be said that Fitzgerald's portrayal was closer to life, since in life too we are often left to guess why this or that person has suffered a breakdown. But this is precisely where the art of fiction, if it is to satisfy us, must be superior to our ordinary knowledge of life. Art cannot stop short at the buzzing confusion of the flux, which is what life about us is most often like. Art must bring illumination, understanding, or it fails. Not that a novelist can spell out the causes of a character's disintegration in the clinical manner of a psychiatrist. But he can, and should, provide us with a key to the understanding of a character, which should show us why the character did what he did or suffered what he suffered. This key to the understanding of Dick Diver, Fitzgerald in the end has failed to give. Thus Fitzgerald's failure in *Tender is the Night* is fundamentally a failure to objectify his material and to fuse its "layers of experience" into an artistically unified whole.[22]

Obviously, any critic's reaction to the depiction of Dick Diver must be fundamentally personal. The critic who finds

Dick Diver an unconvincing or confusing character will not be persuaded otherwise by any amount of argument—or by a detailed reconstruction of the composition of *Tender is the Night*. For the record, this reader feels that Dick Diver is a satisfying character, that the causes of his deterioration are sufficiently probed, that his fall is tragic, and that the novel is unified by Fitzgerald's view of his hero. A study of the manuscripts lends support to some of these claims. Although Fitzgerald did not write long, detailed analyses of his work, the preliminary sketch of Dick Diver prepared in 1932 indicates that he knew the causes of Dick's decline. The first holograph draft for the published version of *Tender is the Night* reveals that Fitzgerald felt he thoroughly understood his hero. There are no discarded sections which show contradictory views of Dick Diver. This evidence, admittedly negative, is supplemented by the revisions of the typed drafts in which Fitzgerald points up his interpretation of his protagonist. In the analysis of the manuscripts I have repeatedly extended the scope of this study to comment on what the drafts reveal about Fitzgerald's view of Dick Diver. In addition, I have attempted to give a running interpretation of his decline as it develops in the story.

The alleged confusion in Fitzgerald's treatment of Dick Diver is frequently connected with the alleged confusion in the structure of *Tender is the Night*. Accordingly, I have also interrupted the account of the composition of the novel to comment on—and to defend—Fitzgerald's original structure. Again the evidence is mainly negative: there is no other discarded structure, and there is no indication that Fitzgerald had any doubts about his narrative plan while he was writing the novel. But there is also the author's summary of Book III in which he flatly states that the withdrawal of Dick Diver from the center of the narrative, which has puzzled some critics, was the intended effect: "All Dick's stories such as are *absolutely necessary* . . . must be told without putting in his reactions or feelings. From now on he is mystery man, at least to Nicole with her guessing at the mystery."[23]

It is not easy to comprehend the basis of the complaints about the narrative difficulty of *Tender is the Night*, which involves one flashback sequence and three obvious shifts in point of view. Its plotting is less elaborate than that of *The Great Gatsby*—the structure of which is always praised—and is far less complex than the novels of James and Conrad. Indeed, Fitzgerald esteemed Conrad as the greatest literary artist of the time and carefully studied him. It is evident that Fitzgerald's use of Nick Carraway in *The Great Gatsby* was learned from Conrad; and Fitzgerald admitted that the "dying fall" technique in *Tender is the Night* was taken from Conrad, too.[24] It is likely that the theory behind the narrative plan of *Tender is the Night* was also learned from Conrad. Although Fitzgerald probably learned his lessons studying Conrad's novels, he may well have read Ford Madox Ford's formulation of the theory in *Joseph Conrad: A Personal Remembrance* (1924):

> For it became very early evident to us that what was the matter with the Novel and the British novel in particular, was that it went straight forward, whereas in your gradual making acquaintanceship with your fellows you never do go straight forward. You meet an English gentleman at your golf club. He is beefy, full of health, the moral of the boy from an English Public School of the finest type. You discover, gradually, that he is hopelessly neurasthenic, dishonest in matters of small change, but unexpectedly self-sacrificing. . . . To get such a man in fiction you could not begin at his beginning and work his life chronologically to the end. You must first get him in with a strong impression, and then work backwards and forwards over his past.[25]

This is the method Fitzgerald selected for Dick Diver—and for the same reasons given by Ford. It is not new or esoteric, and it certainly did not originate with Conrad. Fitzgerald's complication of presenting his opening sequence through the starry eyes of Rosemary Hoyt also has solid precedents. Again, it is not a particularly difficult device. If it fails in *Tender is the Night*, it does so not because the device itself is confusing, but because Fitzgerald's use of it is maladroit. Perhaps, the criticism that the reader is puzzled at the end of Book I when he discovers that the novel is not about Rosemary is a testimonial to the skill with which Fitzgerald has developed her point of view.

Chapter II

Background

SEVENTEEN stages of *Tender is the Night* are represented in the F. Scott Fitzgerald Papers at the Princeton University Library; these stages can be divided into three main groups: The Francis Melarky or matricide group, the Lew Kelly or shipboard group, and the Dick Diver group.[1] The Melarky group is the earliest; Fitzgerald worked longest with it, and much of it ultimately found its way into the published novel. The intermediate and transitional Kelly material bulks the smallest of the three, and little of this was included in the final form of the novel. The Dick Diver group, which became the published novel, is the fullest of the three. Were it all that had survived, it would sufficiently testify to Fitzgerald's painstaking labor on the novel.

As does all of Fitzgerald's best work, *Tender is the Night* draws upon intensely—even painfully—personal material. In tracing the development of the novel, one can readily discern a progression from the relatively impersonal to the acutely personal, both in the author's tone and in the nature of his material. The novel, originally planned as a study of matricide, became a fictionalized account of Fitzgerald's life during the period in which he was writing it. Thus, in the Francis Melarky or matricide version one can see Fitzgerald beginning with sensational tabloid material—which he was ill-equipped by temperament to treat—and gradually shaping it into a highly subjective work of fiction dealing with the deterioration of a talented man. It is obvious that Fitzgerald's struggle to write his novel is mirrored in the protagonist's failure to complete a crucial book on psychiatry. But the most striking indication of the process by which the book became more subjective is, of course, the introduction of material suggested by Zelda Fitzgerald's mental breakdown in 1930.

The Great Gatsby was completed in November of 1924 at St. Raphael on the French Riviera, but there is no evidence that Fitzgerald began work on his next novel until late in the summer of 1925. He had borrowed money from Scribners against the royalties of *The Great Gatsby*, and the disappointing sales—about 25,000 copies—did little more than discharge his debt. His immediate problem was to raise money by writing short stories. In 1925 he published eight stories. One of these, "Love in the Night," contains some writing about the vanished Russian colony on the Riviera, which was incorporated into *Tender is the Night*.[2]

The Fitzgeralds spent November and December of 1924 in Rome, which they abhorred, and then went to Capri where they stayed through March. They spent the spring and early summer of 1925 in Paris; this was a time of heavy drinking and almost no work for Fitzgerald. He began to remain drunk for a week at a time, and his behavior during these periods became increasingly erratic. A number of Fitzgerald's experiences of 1924 and 1925 were written into the Melarky story, and some public events of the period supplied him with the idea for the matricide plot. In January of 1925 Dorothy Ellingson, a sixteen-year-old girl in San Francisco, murdered her mother during a quarrel about the daughter's wild living. The European papers covered the case, interpreting it as a manifestation of the collapse of prohibition society. Fitzgerald was interested by the Ellingson case, and he later mentioned it to Harold Ober, his agent, as a source for his new novel. The Ellingson case followed the Leopold-Loeb case of 1924, another sensational murder, which also excited Fitzgerald's interest. He may also have been influenced in his choice of material by Theodore Dreiser's *An American Tragedy*, published in 1925.

That Fitzgerald had discussed this material with Hemingway is shown by a kidding letter Hemingway wrote him in 1926:

I have tried to follow the outline and spirit of the Great Gatsby but I feel I have failed somewhat because of never having been on Long Island. The hero, like Gatsby, is a Lake Superior Salmon Fisherman. (There are no salmon in Lake Superior.) The action all takes place in Newport, R. I., and the heroine is a girl named Sophie Irene Loeb who kills her mother. The scene in which Sophie gives birth to twins in the death house at Sing Sing where she is waiting to be electrocuted for the murder of the father and sister of her, as then, unborn children I got from Dreiser but practically everything else in the book is either my own or yours. I know you'll be glad to see it. The Sun Also Rises comes from Sophie's statement as she is strapped into the chair as the current mounts.[3]

Another source of material for Fitzgerald's new novel was his friendship with Gerald and Sara Murphy. A sophisticated American couple who had pioneered the summer Riviera, the Murphys were splendid hosts and imaginative party-givers. Their friends included John Dos Passos, Archibald MacLeish, and Philip Barry (the setting of *Hotel Universe* is said to be based on the Murphys' Villa America at Antibes, which also supplied the model for the Divers' Villa Diana). This was American expatriate life at its richest, and Fitzgerald, who was in Antibes in August of 1925, was fascinated by the Murphys. In a gallant way he paid court to Sara Murphy, and he quickly identified himself with Gerald Murphy. So complete was this identification that when Murphy remarked after reading *Tender is the Night* that he was puzzled by the combination of himself and Fitzgerald in the character of Dick Diver, Fitzgerald assured him that this was not a problem because he and Murphy were, in fact, the same person.[4] Striking evidence of the way Fitzgerald borrowed qualities from Murphy for both himself and Dick Diver is provided by a passage in "Handle with Care": "That a fourth man had come to dictate my relations with other people when these relations were successful: how to do, what to say. How to make people at least momentarily happy. . . . This always confused me and made me want to go out and get drunk, but this man had seen the game, analyzed it and beaten it, and his word was good enough for me."[5] The parallels between Murphy and Dick Diver troubled Hemingway, who warned Fitzgerald after the book was published about the self-pity involved in interpolating Fitzgerald's own anxieties into a portrait of Murphy.[6] The Murphys were written into the novel from the very start as the Rorebacks or the Pipers, and ultimately they supplied many of the external or social traits of Dick and Nicole Diver. The dedication page of *Tender is the Night* reads: "TO GERALD AND SARA MANY FÊTES".

As Fitzgerald worked at converting the Murphys into characters in his novel, he shared his insights into their personalities with them. By the summer of 1929 the strain of being analyzed became so great that Sara Murphy was compelled to tell Fitzgerald that he was endangering their friendship.

You can't expect anyone to like or stand a *Continual* feeling of analysis, & sub-analysis & criticism—on the whole unfriendly —such as we have felt for quite awhile. It is definitely in the air,— & quite unpleasant.—It certainly detracts from any gathering, —& Gerald, for one, simply curls up at the edges & becomes someone else in that sort of atmosphere. And last night you even said, "that you had never seen Gerald so silly & rude." It's hardly likely that I should explain Gerald,—or Gerald me—to you. If you don't know what people are like it's *your* loss—and if Gerald was "rude" in getting up & leaving a party that had gotten *quite bad*,—then he was rude to the Hemingways & MacLeishes too. No, it is hardly likely that you would stick at a thing like *manners*—it is more probably some theory you have,—(it *may* be something to do with the book,)—But *you ought to know at your age* that you *Can't have Theories about friends*. If you Can't take friends largely, & without suspicion—then they are not friends at all—We *cannot*—Gerald & I—at our age—& stage in life—*be bothered* with sophomoric situations—like last night. We are very simply people—(unless we feel ourselves in a collegiate quagmire)—and we are *literally & actually* fond of you both—(There is no reason for saying this that I know of—unless we meant it.) And so—for God's sake take it or leave it,—as it is meant,—a straight gesture, *without* subtitles—[7]

According to the late Theodore Chanler, a composer who was studying abroad in 1925, an incident in which the Murphys figured supplied Fitzgerald with the *donnée* for the earliest form of the novel.[8] Chanler had been befriended by the Murphys and the MacLeishes, and although he enjoyed their company, he found himself growing increasingly dissatisfied with the irregularity of his life in France—especially with his drinking—and decided to break with his friends. In this mood he informed the Murphys and the MacLeishes that he was tired of them. Chanler reported this incident to Fitzgerald, who was excited by it and spoke of it as the basis for a novel about a talented young American who is taken up by a brilliant expatriate group and experiences a breakdown. This is the story of Francis Melarky with the matricide omitted.

Another American expatriate may have added to the picture Fitzgerald was then forming of Francis Melarky. While at Princeton Fitzgerald had made Walker Ellis the object of his hero worship. A member of the class of 1915, Ellis had a brilliant undergraduate career. He was elected to Phi Beta Kappa and was Commencement Ivy Orator, but to Fitzgerald his greatest distinction was the presidency of the Triangle Club. Fitzgerald's first Triangle show, *Fie! Fie! Fi-Fi!*, was written in collaboration with Ellis, although Fitzgerald actually did most of the work. After taking a law degree at Harvard, Ellis served as a combat pilot in the war, but after 1918 apparently failed to fulfill the promise of his college years. He abandoned the law for acting, and in 1925 went to Europe. Like Francis Melarky, he was a Southerner and seems to have had a difficult relationship with his mother. Walker Ellis was on the Riviera at the time Fitzgerald was, and Gerald Murphy recalls that "He was much on Scott's mind. He spoke often of him to me."⁹ It would appear likely that Ellis joined Chanler as a model for Francis Melarky.

While they were in Rome in 1924, the Fitzgeralds became friendly with the Americans who were working on the motion picture *Ben-Hur*. The information about the motion-picture industry that Fitzgerald picked up from the *Ben-Hur* crew probably supplied the background he needed for the characterization of Francis Melarky as a motion-picture technician.¹⁰

At the same time that Fitzgerald's imagination was excited by Chanler, Ellis, the newspapers, the Ellingson case, and the motion-picture industry, some of his more personal experiences contributed to his plan for the new novel. The Fitzgeralds attended the *Ben-Hur* studio Christmas party, after which Fitzgerald got into a nightclub brawl by volunteering his opinions of Italians. On another occasion Fitzgerald fought with some taxi drivers and was beaten by the police. These episodes formed the basis for Francis Melarky's experiences in Rome and were later combined into one of the strongest episodes in *Tender is the Night*. Indeed, Fitzgerald's intense dislike of Italians colored his treatment of them from the inception of his novel.

In examining so subjective a writer's selection of a matricide plot, one must consider the author's feelings about his own mother. It is true that relations between them were strained and that Fitzgerald was often acutely embarrassed by his mother. Mrs. Fitzgerald was a mildly eccentric woman whom her son hyperbolically described in 1926 as "a neurotic, half insane with pathological nervous worry."¹¹ She had spoiled him as a child, and he later came to feel that this upbringing had at least contributed to his egocentric and unhappy adolescence. However, he was also grateful to his mother for her devotion to him. He dedicated *Tales of the Jazz Age* to her; when she died in 1936 he wrote a story about her, "An Author's Mother," in which she is sympathetically portrayed as a confused woman, very proud of her author son. At the time Fitzgerald was working on the matricide story, his mother visited him in Paris. Though he expected to be embarrassed by her, her behavior was unexceptionable.

Crucial to an assessment of Mrs. Fitzgerald's influence on the matricide material is whether or not she served as a recognizable model for Charlotte Melarky, Francis' mother. Quite to the contrary, the domineering Mrs. Melarky is a far cry from the rather confused Mrs. Fitzgerald. Nor is there anything to indicate that Fitzgerald was obsessed by the theme of matricide. At the time he was working on the Melarky story he wrote a comic ballad about matricide:

> Just a boy that killed his mother
> I was always up to tricks
> When she taunted me I shot her
> Through her chronic appendix.

Fitzgerald entertained his friends by reciting this poem, and his willingness to burlesque the theme of his novel might well be interpreted as an indication that subconsciously he had developed doubts about the material, which was so alien to his creative temperament. This suspicion is supported by his otherwise inexplicable selection of the name Francis Melarky for the protagonist of a novel that was not to be satiric. The name is doubly puzzling because the given name identifies the character with the author, whereas the surname ridicules him. Fitzgerald was extremely careful about the names of his characters; he often chose names which indicate their personalities—Jay Gatsby, Dick Diver, Anthony Patch, Monroe Stahr. None of the other people in the Melarky version take any notice of the name, although they do jibe at Albert McKisco's comparatively ordinary name.

Fitzgerald worked on the Melarky-matricide version through repeated interruptions from 1925 to 1930. It had four tentative titles. *Our Type* and *The World's Fair* were the earliest; later Fitzgerald considered *The Melarky Case* and *The Boy Who Killed His Mother*, which was suggested by his wife.

First Draft. The holograph third-person draft of the Francis Melarky-matricide version.

Description & Pagination	Corresponds to TITN	Remarks	Location	Key
H: 8½″ x 13″. 1-51.	II, 22-23.	Originally prologue, changed to Chapter I. Francis Melarky in Rome.	Box 2	1
H: 8½″ x 12″, 8½″ x 13″, 8½″ x 10″. 48, (49-50), 51, 51½, 52, [ ], 53, 53½, 54-55, 44½, 56-60, 62-66, 68-69, 71-74, 77-78, 78½, 79-84, 84½, 85-86, (87-91), 92-98, 98½, 99-123, insert A-B, 124-131. 92-96 also numbered <31-32, (33-34), 35-36>.	I, 1-3, 5, 10-11.	Francis' second day on beach. Meets Seth Roreback. Visit to studio. Walter Naamen [Abe Herkimer and Francis Melarky arrange duel. McKisco's duel.	Box 2	2
H: 8½″ x 11″. Trimmed. 1 p.	I, 5.	Discarded from #2?	Box 2	3
H: 8½″ x 13″, 8½″ x 12″. 85½, 87¼, 87½, 88½, 89-96, 100-101.	I, 10-11	Another draft of Francis and Abe Herkimer arranging duel. Seth Roreback.	Box 2	4
H: 8½″ x 13″. 56½, 57-58, 58½, 59-60, [61], 62, 62½, 63-68, 70-74.	....	Alternate material for #2. Francis meets Abe Herkimer. Seth Roreback.	Box 2	5
H: 8½″ x 13″, 8-13, 13½, 14-20, 20½, 21-22.	....	Francis' second visit to studio. Quarrel with mother.	Box 2	6
H: 8½″ x 13″. "Insert for page 80."	....	Francis and mother quarrel about invitation to villa.	Box 2	7

Description & Pagination	Corresponds to TITN	Remarks	Location	Key
H: 8½″ x 13″. [1], 2-18. 16-18 originally numbered <4, 5, 7>.	I, 6-8.	Chapter III. Seth and Dinah Roreback in garden. Dinner party. Herkimer. Several drafts combined here. Narrator on p. 17.	Box 2	8
H: 8½″ x 13″. [ ], [ ], 6, 7.	I, 6.	Chapter III. Another draft of #8.	Box 2	9
H: 8½″ x 13″. 7, 9-10, 12, 12½, 13.	I, 6.	The dinner party. Seth and Dinah Piper. Abe Grant. Another draft of #8.	Box 2	10

The earliest attempt Fitzgerald made to write the novel that became *Tender is the Night* was the third-person account of the Francis Melarky story. This work was probably begun in Paris in the fall of 1925 and continued in the Pyrenees, where the Fitzgeralds stayed from January to April 1926. It was an ideal time for Fitzgerald to work on the novel, for he was temporarily free from financial pressures. *The Great Gatsby* was made into a play which opened in February of 1926 and brought Fitzgerald about $18,000; Hollywood paid him either $15,000 or $20,000 for the screen rights.

Fitzgerald had been hurt by the poor sale of *The Great Gatsby,* and his ambition was to write a novel that would show the public that he was "much better than any of the young Americans *without exception."* His next novel would be "something really NEW in form, idea, structure—the model for the age that Joyce and Stein are searching for, that Conrad didn't find." [12]

As planned in 1925-26, the central figure in the matricide

version is Francis Melarky, a twenty-one-year-old Southerner who is touring Europe, much against his will, with his mother. The narrative opens with their arrival on the Riviera, but at this point Francis has already been involved in a drunken brawl in Rome and been beaten by the police. Before that he had been dismissed from West Point for insubordination and had then worked as a technician in Hollywood—although the nature of his work remains vague—where he had become involved with an actress. Melarky has a quick and violent temper which his domineering mother frequently excites by reminding him of his past failures. Her attempts to control him have long since alienated Francis, so that she must resort to deceit in order to manage him. Her anxiety about her son is partly owing to the circumstance that her husband is serving a prison term for misappropriation of state funds.

No plot summary has survived for the matricide version, and it is unlikely that Fitzgerald ever prepared one; however, the general outline is clear up to a point. After his arrival on the Riviera, Francis is taken up by a brilliant group of Americans led by Seth and Dinah Roreback (also Rorebeck) or Piper. The most interesting of their friends is Abe Herkimer, an alcoholic composer who has squandered a strong talent. Herkimer and Francis act as seconds in a duel between Gabriel Brugerol and Albert McKisco, a writer. Francis attempts to secure work at an American film studio in France, but his plans are frustrated by his mother, who considers film people a bad influence on him. Having nothing better to do, he accepts the Rorebacks' invitation to go to Paris with them to see Abe off for America. In Paris Francis falls in love with Dinah Roreback. She is flattered by his attentions, and allows him a few kisses, but she does not develop any romantic feelings about him. At this point Fitzgerald abandoned the Melarky version, but from Fitzgerald's letters and from the recollections of his friends it appears that Francis would have suffered a nervous breakdown—probably from drinking—and then would have murdered his mother in a fit of rage. There is evidence that

Fitzgerald considered two possible conclusions. One was to leave Francis in the hands of the law; and in 1926 Fitzgerald requested legal information from Maxwell Perkins:

> In regard to my novel. Will you ask somebody what is done if one American murders another in France. Would an American marshall come over for him? From his state of residence? Who would hold him meanwhile—the consul or the French police? Why isn't that so if one Italian kills another Italian in America?
> Its important that I find this out and I can't seem to.
> In a certain sense my plot is not unlike Dreisers in the American Tragedy. At first this worries me but now it doesn't for our minds are so different.
> I should be writing this afternoon but I'm nervous as hell and can't. Zelda is much better. My novel will be called *The World's Fair* or *Our Type*. I don't know which.[13]

Fitzgerald told Edmund Wilson that Melarky would have been hunted down and killed by a shot from a "squirrel gun."[14] According to Wilson, Fitzgerald considered it ironic that someone who had committed the grave crime of matricide should be punished with what Fitzgerald considered a childish weapon. Perhaps both episodes were to have been retained.

The manuscripts are not dated, and there is little outside information available about the stages of Fitzgerald's work on this material; nevertheless it is possible to establish a chronology on internal evidence. Fitzgerald's practice at this time was to begin with fragmentary scenes which he expanded; from the incomplete condition of the material and from changes in the names of the characters, it is evident that the holograph sections listed above form the earliest draft of the matricide version. This is the briefest and the most disjointed draft, but it is possible to identify parts of three chapters.

The earliest surviving section of the matricide version is the "Prologue" (#1, fifty-one pages), which was subsequently headed "Chapter I." It is unlikely that Fitzgerald first wrote #1 as it now stands, for this section is a finished piece of work. The pagination is continuous—there are no inserts—which is extremely unusual in a Fitzgerald first draft. Nothing earlier than this draft has survived, though.

The idea of introducing a novel with a prologue describing an earlier period of the hero's life had appealed to Fitzgerald at least from the time he wrote *The Great Gatsby*, for that novel at one time had a prologue which was separately published later as the short story "Absolution." The prologue to the matricide story is an account of Francis Melarky's adventures in a Roman nightclub and of his drunken brawl with some cabdrivers. He is beaten by the police and rescued by his mother, who has sought aid at the American Embassy and the American Consulate. These events were included in every draft of the Melarky and Diver versions, and eventually they appear in *Tender is the Night* as Chapters 22 and 23 of Book II. Except for the shift from Charlotte Melarky to Rosemary to Baby Warren in the role of rescuer, this block changes very little throughout its history. All the details are retained; for example, both Francis and Dick are mistaken for a rapist by the crowd outside the court.

In *Tender is the Night* the episode is a painfully effective one, indicating the full extent of Dick's deterioration. There can be no doubt about his condition when the infinitely promising young psychiatrist of Book I is shown in a drunken brawl in Book II. The effectiveness of this contrast in Dick's case may owe something to the fact that the scene was originally written about a young man who lacked self-discipline. As has been noted, this episode was based on Fitzgerald's own experience in Rome, an experience which he later referred to as "just about the rottenest thing that ever happened in my life." [15] The prologue was probably written in the fall of 1925, after he had used the brawl in a humorous article, "The High Cost of Macaroni." This article remained unpublished during his life, and he described it to his agent as "the lousiest thing I'd ever written." [16] In this account, which also includes an argument about a reserved table, Fitzgerald knocks down "John Alexander Borgia, the chief of the secret police of the carbonieri"; Fitzgerald is not beaten, but instead departs for Capri "where the Emperor Tiberius used to go when Rome got too hot for him. People have been going there for much the same reasons ever since. . . ." [17]

Fitzgerald's experiences in Italy left him with a deep animosity toward the country and its people; this prejudice is evident in *Tender is the Night,* where Dick's outrageous behavior in Rome is partly provoked by the Romans. In 1925 Fitzgerald wrote to his agent, "I hate Italy and Italiens so violently that I can't bring myself to write about them for the Post." [18]

The next section (#2, eighty-three pages) is a fragment that begins with Francis' second day on the beach at Gausse's hotel. (The name for the hotel was taken from Dean Christian Gauss of Princeton.) The opening of this chapter, describing Francis' arrival, is missing. It was probably lost or destroyed after Fitzgerald used it in writing a later draft. In #2, Francis meets a group of Americans which includes Albert and Violet McKisco; the two homosexuals, Dumphries and Settig (who became Dumphry and Campion in *Tender is the Night*); and Mrs. Abrahams or Abrams. The McKiscos are a beacon shining over the seas of change in the manuscripts; their characters and actions are unalterably fixed in their first appearance in the manuscripts. Violet makes her joke about "the plot" and brags about Albert's literary work; and she is rudely silenced by him.[19] Francis learns from them about the Rorebacks and Walter Naamen (who is quickly rechristened Abe Herkimer). Francis then visits Earl Drowne (who becomes Earl Brady) at his Monte Carlo movie studio to seek employment. Up to this point, Francis' experiences—except for the Rome flashback—exactly parallel those of Rosemary Hoyt in *Tender is the Night.* In comparing the drafts for the Francis Melarky version with the published novel, one is struck by the way Fitzgerald salvaged the Melarky material. None of the actions of Melarky which are transferred to Rosemary in *Tender is the Night* is inappropriate to her, although she and Francis have entirely dissimilar natures.

After his second meeting with the McKisco group, Francis absents himself from the beach for a week, but he becomes involved with the beach people when he agrees to serve as Albert McKisco's second in a duel with Brugerol over Violet McKisco. Francis then meets Abe and Mary Herkimer, for Abe is Brugerol's second. Francis immediately likes Herkimer for his dignity and dry wit. Herkimer, who is planning to resign from the State Department in order to concentrate on music, is, of course, the same person as Abe North in *Tender is the Night*. The figure was based on Ring Lardner, who was one of Fitzgerald's closest friends, and Abe's bitter humor is Lardnerian. Fitzgerald felt that Lardner represented a tragic waste of talent through a sense of the futility of effort, and that Lardner's heavy drinking was a manifestation of the tragedy and not its cause.[20] That Herkimer is a musician probably derives from the fact that Lardner had musical ability and was disappointed in his attempts to write a musical comedy. The fact that Chanler was a composer may also be reflected in Abe's occupation. Despite Francis' admiration for Abe, he considers an attempt to seduce Mary Herkimer, a former actress and a beauty. The outcome of the duel between McKisco and Brugerol is the same as the outcome of the duel between McKisco and Tommy Barban in *Tender is the Night:* no harm is done, and McKisco develops a feeling of self-confidence.

There are two additional accounts of the meeting between Francis and the Herkimers, both fragmentary. Section #4 (fourteen pages) is another version of the arranging of the duel by Francis and Abe. The other account (section #5, twenty pages) does not involve the duel at all. Here Abe asks Francis for permission to show him a list of funny names of tourists in the *Paris Herald,* a piece of business that was finally transferred to Barban in *Tender is the Night.* Mary Herkimer tells Francis about her admiration for Seth and Dinah Roreback, and Abe invites him to the Roreback villa.

On the next day (section #6, seventeen pages), Francis goes to Brady's studio again and receives encouragement about a job. He returns to the hotel, and an argument begins when his mother criticizes the movies and reminds him of his past failures; but the scene breaks off in mid-sentence. Related to this is a single page, section #7, in which Francis and his mother quarrel over Abe's note inviting them to the Rorebacks' villa. Although it is headed "Insert for page 80", there is no place in the manuscripts where it properly fits.

The next section (#8, eighteen pages) is headed "Chapter III"; but because it is impossible to determine when Fitzgerald changed the Rome episode from "Prologue" to "Chapter I," it is also impossible to tell whether he regarded the beach, motion-picture studio, and duel scenes as constituting one or two chapters.

"Chapter III" opens with Seth and Dinah Roreback in their garden on the afternoon before their dinner party. The garden scene here is the original for one in Chapter 6 of the first book of *Tender is the Night*. The Rorebacks' characters, their way of life, and their home are all duplicated by the Divers'. Both the Rorebacks and the Divers have two children—named Ginevra and Lanier here, and Topsy and Lanier in *Tender is the Night*. The one real difference between Seth and Dick at this point is that Seth is apparently a man of leisure, whereas Dick is at least nominally occupied with his text on psychiatry. Seth does have a work-house like Dick's, but what he does there remains a mystery. Perhaps he paints, like Gerald Murphy.

In the evening the Herkimers, Francis, and Charlotte Melarky arrive at the villa; and at this point it is Seth Roreback who reads the names in the *Paris Herald* to them. There are several layers or stages represented in the account of the dinner party. Pages 12-15, which repeat the quarrel between Francis and his mother, were written at another time and then inserted here, for the handwriting, though Fitzgerald's, is unlike that of the rest of the section. Even more clearly a later insertion are pages 16-18, for here the dinner party is described by a narrator who is a guest there.

Section #8 includes instructions for a typist—"trip no car" (triple space, no carbon copy)—but no typescript has survived.

Section #9 (four pages) presents a different but disjointed version of the opening of Chapter 3, the garden scene. Another account of Francis' arrival at the villa is in section #10 (six pages). It was written later than anything else described here, for the characters are named Abe Grant and Seth and Dinah Piper. This has been included with the first draft only because it represents an abortive attempt to revise section #8.

Second Draft. The typescript third-person draft of the Francis Melarky-matricide version.

Description & Pagination	*Corresponds to* TITN	*Remarks*	*Location*	*Key*
T & RH inserts: 8½″ x 11″, 8½″ x 12″. Pica. 1-17, insert 17, 18-20, 20a, 21-23, insert 23, 24-27, 27½, 28-43. Also numbered <31-71>.	I, 1-5.	Chapter II [Chapter I. Abe Grant, Seth and Dinah Piper. This covers Francis' arrival through invitation to the villa.	Box 2	11
RTX: 8½″ x 11″. Pica. 3.	....	Discarded from #11?	Box 2	12
CC: 8½″ x 11″. Pica. 31-66.	I, 1-5.	CC. of most of #11.	Box 2	13
CC: 8½″ x 11″. Pica. 45, 45½, 46-71, 71½, 72, 72½. Originally <1-30>.	II, 22-23.	Chapter I? [Chapter II. [Chapter VII. Francis in Rome [Dick in Rome. Charlotte [Rosemary.	Box 2	14
T & H short form pagination: 1-53.	I, 1-5.	Chapter I, Chapter II. This was revised into first draft of final	Box 4	15

Description & Pagination	Corresponds to TITN	Remarks	Location	Key
		version—see below under *The Drunkard's Holiday.*		
RT & H short form pagination: 92-127.	I, 8-11.	Pp. 113-114, 116, 124-127 deal with duel. This was revised into first draft of final version—see below under *The Drunkard's Holiday.*	Box 1	16

From the Pyrenees the Fitzgeralds went in May of 1926 to Juan-les-Pins on the Riviera, where they remained until December. Situated at the principal locale of his novel, Fitzgerald tried hard to push ahead with the project. In May he wrote a sanguine report to Harold Ober, who was then with the Reynolds Agency and later became Fitzgerald's agent, predicting that the novel would be completed by about the first of the year. Fitzgerald said that the book was "about one fourth done," and that the finished work would be 75,000 words long and consist of twelve chapters. The novel would deal with "such a case as that girl who shot her mother on the Pacific coast last year." [21] Allowing for the fact that Fitzgerald was probably trying to send an optimistic account of his work, this letter is still useful. It tells us that Fitzgerald had planned a short, dramatic novel resembling *The Great Gatsby*. If "about one fourth done" was calculated in terms of chapters, the report most likely refers to the first two drafts, where there are at least three chapters in various stages of completion. This was not much to show for ten months of writing, but Fitzgerald continued to be optimistic. In June he opened negotiations with *Liberty* for the serial rights and even allowed them to advertise it in their December 11, 1926, issue.

It was Fitzgerald's habit to write out one or more pencil drafts until he had achieved something he considered good enough to have typed by a secretary. The typescript, almost always triple-spaced, was then revised in pencil—usually with inserted pages—and retyped. In the course of preparing a work for publication, a considerable body of drafts might accumulate. Although Fitzgerald attempted to save all his papers, he was hardly a methodical man; and even a well-ordered household would have suffered losses when exposed to the Fitzgeralds' peripatetic life. Moreover, there are apparently reliable accounts of Fitzgerald's burning his manuscripts in moods of depression. Gerald Murphy remembers witnessing one such scene during the time Fitzgerald was writing the matricide version of the novel.[22] These circumstances may account for a few of the gaps in the unusually full body of material for the versions of *Tender is the Night*, although it is unlikely that Fitzgerald ever deliberately destroyed any important material. One gap is indicated by the fact that there is a complete typescript for which there is no corresponding holograph material. This is section #11 (forty-seven pages), the true beginning of the story at Francis' arrival on the Riviera. It describes his first day on the beach, his meeting with Abe Grant through the list of funny names, the two trips to the motion-picture studio at Monte Carlo, and the invitation to the Pipers' villa. Though this is all related to sections #2, #4, and #5 in the first draft, its degree of finish indicates that it could only have been prepared from a lost intermediate draft. Additional evidence for a time lag between this typescript draft and the surviving holograph draft is provided by the names of the characters: Herkimer and Roreback do not occur at all.

It must be emphasized that the division of the manuscripts into holograph and typescript drafts is something of a convenience. Fitzgerald worked on both at the same time. His system of work was to write out a draft of, for example, Chapter 1, which he turned over to a typist. He would go ahead with a pencil draft of Chapter 2, and then revise the typescript of Chapter 1.

The duel has been cut from section #11, but the quarrel between Francis and his mother over his desire to work for the movies has been developed so that a clear picture of Francis' capacity for violence emerges. The hasty character sketch of Francis supplied in the first draft is now filled in. Francis is portrayed not unsympathetically as a person who wants to resolve conflicts he recognizes in his nature, but is inevitably defeated by the helpless rage his mother excites in him through her attempts to manage his life. After his second trip to the studio, he returns in a mood of elation at the prospect of resuming his career; but Charlotte Melarky provokes him into throwing his shoe through a window. Fitzgerald analyzes Francis' predicament as follows in section #11:

He did not feel ill-adjusted to the world, but if he was, if his heart was black, if he did not appear to others as he did to himself, he had no intention of paying for it in any way.

"In any way!" he repeated to himself furiously.

Thinking this way, the Grace of God withdrew <out of> from him, and he was fit for accomplishing nothing, but only for distracting himself desparately with <anything> whatever that came to hand.

In terms of the ultimate development of *Tender is the Night*, the most interesting thing about section #11 is the way it anticipates the beginning of the published novel. All the important events—and many minor ones—that Rosemary Hoyt experiences during her first days on the Riviera are here—including the warning about sharks, the reference to dope at the studio, the evocation of the vanished Russian colony.

The metamorphosis of Francis Melarky into Rosemary Hoyt and Dick Diver is one of the most intriguing aspects of these manuscripts, for it is accomplished without awkwardness. That the experiences of a violent young man should be converted into the experiences of both an ingenuous actress and a profoundly intelligent psychiatrist seems, on the surface, absurd. Yet when it is done, there is no patchwork discernible. Indeed, the brilliant Americans on the Riviera are even more interesting when observed through Rosemary's eyes; and the Rome episode is certainly more powerful when Dick Diver is involved.

The chapter headings and paginations of sections #11 and #14 show that Fitzgerald changed his mind about the use of the Rome flashback, first including it and then deleting it. Section #11, the beach scene, was originally called Chapter II. Its pages were numbered 31-71, and it was to follow a thirty-page prologue dealing with the Rome episode. But it was redesignated Chapter I, and its pages renumbered 1-43.

Section #14, a carbon copy, is the earliest surviving typescript of the Rome prologue. From differences between the holograph draft, section #1, and section #14, it is clear that there was an intermediate draft, now lost. The original chapter heading of section #14 is indecipherable, but it was intended as the opening of the novel; this is indicated by the original pagination of 1-30. It was subsequently labelled "Chapter II," with a pagination of 45-72½. It seems likely that the change was made because Fitzgerald came to prefer the beach scene as an opening, and intended to follow it with the Rome episode introduced as a flashback. Since the pagination of the beach scene was changed to 1-43, and the Rome episode to 45-72½, it is probable that the missing page 44—if one may assume that such a page was written—prepared for the flashback. At some time after 1932, when he conceived the final version of the plot, Fitzgerald redesignated section #14 as "Chapter VII" and added a note to his secretary: "Substitute the name Rosemary for Charlotte Melarky all through, and the name of the young southerner for that of Adams. And Dick for Francis." In its revised form section #14 belongs with the material for the first Dick Diver draft, and it will also be discussed with that material.

At some time after he had abandoned the second draft, Fitzgerald prepared another draft of the opening of the novel, based on section #11. This is included in section #15, which is the original Melarky version revised into the first draft of the final version—*The Drunkard's Holiday*. Section #15 had an involved history. In 1930 it was made part of the sixth draft, which was an attempt to return to the Melarky version after a start had been made on the Kelly version. Finally, in 1932, it was considerably augmented with holograph material and became the first five chapters of the final version. The twenty-five typed pages of section #15, which was originally part of the second draft, cover Francis' arrival on the Riviera through his first trip to the studio. His meeting with the McKisco group is described in detail, but there is no account of his meeting with the Grants or the Pipers. This section will be discussed more fully with the sixth and seventh drafts.

The foregoing comments on section #15 apply as well to section #16, which was also used in the sixth draft and finally incorporated into *The Drunkard's Holiday*. Only seven pages of typescript survive from what was once a full chapter. These seven pages describe the duel; Fitzgerald's attempts to salvage them are shown by the variant sets of pagination they bear:

p. 113	also numbered	102	90	33
p. 114			92	23
p. 116			95	29
p. 124		104	87	35
p. 125		105	88	36
p. 126		106	89	37
p. 127		107		38

This section is more fully treated with the sixth and seventh drafts.

Third Draft. The holograph narrator draft of the Francis Melarky-matricide version.

Description & Pagination	Corresponds to TITN	Remarks	Location	Key
H: 8½" x 12", 8½" x 13". [1], 2-21, 23-25.	I, 1, 2.	Chapter II. Abe Caswell.	Box 2	17
H: 8½" x 13". 29, 29½.	....	Francis meets Abe Grant.	Box 2	18
H & RT: 8½" x 13". 34-35, 35½, 36, 37½, 38-39.	....	Seth and Dinah Piper. Abe Grant.	Box 2	19
H, RT & RCC: 8½" x 11", 8½" x 12", 8½" x 13". 73, 73½, 74-77, 77½, 78-89, 89½, 90-90 a-c, 91, insert 91, 91½, 92-93, insert 93, 94-97, 97½, 98-114, 114½, 115-116, 116½, 117-118, 118½, 119, 119½, 120-124, insert 124, 125-129, 103-106.	I, 6-11.	Chapter III. Piper, Grant.	Box 2	20
H: 8½" x 13". 11.	I, 7.	Dinner at villa.	Box 2	21
H: 8½" x 9¾". insert 18.	I, 7.	Dinner at villa.	Box 2	22
HX: 8½" x 13". 6 unnumbered pages.	I, 17, 13.	Opening of Chapter IV. Paris.	Box 1	23
H: 8½" x 13". 1-3, 3½, 4-11, 11½, 12-17, 17½, 18-25, 25½, 26-28, 28½, 29-40, 40-62.	I, 12, 17, 19.	Chapter IV.	Box 2	24
H: 8½" x 13". 40-62, 1-6.	I, 17.	Lesbian material.	Box 2	25

The most likely date for the introduction of the narrator into the novel is the summer or fall of 1926. Fitzgerald must have been working steadily on the novel at this point, for he appears to have made a good start into the second draft by May, and he promised to meet a January deadline. If he still planned a twelve-chapter novel, he was able to prepare only one-third of the book before departing for America and a Hollywood assignment in December of 1926. In Hollywood he met Lois Moran, a young star, who became the model for Rosemary Hoyt.

Fitzgerald began the matricide novel after publishing *The Great Gatsby*, technically his most nearly perfect novel. Before *The Great Gatsby*, Fitzgerald showed little interest or aptitude for problems of form. That the man who wrote *This Side of Paradise* could have written *The Great Gatsby* is impressive and surprising. In *The Fictional Technique of F. Scott Fitzgerald*, James E. Miller characterizes the change as a switch in allegiance from the novel of saturation to the novel of selection.[23] Miller's idea is certainly sound, and it is supported by Fitzgerald's attempt to urge "the novel of selected incident" on Thomas Wolfe in 1937;[24] however, it is important to recognize that the formal excellence of *The Great Gatsby* derives mainly from the skillful use of Nick Carraway, the narrator. Though the use of the partly involved narrator is not uncommon before Joseph Conrad, it is generally identified with him because he used it regularly and with greater flexibility than anyone before or since. There can be little doubt that in *The Great Gatsby* Fitzgerald copied Conrad's technique, for he studied Conrad carefully and considered him the greatest literary craftsman of the century.[25]

It would have been natural for Fitzgerald to attempt to capitalize on the success of the narrative technique in *The Great Gatsby* when he began his next novel. But in fact he did not begin the matricide version with a first-person narrator, for the manuscripts show that Fitzgerald did not introduce this figure until after he had tried to write a straight third-person narrative. The draft with the narrator is so much more detailed and stylistically polished that it clearly postdates the two drafts already discussed.

It is not easy to quarrel with the critics who contend that Nick Carraway, the participating narrator of *The Great Gatsby*, is really the most important figure in that novel. In addition to documenting the events in the book and supplying the reader with a trustworthy moral guide, Nick is the only character who learns from the events. Conrad, of course, experimented widely with his narrators; they vary from mere personae for the author to leading figures in their own right. Nick's role is similar to that of Marlowe in "The Heart of Darkness" in that each becomes morally involved in the story he narrates.

The narrator invented for the matricide story is a very different figure from Nick and a much weaker technical device. He is unimportant as a character. Indeed, Fitzgerald does not even give him a name; he is merely a convenience for the author. The main function of this narrator is to interject an observation or an anecdote, and this is no more skillful or economical here than the use of omniscient third-person narrative form. Although the narrator is basically a device for supplying verisimilitude, unlike Nick he does not document each event, for he describes whole scenes he did not witness and for which he does not give a source.

Had Fitzgerald retained the narrator, it is very likely that the man's character would have been developed—that his role would have resembled that of Cecilia Brady in *The Last Tycoon*. Fitzgerald set forth the function of this type of narrator in an outline of the novel: ". . . by making Cecilia, at the moment of her telling the story, an intelligent and observant woman, I shall grant myself the privilege, as Conrad did, of letting her imagine the actions of the characters. Thus, I hope to get the verisimilitude of a first-person narrative, combined with a Godlike knowledge of all events that happen to my characters." [26]

Though the finished version of *Tender is the Night* does not have a narrator, its first third has a decided point of view. It is seen through Rosemary's eyes, and it may well be that Fitzgerald's experiment with the narrator of the matricide version was at least in part responsible for the use of Rosemary as an observer.

The manuscripts of the narrator draft are fuller than those for the third-person account, and the plot is advanced a full step to include Francis' trip to Paris, where he falls in love with Dinah Piper. Nevertheless, the third draft is a rough working draft, for there are lacunae which are only partly filled by very disjointed fragments.

The first chapter of this draft, section #17 (twenty-four pages), is probably the earliest writing Fitzgerald did for the first-person narrator stage. This account of Francis' arrival on the Riviera is headed Chapter II, indicating that at this point Fitzgerald had temporarily returned to the plan of opening the novel with the Rome episode. The narrator addresses the reader in a formal, authorial manner and sets the time of writing as three years after "The Melarky Case." After describing the beach and the arrival of the Melarkys, the narrator interrupts his story to tell about his first meeting with Francis on an ocean liner "some years before this tale begins." On the Riviera, after swimming and getting sun-burned, Francis goes to Cannes where he sees the *Tour de France*. He does not seek employment at the studio. Additional evidence that this draft of the chapter is distinct from those already discussed is provided by the fact that this is the only place where Abe is surnamed Caswell.

In section #18, a two-page fragment, the narrator renews his acquaintance with Francis, and Abe Grant shows Francis the list of funny names. This is followed by another fragment, section #19, seven pages of revised typescript and holograph in which the Grants, Francis, and the narrator go to a café in Cannes. In this section the narrator informs the reader that he is in the process of obtaining a French divorce.

Section #20 (seventy-six pages), Chapter III, was pieced together from holograph, heavily revised typescript, and carbon copies. This is a third-person account of the dinner at the villa and the duel—revised to a first-person account by the insertion of the narrator in one place. Several levels of work are involved here, and much of the material may have been removed from the second draft. The description of the dinner and the duel is much more detailed than in section #8. In section #20, for example, Dinah gives Mrs. Melarky a yellow evening bag, a gift which Nicole Diver makes to Mrs. Speers. There is no indication of mental instability in Dinah Piper, for this detail does not enter the novel until after Fitzgerald replanned it in 1932. But the fight which breaks out in the car on the way back from the Pipers' villa and the picture of McKisco's ordeal before the duel are quite close to the published novel. Some background information is provided about Brugerol, but he does not change into Tommy Barban until the Dick Diver version. At this stage, the only characteristic shared by the two is a fierce pride which prompts them to travel with duelling pistols.

The duel is made the occasion for an exhibition of Francis' explosive temper in section #20, when Brugerol complains about the conditions which Francis and Abe arrange to prevent bloodshed. At "Insert for p. 124" in section #20 Francis nearly challenges Brugerol to a duel, but Abe calms him. Mrs. Melarky is annoyed when Francis insists on acting as McKisco's second. She retaliates by intercepting an offer from the studio to take Francis to Corsica. Francis becomes literally sick with rage; having nothing else to do, he agrees to go along with the Pipers to see Abe off in Paris.

Two one-page fragments, sections #21 and #22, belong with Chapter III, for in these the narrator describes the dinner party.

Before Fitzgerald wrote out Chapter IV, he prepared a sketch, which has survived in part. This is section #23 (six pages), which deals mainly with the party given by the Pipers in Paris; it includes the ride in the carrot wagon, the waiter trap, and the Indian. A tipsy argument between Francis and Abe about Seth Piper is made the occasion for the narrator to describe a trip by the group to the Somme battlefield. In pages [5-6] of section #23 there is a description of an American girl who is unable to locate her brother's grave at the Somme.

Considerably expanded, the sketch became Chapter 13 of Book I of *Tender is the Night*. This chapter is thematically significant, for it is one of the places where Fitzgerald unmistakably indicates that the novel is a commentary on the post-war world. Fitzgerald excelled at conveying moods; the mood that emanates from the visit to the battlefield is one of sadness and regret—a sense of loss. This is a far cry from the bitter disillusionment that characterizes so many post-war novels of the period.

Chapter IV, section #24 (sixty-eight pages), is a very full account of Francis' trip to Paris with the Pipers and the Grants. It includes most of the scenes which later make up Rosemary's trip to Paris with the Divers and the Norths in *Tender is the Night*; and Francis and Dinah play the lovers' roles that Rosemary and Dick play in the published novel. After a luncheon at which Seth proves he is the only person in the restaurant with composure, Francis and Dinah go shopping. She then takes him to the salon of a wealthy American, Miss Retchmore. During the course of this day Francis falls in love with Dinah. She does not reciprocate his passion, but she allows him to kiss her. The Melarky story was not written beyond the trip to Paris, but it seems likely that Francis' love for Dinah was to be a precipitating factor in his final breakdown.

That evening the Pipers give a splendid party which, as in *Tender is the Night*, includes the joke about General Pershing, the waiter trap, and the Indian (here named John Spotted-Bear). The party—including the King of Sweden and a manufacturer of dolls' voices from Newark—moves on to a homosexual hangout. At pages 19-20, section #24 includes a description of the homosexuals which Fitzgerald shifted to several places in the Melarky and Diver versions before deleting it from the novel: [27]

Mary was trying to get him home

The place was full of fairies — I never so many or such a variety together. There were tall gangling ones and little pert ones with round thin shoulders ~~and delicate gestures,~~ ~~broad~~ broad ones with the faces of hero and Oscar Wilde, fat ones with sly smiles that ~~folded~~ ~~widened~~ broadened into leers, nervous ones who hitched and jerked, opening their eyes very wide, handsome, passive dumb ones who turned their profiles this way and that; nobled faced ones with the countenances of senators that dissolved suddenly into girlish fatuity; pimply stodgy ones with the most delicate gestures of all; raw ones with red lips and frail curly bodies, shrill voluble ones ~~piping above the hot oolong of american tea shops Piccadilly~~ ~~who shrieked and chattered~~ opening their eyes very wide; self conscious ones who looked with

eager politeness toward every noise;
satyrs whose lips curled horribly;
English ones with great racial
self-control, Balkan ones — a
small cooing Japanese.

The others must have ~~looked~~ maybe been around
simultaneously, for we all said "Let's
get out" together. After that we ~~rode~~
in the Bois, I think — Then Francis, and
Abe and I, ~~were drinking~~ the last
survivors ~~were drinking~~ went on to drink coffee ~~by
the Ritz Bar, bought midnight~~ in the
Ritz Bar

They were talking They were ~~big~~ tall
fine looking men, neither of them themselves
just now. They shouldn't have been there
just talking — Abe ~~ought to have been
in bed~~ should have had all this behind
him, and Francis off should have been sleeping with
some girl. ~~Neither of them was having a
good time. And what they had in
common that was keeping them~~ and it seemed to all

The narrator is very much before the reader in section #24; the luncheon and the party are described from his detached point of view. But he himself never becomes a figure in the story.

The next morning Dinah meets Abe at the railroad station. As in the published version of *Tender is the Night,* Abe is in bad shape from drinking; he is very bitter and tells Dinah of his love for her. He urges her to teach her son to love trees, a plea which Abe North also makes to Nicole Diver. The only significant difference between this account of the station scene and that in *Tender is the Night* is the absence here of the shooting. Apparently, Fitzgerald had not yet worked out the idea of punctuating the sections of the novel with shots.

Section #25 (twenty-nine pages) continues Chapter IV, and describes Francis' activities after Abe's departure. Dinah Piper allows Francis to continue his advances. Their kisses become more passionate, and she appears to enjoy the kissing game they play on the stairway of her hotel. The affair—if it can be called that—between Francis and Dinah in this draft is much less convincing than the affair between Rosemary and Dick in *Tender is the Night* because Dinah's participation is unmotivated. Dick's response to Rosemary's love is an act of self-indulgence, and it is the first clear indication that this brilliant man has begun to crack beneath his urbane manner. But Dinah's interest in Francis is inexplicable, for she is a self-controlled, self-sufficient person; she is certainly not a woman to yield to an impulse of this sort.

Section #25 goes on to describe Francis' date with an American girl, Wanda Breasted—another curious name. Although the circumstances of their first meeting are not given, Fitzgerald probably planned to connect it with Miss Retchmore's salon. Wanda Breasted is waiting for Francis with three women who, uninvited, go along on the date. His annoyance is increased when the women disparage the Pipers. The women are clearly Lesbians, and when one of them embraces Wanda in a cab, Francis dumps the woman into the street. Wanda makes a halfhearted attempt at suicide when Francis takes her home, and he is obliged to stay with her until she calms down. This is a powerful episode with thematic significance, supporting the impression Fitzgerald was trying to convey of the moral decline of post-war society, a condition particularly evident in Americans abroad. If Fitzgerald's title at this point was *The World's Fair,* the Wanda Breasted episode underscores the irony of the title. Fitzgerald was able to salvage very little of this material in *Tender is the Night;* the three women with heads like cobra hoods appear in the salon Dick and Rosemary visit, and there Rosemary is approached by a young American Lesbian. The Wanda Breasted episode was published in 1948, and it holds up very well separated from the rest of the Francis Melarky material.[28]

At one time Fitzgerald may have considered ending the novel with a retrospective summary delivered by the narrator, as in *The Great Gatsby.* Section #46, a body of general notes for the Dick Diver version, includes a typed sheet headed VIII which bears one sentence: "But things like Melarky's death and my having to explain to that damn Frenchman who I was stick in one's mind."

Fourth Draft. The typescript narrator draft of the Francis Melarky-matricide version.

Description & Pagination	*Corresponds to* TITN	*Remarks*	*Location*	*Key*
RTX: 8½″ x 11″. Pica. 29-44, 44½.	....	The Riviera. Francis and Abe Grant.	Box 2	26
T & H short form pagination: 54-91.	I, 6-8.	Chapter III [Chapter II Pp. 54-61, 74, 79-80, 90 describe dinner party. This was revised into first draft of the final version.	Box 4	27

Description & Pagination	Corresponds to TITN	Remarks	Location	Key
		See below under *The Drunkard's Holiday.*		
RTX: 8½" x 11". Pica. 81.	I, 7.		Box 2	28
RT: 8½" x 11". Pica. 82, 84-85, 85½, 88-91, 93-97, 99-101, 103, 108-112.	I, 7-11.	Transitional stage: 3rd person [narrator; Francis [Rosemary. Corresponds to Chapter III.	Box 2	29
T: 8½" x 11". Pica. 1 p.	....	Notes for Chapter IV. Abe's departure.	Box 1	30
RT & H: 8½" x 11". Pica. [1], 2-5, 5½, 6, 6½, 7-10, 10½, 11, 11½, 12, 12½, 13-19, 20, 19½, 20, 22, [ ], 23-24, 24½, 25-26, 26½, 27-28, 25-30, 30½, 31, 31½, 32-33.	I, 12, 17-19, 24.	Chapter IV. Paris.	Box 2	31
TX: 8½" x 11". Pica. 40, 42-43, 45-46, 48, 50-52, 56, 58-65.	I, 19.	Continues Chapter IV. Includes Lesbian episode.	Box 2	32
TX: 8½" x 11". Pica. [1], 2-3, 7, [8], 9, 11, 14-16, 19-20, 22, [ ], 23, 26-38.	I, 12,	Revised typescript of #31. Chapter IV.	Box 2	33
H & RT short form pagination: 1-7.	I, 12.	Includes 2 pp. RT removed from #33. Originally numbered pp. 4 & 6. Lunch at Voisins. See below	Box 2	34

Description & Pagination	Corresponds to TITN	Remarks	Location	Key
		under *The Drunkard's Holiday*.		
H & RT short form pagination: 1-9.	I, 12.	Includes 1 p. RT removed from #33. Originally numbered p. 10. Shopping in Paris. See below under *The Drunkard's Holiday*.	Box 1	35
H & RT short form pagination: 1-85.	I, 13-18.	Includes 5 pp. RT removed from #33, originally numbered pp. 5, 12, 24, 17, 18. Includes Amiens, Miss Retchmore, homosexuals, and Paris party. See below under *The Drunkard's Holiday*.	Box 1	36
TX: 8½″ x 11″. Pica. [ ].	, I18.	Notes.	Box 1	37
TX: 8½″ x 11″. Pica. 2-3, [ ].	I, 13.	Notes.	Box 1	38
H & RT short form pagination 1-55.	I, 19-22.	Includes 3 p. T, numbered p. 39 a-c. Francis & newsvendor moved from Riviera to Paris. See below under *The Drunkard's Holiday*.	Box 1	39

It is at this point that Fitzgerald became bogged down for two and one-half years. The years 1927, 1928, and half of 1929 saw him making no progress at all on the matricide version. In March of 1927 the Fitzgeralds settled at "Ellerslie" near Wilmington, Delaware. They remained here until March of 1929, except for a trip to France in the summer of 1928. This period was punctuated by optimistic reports from Fitzgerald to his editor and his agent, but the manuscripts do not support his claims.

In January of 1927 Perkins resorted to a little gentle prodding and urged Fitzgerald to announce the title *The World's Fair* in order to gain "a sort of proprietorship" over the material.[29] Fitzgerald replied by wire from Hollywood: . . . DONT GIVE OUT TITLE YET STOP EXPECT TO DELIVER NOVEL TO LIBERTY IN JUNE STOP. . . .[30] As late as April, Fitzgerald was promising June delivery, probably really believing that he could finish the job in an extended burst of hard work. He even asked for and received a $6,000 advance in 1927.

Everything considered, 1927 was a wasted year for Fitzgerald. The matricide version remained at a standstill, and Fitzgerald's short-story output hit a low of four for the year. Yet one of these, "Jacob's Ladder," plays an important role in the gestation of the Dick Diver plot. This story is discussed below in connection with the Kelly-shipboard version.

The typescript draft of the narrator account represents a transitional stage. It is fragmentary, and the pencilled revisions indicate that details of the story were still developing in Fitzgerald's mind.

The earliest surviving section of this draft is section #26 (seventeen pages), which begins after Francis' arrival on the Riviera. This section is based on holograph sections #18 and #19 of the third draft. Each page of section #26 is covered with a large cross, but many passages are underlined, indicating that Fitzgerald decided that these pages were not worth revising, but that the underlined passages were to be salvaged. Section #26 is, nonetheless, informative. In it Francis' character is more fully analyzed, and the role of the narrator is slightly augmented.

After Abe shows him the list of funny names, Francis goes with the Grants and the narrator to a café in Cannes. The narrator describes this scene from his point of view and freely comments on his companions. The next day Francis is promised work at the movie studio; this results in a quarrel with his mother. The narrator does not witness the quarrel, which is described in straight third-person narrative.

As characterized in section #26, Francis is not just a puerile, charming young man with a violent streak. Real complexities and tensions in his personality are adumbrated. Although Francis' role is chiefly assumed by Rosemary in *Tender is the Night*, some of his personality problems foreshadow Dick's. The heart of Dick's tragedy is his desire to be all things to all people: husband and physician to Nicole, physician to his patients, and spiritual guide to the American colony. In a crude form this tendency may be seen in Francis at page 39 of section #26, where Fitzgerald analyzes Francis' desire to resolve the opposing drives in his personality:

To achieve and to enjoy, to be strong and yet to miss nothing . . . to be both light and dark?

To harmonize this, to melt it all down into a single man—there was something to be done. The very thought of such perfection crystallized his vitality into an ecstacy of ambition.

Fitzgerald underlined this material, indicating that it was worth salvaging. Some phrases from this passage are applied to Dick Diver in the early stages of *Tender is the Night* proper, and the tone survives in the fourth chapter of Book II, when Dick is taking stock of himself: ". . . he used to think he wanted to be good, he wanted to be kind, he wanted to be brave and wise, but it was all pretty difficult. He wanted to be loved, too, if he could fit it in" (p. 176).

What corresponds to the third chapter—the dinner party at the Pipers' villa and the duel—is fragmentary in this draft.

The first piece of Chapter III here is a single page, section #28, which is a typescript of holograph section #21. In this the narrator describes the mood of the party. Section #29 repeats the action of holograph section #20, including the duel and Mrs. Melarky's interception of the message from the studio. The narrator is present at most of the scenes, but only as a witness; he does not interpret the events for the reader. Fitzgerald tried to remedy this by inserting in pencil a few speeches and observations made by the narrator. Later, he tried to incorporate section #29 into *Tender is the Night,* for at one point the name Francis is changed to Rosemary.

That there was a later typescript of section #29 is indicated by twelve typed pages in section #27, in which the first-person pronouns are integral—and not inserted. These pages are numbered 54-61, 74, 79-80, 90; but were previously numbered [1], 2-7, [ ], 11, 14-15, [ ]. They describe only certain scenes from the dinner party, and it is very likely that they were removed from a fuller manuscript. The surviving fragment was used in the sixth draft and was then incorporated into *The Drunkard's Holiday*. Section #27 is more fully discussed in connection with these two later drafts.

The single typed page headed "Notes for Chapter IV" has dialogue between Abe and Noel in the station before his departure. "Chapter IV", section #31 (forty-eight pages), is based on holograph section #24 and describes Francis' trip to Paris with the Pipers. It is heavily revised and includes new holograph material on inserted pages. For example, Francis is here shown making the date with Wanda Breasted at Miss Retchmore's salon. The most significant material that has been added involves Francis' attack on a Negro, which brings from Abe Grant an anecdote about his own experiences with Negroes in Paris. This anecdote at page 20 of section #31 was expanded into a major episode in *Tender is the Night,* revealing the full extent of Abe's deterioration: [30A]

"I'm all through with niggers—no more niggers," said Abe, "Once I had two many, more than you ever saw so I had to hide in my appartment and the maids were all furnished with a color chart so nobody could get in below a certain shade of tan. There was a nigger that I thought had stolen a thousand francs from me, and another one that I thought was him when I came back with the gendarme, and Mitchell — you knew Mitchell — who they kept in jail all next morning, when he went to get his friend out, because they might be the one. He was the maddest because he's a very proud fellow. But the most trouble was a Copenhagen nigger named Hedstrum who had helped me get a gend'arme and who I'd promised to set up in business. The shoe polish manufacturing business. He left all his materials in the appartment. I got so I wouldn't see any of them, innocent or guilty..."

Mary Grant repeats this story about Abe in another holograph insert which is crossed out. Abe's account, as far as it goes, includes the basic details which appear in Chapter 24 of Book I: a thousand-franc note is involved; Abe is aided by a Scandinavian Negro (Peterson from Stockholm) who hopes to manufacture shoe polish; and a prominent Negro is falsely arrested (the name was later changed to Freeman because there actually was a Negro named Mitchell who operated a Paris club).

Sections #34, #35, and #36 include eight pages of revised typescript which originally belonged to section #33. These pages were included in the first complete draft of the published version.

Section #33 is a typescript of section #31, including the revisions and inserts. The insertion of the name Rosemary on page three indicates that Fitzgerald at one time considered the scheme of revising section #33 to fit into the final version. It is clear that he rejected the scheme in favor of rewriting the chapter, for each page is crossed out, and many passages are underlined for copying.

Although there is a hiatus in pagination between sections #31 and #32, "Chapter IV" is continued in section #32 (eighteen pages). It describes Francis' afternoon with Dinah after Abe's departure and includes an account of his date with Wanda Breasted. Here again, the pages are crossed out and underlined.

Typescript sections #37 and #38, both fragmentary, contain notes and rough dialogue for Chapter IV. Section #39, from *The Drunkard's Holiday*, includes three pages of revised typescript which originally formed part of the fourth draft. These pages originally described the encounter between Francis and the newsvendor on the Riviera; the revisions change Francis to Dick and move the meeting to Paris.

The disappointments of 1927 were repeated in 1928. Edmund Wilson visited Fitzgerald in February, and in 1952 wrote an account of the visit, "A Weekend at Ellerslie." Wilson pictures Fitzgerald as very defensive about his failure to complete the novel and remarks:

> He had now gone on to tackle a subject that might well have taxed Dostoevsky, and he was eventually to find it beyond him. It must have been a psychological "block" as well as the invincible compulsion to live like a millionaire that led him even more than usual to interrupt his serious work and turn out stories for the commercial magazines.
>
> . . . .
>
> I remember his sitting around in his bathrobe and reading to Gilbert Seldes and me what must have been one of the early Riviera chapters from his novel then in progress, which was to turn into *Tender is the Night*. There was especially one dazzling passage with which he had evidently taken much pains and on which he must have counted to stun us. It presented a group of attractive girls—on a beach or in a room, I can't remember—but in any case floating and glowing in richest Fitzgerald glamor. "What do you think of that description?" he asked. We told him we thought it was splendid. "I read this chapter to Dos Passos, when he was here," he said, "and afterwards he said that he liked it 'all except that part,' he said, 'that's so wonderful.' I asked him what he meant, and he said, 'Oh, you know: that part that's so wonderful—that part that's so perfectly marvellous.'" This may have led him to leave it out, or he may have had to scrap it with his original subject, for I cannot now find this passage, in any form I can recognize, in *Tender is the Night*.[31]

The dazzling passage described by Wilson does not survive in the manuscripts, and one can only wonder whether it was destroyed—or if, after twenty-four years, Wilson's memory played him false. By 1928 the windfall from the Broadway and Hollywood versions of *The Great Gatsby* had been spent, and Fitzgerald was compelled to increase his magazine work. He published two articles and nine stores in 1928. Five of the stories deal with Basil Duke Lee. This series, which ran to nine stories (one, "That Kind of Party," was first published in

1951), forms an episodic autobiographical novelette. The Basil stories include some excellent writing, and the time and creative energy that went into them partially account for the lack of progress on the novel in 1928-29.

The Fitzgeralds went in May of 1928 to France where Fitzgerald apparently planned to complete the novel. In June he wrote Reynolds: "Two more chapters finished all completed August." [32] And in August he informed Ober: "Novel nearly finished." [33] The manuscripts include no writing on the matricide story which justifies Fitzgerald's optimism. One can only suspect that he was greatly exaggerating his progress, for at no stage does the matricide story survive in more than four chapters. In point of fact, it is doubtful if Fitzgerald did any serious work at all during the summer of 1928, for he drank heavily and was jailed twice.

In the fall of 1928 the Fitzgeralds returned to Ellerslie. He had made no progress on the novel during the summer; fall brought no improvement in the situation. The escapades of the summer were continued, and Fitzgerald's drinking landed him in jail several times. Early in November he admitted to himself that he lacked the self-discipline to bring the book to completion; therefore he devised a scheme for keeping himself to a work schedule. At this time Fitzgerald made Perkins a proposal for sending him two chapters each month until February: "I think this will help me get it straight in my own mind—I've been alone with it too long." [34] Perkins wrote on November 5 agreeing to this plan. On November 28 (more than three weeks later) Fitzgerald sent the first two chapters along with the fullest known letter about the novel:

> It seems fine to be sending you something again, even though its only the first fourth of the book (2 chapters, 18,000 words). Now comes another short story, then I'll patch up Chaps. 3 & 4 the same way and send them, I hope, about the 1st of December.
> Chap. I here is good.
> Chap. II has caused me more trouble than anything in the book. You'll realize this when I tell you it was once 27,000 words

long! It started its career as Chap. I. I am far from satisfied with it even now, but won't go into its obvious faults. I would appreciate it if you jotted down any critisisms and *saved them until* I've sent you the whole book, because I want to *feel* each part is finished and not worry about it any longer, even though I may change it enormously at the very last minute. All I want to know is if, in general, you like it & this will have to wait, I suppose, until you've seen the next batch which finishes the first half. (My God its good to see those chapters lying in an envelope!

Remember, novel is confidential, even to Ernest.[35]

This reveals a good deal about Fitzgerald's attitude toward the novel, but it also raises a few puzzles. It is very clear that Fitzgerald did not really have complete confidence in the chapters he was sending to Perkins. He was no longer trying to prepare printer's copy; he was just trying to force himself to complete a draft in any condition. The admonition about not discussing the novel with Ernest Hemingway indicates that professional tensions had developed in their friendship, and that Fitzgerald was concerned that his difficulties with the novel were costing him the respect of his fellow writers.

The letter also indicates that Fitzgerald had altered the physical shape of the novel since his 1926 letter to Ober in which he said that it would have twelve chapters or 75,000 words total. This inference is based on the calculation that the chapters sent to Perkins were one-quarter of the novel. The calculation is supported by Fitzgerald's earlier letter to Perkins in which he proposed to send two chapters per month for four months.

The chief problem with regard to the scheme for sending the novel to Perkins piecemeal is to identify the two chapters Fitzgerald sent him. There is no surviving typescript of the matricide version in a finished enough condition for Fitzgerald to have sent to his editor. It is virtually certain that Perkins returned the chapters to Fitzgerald; they were either discarded by Fitzgerald or incorporated in a later draft in such a way as to defy isolation. In October of 1933 Fitzgerald asked Perkins to return "that discarded beginning I gave you," but this could just as well refer to the Dick Diver version.[36]

From Fitzgerald's work up to this point it is safe to suppose that the two chapters represented the latest form of the opening of the matricide plot. The loss of these chapters would explain why the typescripts for the fourth draft are so fragmentary—they are the foul papers left after Fitzgerald sent a fair typescript to Perkins. From Fitzgerald's remarks about the chapters, it is likely that the Chapter I sent was the chapter about Rome; Chapter II was probably the description of Francis' first days on the Riviera, which had been labelled I or II at different times and had grown as Fitzgerald added details about Abe. The other two chapters which Fitzgerald said were nearly ready are Chapters III and IV in the fourth draft.

Even the threat of disappointing Perkins failed to keep Fitzgerald on schedule, for he went to Europe in March of 1929 without having delivered anything more. In a note which he seems to have left at Scribners before sailing, Fitzgerald explained that he would finish the next installment on the ship and mail it from Genoa. Despite his chagrin at his inability to keep to the schedule—"I hate to leave without seeing you—and I hate to see you without the ability to put the finished ms in your hands"—Fitzgerald did not send the next two chapters.[37]

The Fitzgeralds remained abroad until September of 1931. Although Fitzgerald continued to send optimistic letters to Perkins and Ober, the matricide material proved as recalcitrant as before; however, the gestation of the Dick Diver version is readily seen during this period.

Chapter III

Fifth Draft. The Kelly-shipboard version.

Description & Pagination	Corresponds to TITN	Remarks	Location	Key
H: 8½″ x 14″. [1], 2-14.	....	Chapter I.	Box 4	40
H: 8½″ x 14″. 15, 15½, 16-34, insert 34, 35-40, two-page insert 40, 41, 41½, 42-44, 44½, 45-47.	....	Chapter II.	Box 4	41
T: 8½″ x 11″. Pica. 15, 17.	....	Material for second chapter.	Box 1	42

To finance the year 1929 Fitzgerald published eight stories and two articles. This work reduced the amount of time he could give to the novel, even if he had been wholly determined to complete it. One of these stories, "The Rough Crossing," published in June, has an intimate connection with both the Kelly and the Dick Diver versions. In this story a successful young playwright and his wife are going to Europe so that he may recharge his artistic batteries. During the trip he is attracted to a pretty young woman, temporarily upsetting the equilibrium of his marriage—just as the storm at sea upsets the order of the ship.

In or very close to June, after "The Rough Crossing" had been written, Fitzgerald wrote to Perkins: "I am working night and day on novel from new angle that I think will solve previous difficulties."[1] This message has been interpreted by Mizener to mean that Fitzgerald had started the Dick Diver version, but it is exceedingly unlikely that the Dick Diver version could have taken shape before Mrs. Fitzgerald's breakdown in 1930.[2] It is equally unlikely that Fitzgerald began work on the Diver story much before 1932, when he plotted out the published version of the novel.

At about the same time that Fitzgerald informed Perkins of the "new angle," he wrote Ober a practical letter about his plans for the summer of 1929, stating that he had enough money to work on the novel for two months.[3] Even allowing for Fitzgerald's custom of exaggerating his progress, he must have made a good start on the Kelly version, for in August he wrote Reynolds that the novel would be three-quarters done by the end of September.[4] This can be interpreted to mean that he had completed the two surviving chapters of the draft and expected to complete several more chapters by the end of September. In a letter received by Ober on September 1, Fitzgerald announced that he had another month to devote to the novel.[5] Late in October Fitzgerald reported to Ober that the novel was approaching completion.[6]

The "new angle" for the novel involves a brilliant young motion-picture director and his wife, Lew and Nicole Kelly, who leave for Europe on an extended vacation at the peak of his success because he feels drained. Also on the ship is a young woman named Rosemary who hopes to get a break in the movies by impressing Kelly. The remaining material for this version is in section #42 and consists of two crossed-over pages of typescript which describe Rosemary's sneaking into first class from tourist class. There are no notes or outlines to indicate the direction of the story after the first two chapters. It is probable that the Kelly version would have resembled the Melarky version in that Lew Kelly would have experienced a process of deterioration in Europe.

The shipboard version may have been suggested by the career of Rex Ingram, the director, whom Lew Kelly resembles. Kelly is Irish, a Yaleman, and has achieved great success early in life by hard work. He has artistic ambitions and hopes that his trip to Europe will enlarge his intellectual horizons. Rex

Ingram (born Hitchcock) attended Trinity College, Dublin, and the Yale School of Fine Arts. He had worked at a series of jobs—in and out of the movies—before achieving resounding success as the director of *The Four Horsemen of the Apocalypse* in 1921 when he was twenty-nine. Ingram followed this film with such successes as *The Prisoner of Zenda* and *Scaramouche* and then went to Europe in search of greater artistic freedom in making his films. He had a studio at Nice in 1927, where he made *Mare Nostrum* and *The Garden of Allah*, which some critics regarded as pretentious. Ingram's career went into an eclipse with the introduction of sound movies. Fitzgerald was on the Riviera at the same time as Ingram, and it is more than likely that they met. There are only a few references to Ingram in Fitzgerald's letters and ledgers, but Ingram was the kind of person who would have interested Fitzgerald.[7]

These two chapters represent an unmistakable transitional stage between the matricide version and the Dick Diver version. The most obvious link is the names: Kelly is first called Melarky; and the names Nicole and Rosemary prefigure the female leads in *Tender is the Night*. Rosemary's method of gaining an entree into the movies and her dependence on her mother's judgment were written into the published version. The description of the pier (taken from "The Rough Crossing") and Kelly's attempt to help the youth named Curly who had jumped overboard are in *Tender is the Night*—but the Curly material was deleted after the novel was serialized.

The opening of the Kelly version in section #40 includes material which formed the basis for two important free-association passages in *Tender is the Night:*

Chapter I

"Oh – oh – oh – oh
Other flamingoes than me
Oh – oh – oh – oh
Other flamingoes than me –

Their heels hit the deck together. There was a blowy corner and each time they turned it ~~she beat go~~ slanting forward against the wind ~~but her coat~~ and pulled her coat together ~~but~~ without ~~getting~~ losing step

"Oh – oh – oh – oh
Other flamingoes than me
Oh oh – oh – oh
Other flamingoes than me."

On the starboard ~~outside~~ side the sea was fair and they ~~looked~~ found it ~~seeing~~ different things; ~~she~~ the young woman ~~seeing~~ saw it ~~immediately~~, objectively, ~~sweep~~ aesthetically – the man searched it for ~~the~~ what power of evocation it might ~~possess~~ – the isles of

(2)

Greece, the lost girl on the shore, unfamiliar ports, secret waters, greener foliage, bluer skies, lighter sands, and always the girl waiting; searched it still for the mandolins and the night voices heard outside his window in childhood, the brave events of romantic books, the spanish main on a backdrop, the moon of a popular song. His mind was made up of all tawdry souvenirs of his time, things given away, unearned, like the pictures of celebrities he had once collected from cigarette packages. Somewhere in the littered five-and-ten glowed the low, painful fire of his talent.

"Oh — oh — oh — oh
Other flamingoes than me—"

As they swung along a man and woman in deck chairs swayed together and the woman asked:

"What are they singing? I get the word flamingo every time. It's something about flamingos."

"I thought it was something about mingle," said the man, "mingle with me or something

The promenade around the deck to the beat of the same nonsense song is used skillfully in Book II, Chapter 10, of *Tender is the Night* as the introduction to an extended free-association reverie in which Nicole reviews the events between her marriage to Dick and the arrival of Rosemary on the beach.

In Book II, Chapter 16, of *Tender is the Night* Dick's thoughts in the plane when leaving on a trip after Nicole's breakdown echo Lew Kelly's thoughts above and suggest Dick's sense of loss:

—he must press on toward the Isles of Greece, the cloudy waters of unfamiliar ports, the lost girl on shore, the moon of popular songs. A part of Dick's mind was made up of the tawdry souvenirs of his boyhood. Yet in that somewhat littered Five-and-Ten, he had managed to keep alive the low painful fire of intelligence. (p. 255)

The Kelly and Diver forms of the Isles of Greece reverie provide a good example of Fitzgerald's revision technique. It is a commonplace of Fitzgerald criticism that he was an undisciplined writer, lacking the ability to strike out the dazzling phrases his fruitful fancy supplied; however, an examination of his papers indicates that he was a diligent self-critic whose chief concern was for the balance and movement of each sentence. The passages at hand show Fitzgerald deleting the romantic, evocative phrases he was so fond of and which were his literary trademark. In reducing "His mind was made up of all tawdry souvenirs of his time, things given away, unearned, like the pictures of celebrities he had once collected from cigarette packages" to "A part of Dick's mind was made up of the tawdry souvenirs of his boyhood" Fitzgerald sacrificed a good simile for the sake of a leaner, more emphatic sentence. He was a stylist with a sensitive ear for English. For all that his prose sparkles with wit and surprises with its power to evoke moods, it is lucid. Gertrude Stein complimented him on this quality in a letter about *The Great Gatsby:* "You write naturally in sentences and one can read all of them and that among other things is a comfort."[8]

It is important to recognize that the two chapters of the Kelly or shipboard version do not represent a false start and wasted time, for they really mark an important state in Fitzgerald's slow advance toward a mature and personally meaningful conception of the expatriate material he was attempting to deal with.

If June 1929 is the correct date for the new version, it had been preceded by more than three years of frustrating work on the matricide version. The fact that Fitzgerald was unable to push beyond the trip to Paris—at best, the halfway point—indicates that at some level of consciousness the matricide material had long since been rejected. Fitzgerald was well equipped to write a serious novel about expatriate life, but the superimposed matricide plot was alien to his genius. Another fault in the material was Fitzgerald's conception of the protagonist. Although Fitzgerald tried to indicate some fundamental worth in Francis, he is the least prepossessing of Fitzgerald's heroes. Consequently, Francis' experiences are only a better-written version of the now-familiar chronicles of Europe in the twenties.[9]

Social distractions and interruptions for magazine work are not wholly to blame for Fitzgerald's failure to complete the novel. In Fitzgerald's character the playboy bulked no larger than the dedicated man of letters. He was determined to achieve literary stature, and he was capable of hard work. It is difficult to avoid the conclusion that Fitzgerald had trapped himself: having wasted so much time on the matricide plot, he was unwilling to abandon it; but at the same time he was concerned about damaging his reputation with a novel which would justify the critics who had damned his work as adolescent, flashy, and sensational. Fitzgerald's anxiety about his position in the world of letters can be seen in his reply to Harold Ober's suggestion that the Basil Duke Lee stories be published as a book:

I could have published four lowsy, half baked books in the last five years & people would have thought I was at least a worthy young man not drinking myself to pieces in the south seas—but I'd be dead as Michael Arlen, Bromfield, Tom Boyd . . . & the others who think they can trick the world with the hurried and the second rate.[10]

The attempt to replot the novel around Lew Kelly and Rosemary indicates that Fitzgerald had to some extent, at least, faced up to the limitations of the Francis Melarky material. The "new angle" can be traced back to 1927 when he had written "Jacob's Ladder," a story which deals seriously with an affair between a cultured man of thirty-three and a seventeen-year-old actress.

With the Kelly version Fitzgerald made a distinct advance towards the final version of the novel, for Lew and Nicole Kelly and Rosemary are readily recognized as sketches for Dick and Nicole Diver and Rosemary Hoyt. The next step was to conceive the nature of the hero's disintegration, and this Fitzgerald began to work out in 1930 in a short story, "One Trip Abroad." The complete cycle is: Melarky Version (1925-1930)—"Jacob's Ladder" (1927)—"The Rough Crossing" (1929)—Kelly Version (1929)—"One Trip Abroad" (1930)—Dick Diver Version (1932-1933).

Chapter IV

Sixth Draft. The second typescript third-person draft of the Francis Melarky-matricide version.

Description & Pagination	Corresponds to TITN	Remarks	Location	Key
T & H short form pagination: 1-53.	I, 1-5.	Chapter I. See also under 2nd draft and 7th draft.	Box 4	15
T & H short form pagination: 54-91.	I, 6-8	Chapter II (originally Chapter III). See also under 4th draft and 7th draft.	Box 4	27
RT & H short form pagination: 92-127.	I, 8-11.	Matricide version. See also 2nd draft and 7th draft.	Box 1	16

The sixth draft does not exist as such in the manuscripts; but there is evidence that it was prepared—or rather, assembled—in April of 1930. This draft was a last attempt to salvage the matricide version by patching together the best sections of the second and fourth drafts. After Fitzgerald abandoned this project, the material was incorporated into the seventh draft (holograph draft for the Dick Diver version).

After drafting the two chapters of the Kelly version (fifth draft) in the spring and summer of 1929, Fitzgerald gave up on it. In February of 1930 the Fitzgeralds took a trip to North Africa, which was subsequently written into *Tender is the Night*. After he returned to Paris, Fitzgerald revived the disciplinary scheme, which he had tried with Perkins in 1928, of submitting the novel by chapters. But this time the recipient was to be Harold Ober. On April 8, 1930, Ober communicated his agreement to the arrangement.[1] Nothing was sent to Ober, though, and in May Fitzgerald explained his failure to live up to the agreement:

> At one time I was about to send four chapters out of eight done to you. Then I cut one of those chapters absolutely to pieces. I know you're losing faith in me & Max too but God knows one has to rely in the end on one's own judgement. . . . The novel is a different thing [from *Saturday Evening Post* stories]—if, after four years I published the Basil Lee stories as a book I might as well get tickets for Hollywood immediately.[2]

This letter establishes that the Melarky version—and not the Kelly or Diver versions—was involved. Although Fitzgerald's claim that he had completed eight chapters is almost certainly a face-saving exaggeration, his claim that four chapters were ready (at least ready to be retyped) is probably true. Since the Kelly version had never advanced beyond two chapters, and since the Diver version was not conceived before 1932, these four chapters must have been a return to the matricide version.

It is difficult to determine how extensive the sixth draft was, for when Fitzgerald incorporated it into the seventh draft he dismantled it and discarded a considerable amount. He never had the sixth draft retyped, and it can only be roughly reconstructed on the basis of the crossed-out paginations in the seventh draft.

As they now stand in the seventh draft, section #15 consists of twenty-five typed pages of Melarky material from the second draft and thirty-nine holograph pages which were added in 1932 when Fitzgerald prepared the seventh draft; section #27 consists of twelve typed pages from the fourth draft and twenty-seven holograph pages added in the seventh draft; section #16 consists of seven typed pages from the second draft and thirty holograph pages added in the seventh draft. Some of the typed pages have three and four sets of paginations. The typed material covers Francis' arrival on the Riviera, his meeting with McKisco, the trip to the studio, the Pipers' dinner party, and the duel. It was probably reckoned as three chapters; the chapter which Fitzgerald cut "absolutely to pieces" probably described the trip to Paris. There is no indication of whether the prologue was included in this draft.

These three sections as they now stand, including the Dick Diver material, could not have been prepared in 1930. The reasons for this are detailed with the seventh draft; but the most important clue is that some of the holograph work is on Johns Hopkins Hospital case history sheets, which Fitzgerald scarcely could have obtained in Paris. Moreover, the impetus for the Dick Diver plot was provided by Zelda Fitzgerald's mental breakdown, which occurred on April 23, 1930—two weeks after Ober agreed to accept the novel chapter-by-chapter.

Zelda Fitzgerald's illness brought to a halt Fitzgerald's work on the sixth draft. The interruption was to last until the spring of 1932. At first he was too disturbed to continue with the novel, and when it became apparent that her treatment would be long, he was compelled to return to writing magazine stories for ready money. In 1930 Fitzgerald published eight stories, four of which—"First Blood," "A Nice Quiet Place," "A Woman with a Past," and "A Snobbish Story"—belong to the Josephine series. The Josephine stories, which were started before Mrs. Fitzgerald's breakdown, have some connection with the development of *Tender is the Night*. In these stories Fitzgerald rather superficially worked out his theory of emotional bankruptcy, which is at the heart of *Tender is the Night*. But for the purposes of this study, the most significant of the 1930 stories is "One Trip Abroad," published in October. This story might almost be called a miniature of *Tender is the Night*, and in it Fitzgerald presented an intriguing picture of emotional bankruptcy.

The relationship between Fitzgerald's novels—his avowedly serious work—and his short stories has not always been clearly understood. In general, critics have been satisfied to take Fitzgerald's word for it that most of the stories were potboilers. But when read with the novels in mind, the stories reveal themselves as the equivalent of a more orderly writer's notebooks. In his stories Fitzgerald frequently experimented with themes, characters, and settings that he subsequently developed in his novels. Bits of description were often removed from a story, polished, and then inserted into a novel. For example, the description of the newsvendor at page 120 of *Tender is the Night* originally appeared in "A Short Trip Home" (1927).[3]

Indeed, the comments that have been made about the sad spectacle of this gifted writer wasting his talent on hackwork utterly disregard the fact that the stories served a literary purpose as well as a financial one. True, Fitzgerald's magazine writing interrupted his serious work, but the cause for the interruptions was Fitzgerald's inability to manage money and not his lack of dedication. The point is that the stories enforced a discipline on Fitzgerald to keep him practicing his craft. It was hard work, too, for his stories were published in the toughest magazines in America. It is one thing to publish work-in-progress in expatriate journals, but it is something else again to publish 160 stories in *Smart Set, American Mercury, Scribner's Magazine,* and *The Saturday Evening Post*. Granted, *The Saturday Evening Post*, where most of his stories appeared, was hardly a magazine of literary distinction—even though it boasted a roster of distinguished contributors during the twenties—but it is unfair to assume that Fitzgerald was compelled to compromise regularly in order to make his work acceptable to that publication. When he collected his magazine stories, Fitzgerald made only minor revisions in them. He never wanted to be an avant-garde writer, and he never wished to appeal to the celebrated "fit audience though few."

In an unfriendly article, T. S. Matthews makes this perceptive comment on the place of the stories in the Fitzgerald canon:

Scott Fitzgerald is supposed to be a case of split personality: Fitzgerald A is the serious writer; Fitzgerald B brings home the necessary bacon. And *Taps at Reveille,* a collection of avowed potboilers, was written with his fingers crossed by Fitzgerald B. There seems to be a feeling abroad that it would be kinder not to take any critical notice of the goings-on of Fitzgerald B, since his better half is such a superior person and might be embarrassed. Mr. Fitzgerald himself, however, obviously doesn't feel that way about it, for he signs his moniker to all and sundry, and even collects the offerings of his lower nature in a book. He is right: there is no real difference in kind between *Taps at Reveille* and *Tender is the Night;* the creatures whom he has sold down the river for a good price are a little cruder, that's all.[4]

Fitzgerald himself understood that his stories, for all their slickness of plot, entailed real creative effort. In *The Crack-Up* he noted:

I have asked a lot of my emotions—one hundred and twenty stories. The price was high, right up with Kipling, because there was one little drop of something—not blood, not a tear, not my seed, but me more intimately than these, in every story, it was the extra I had. Now it has gone and I am just like you now.[5]

"One Trip Abroad" is a perfect example of the relation of Fitzgerald's stories to his novels. It is a case history of an attractive young American couple, *Nicole* and Nelson *Kelly,* who come into money and go to Europe to improve themselves. Gradually they are drawn into the society of frivolous expatriates. They have affairs; they quarrel; Nelson drinks heavily; and they eventually become patients in a Swiss sanatorium. To underline the moral decline of the Kellys, Fitzgerald employed the *Doppelgänger* device. The Kellys repeatedly encounter another young couple who undergo a process of deterioration until Nicole realizes that "They're us! They're us! Don't you see?" [6]

In chronicling the experience of the Kellys, Fitzgerald was obviously forming the concept of emotional bankruptcy which is at the heart of *Tender is the Night*. According to this concept, a person has a certain store of emotion or vitality to draw upon; when it has been consumed, he is an emotional bankrupt. Fitzgerald saw himself as a case in point, and in *The Crack-Up* he wrote: ". . . I began to realize that for two years my life had been a drawing on resources that I did not possess, that I had been mortgaging myself physically and spiritually up to the hilt." [7] This is the predicament of Dick Diver, who suffers a lesion of the spirit in consequence of giving too much of himself to his wife, friends, and patients. On a reduced scale, the Kellys are victims of emotional bankruptcy, for they squander their emotional resources on trivialities and become spiritual and physical invalids. But since the Kellys are initially less promising than Dick Diver, their descent is less tragic.

In addition to the thematic link between "One Trip Abroad" and *Tender is the Night*, there are several details which occur in both: the trip to North Africa involving the locusts and the Ouled Naïls; T. F. Golding's yacht; and the use of cannon fire to break up hail-bearing clouds. Particularly striking is the depiction of Switzerland as a country where a resort mood attracts the physical and moral invalids of the world, an attitude developed more explicitly in "Hotel Child" (1931). This view of Switzerland permeates *Tender is the Night*.

In the summer of 1930 Mrs. Fitzgerald was moved from Paris to Montreux in Switzerland for treatment. She remained there until September of 1931, and Fitzgerald stayed with her most of that time. He made visits to Munich and Gstaad, and in January of 1931 he came to America for his father's funeral. These trips were written into *Tender is the Night*, and Dick's reaction to the death of his father is an important element in the novel.

No work was done on the novel in 1931. During this year Fitzgerald published eight stories, including the last story in the Josephine series, "Emotional Bankruptcy." Two other stories, "Hotel Child" and "Indecision," have details which were used in *Tender is the Night*. One of Fitzgerald's best stories, "Babylon Revisited," was also published in 1931. Although it has no specific links with *Tender is the Night,* the story's mood of loss and regret informs much of the novel.

The period of Mrs. Fitzgerald's treatment at Montreux, during which Fitzgerald did no writing on *Tender is the Night,* was probably the time when he conceived the Dick Diver version of the novel. Whether or not Fitzgerald's inability to complete the matricide story can be charged to the incompatibility of author and subject, it is certain that after April 1930 he had new material which he felt deeply. There was nothing bogus about Fitzgerald's anxieties for his wife; and when transferred to Dick Diver, they gave the new version an integrity which was missing in the matricide version. Whatever else is wrong with the matricide chapters, they clearly want a unifying tone. Fitzgerald vacillates between condoning and condemning Francis. When the material is focused, it is focused on young Melarky, who is at best a superficially charming, neurotic, and immature character. Though individual scenes successfully evoke a mood, the body of the matricide material fails to sustain a mood. These criticisms cannot be made of the Dick Diver version. In *Tender is the Night* the reader is compelled to admire a character whose appalling decline is traced. The dominant mood, a compound of regret and disenchantment, is carefully built up to the marvelous final chapter.

Fitzgerald's concern for his wife was matched by his fears for himself. Dick Diver is what Fitzgerald was afraid of becoming. From his anguished broodings of 1930-31, *Tender is the Night* took shape.

Chapter V

General Notes for the Dick Diver Version—*The Drunkard's Holiday*

Description & Pagination	Remarks	Location	Key
H: 8½″ x 13″. 1 p.	Instructions to typist for copying notes.	Box 1	43
TX: 8½″ x 11″. Pica. 1 p.	"Plot of Chapter," "Notes."	Box 1	44
CC: 8½″ x 11″. Pica. 1 p.	"The Blue Grotto."	Box 1	45
TX, H: 8½″ x 11″. 18 pp.	General Notes & material salvaged from stories.	Box 1	46
H: 8½″ x 13″. 4 pp.	General notes—chiefly about Dick.	Box 1	47
H: 8½″ x 13″. 1 p.	Note on deck scene.	Box 1	48
H & T: 8½″ x 11″, 8½″ x 13″. 16 pp.	General plan for novel, character sketches, charts, and work schedules.	Box 1	49
H: 8½″ x 11″. 1 p.	Analysis of *Gatsby*.	Box 1	50

In September of 1931 the Fitzgeralds returned to America, and Fitzgerald accepted a writing assignment in Hollywood. His script was rejected, but the money he earned allowed him to begin work on the new version of the novel.

While Fitzgerald was in Hollywood, Mrs. Fitzgerald's father died; this was followed in January 1932 by her second breakdown. She was taken to Baltimore for treatment. Fitzgerald remained in Montgomery, Alabama, until the spring, when he rented La Paix at Roger's Forge, Maryland. Here he wrote *Tender is the Night*.

On January 15, 1932, Fitzgerald notified Perkins of his plans for the novel:

At last for the first time in two years & ½ I am going to spend five consecutive months on my novel. I am actually six thousand dollars ahead. Am replanning it to include what's good in what I have, adding 41,000 new words & publishing. Don't tell Ernest or anyone—let them think what they want—you're the only one whose ever consistently felt faith in me anyhow.[1]

On the twenty-fifth of the month he wrote to a scholar who had written an article about him: "I am in mid-channel now in a double decker novel which I hope will justify some of the things that you say. . . . for the moment I am vieuxjeu and completely forgotten by the whole new generation which has grown up since I published my last book in '26."[2] Of course, he was not in "mid-channel" at this time.

Fitzgerald's ideas about the size of the novel must have changed between the writing of these two letters. The letter to Perkins indicates that Fitzgerald was still thinking in terms of a short, dramatic novel on the order of *The Great Gatsby*; that is, about 75,000 words. There were only about 35,000 words of salvageable material in the matricide and Kelly versions; and Fitzgerald was planning to add 41,000 words. When published, *Tender is the Night* ran to about 150,000 words. The second letter indicates that he had decided on a longer novel. The reference to "a double decker novel" is puzzling if it was meant in the sense of two volumes rather than just large. Nothing in the outlines for the novel suggests that Fitzgerald planned a two-volume work. Several years after the novel was published, he told Sheilah Graham that "he hoped to rewrite it, for it should have been two books"; but this seems to mean two separate works.[3]

When he began the new version in 1932, he tried to work it out by drawing up plot summaries and character sketches. This was probably done in Montgomery—or at the very latest at La Paix in the spring. In August of 1932 Fitzgerald made this entry in his ledger: "The Novel now plotted & planned, never more to be permanently interrupted." [4]

All the important working notes are in section #49, here reproduced in full.

GENERAL PLAN*

Sketch

1

The novel should do this. Show a man who is a natural idealist, a spoiled priest, giving in for various causes to the ideas of the haute Burgeoise, and in his rise to the top of the social world losing his idealism, his talent and turning to drink and dissipation. Background one in which the liesure class is at their truly most brilliant & glamorous such as Murphys.

The hero born in 1891 is a man like myself brought up in a family sunk from haute burgeosie to petit burgeoisie, yet expensively educated. He has all the gifts and goes through Yale almost succeeding but not quite but getting a Rhodes scholarship which he caps with a degree from Hopkins, & with a legacy goes abroad to study psychology in Zurich. At the age of 26 all seems bright. Then he falls in love with one of his patients who has a curious homicidal mania toward men caused by an event in her youth. Aside from this she is the legendary *promiscuous*

2

woman. He "transfers" to himself & she falls in love with him, a love he returns.

After a year of non-active service in the war he returns and marries her & is madly in love with her & entirely consecrated to completing the cure. She is an aristocrat of half American, half European parentage, young, mysterious & lovely, *a new character.*

[* In this section no attempt has been made to provide an exact transcript of the holograph material; some cancelled words have been ignored.]

He has cured her by pretending to a stability & belief in the current order which he does not have, being in fact a communist-liberal-idealist, a moralist in revolt. But the years of living under patronage ect. & among the burgeoise have seriously spoiled him and he takes up the marriage as a man divided in himself. During the war he has taken to drink a little & it continues as secret drinking after his marriage. The difficulty of taking care of her is more than he has imagined and he goes more and more to pieces, always keeping up a wonderful face.

At the point when he is socially the most charming and inwardly corrupt he meets a young actress on the

3

Rivierra who falls in love with him. With considerable difficulty he contains himself out of fear of all it would entail since his formal goodness is all that is holding his disintegration together. He knows too that he does not love her as he has loved his wife. Nevertheless the effect of the repression is to throw him toward all women during his secret drinking when he has another life of his own which his wife does not suspect, or at least he thinks she doesn't. In one of his absences during which he is in Rome with the actress having a disappointing love affair too late he is beaten up by the police. He returns to find that instead of taking a rest cure she has committed a murder and in a revulsion of spirit he tries to conceal it and succeeds. It shows him however that the game is up and he will have to perform some violent & Byronic act to save her for he is losing his hold on her & himself.

He has known slightly for some time a very strong & magnetic man and now he deliberately brings them together. When he finds under circumstances of jealous

4

agony that it has succeeded he departs knowing that he has cured her. He sends his neglected son into Soviet Russia to educate him and comes back to America to be a quack thus having accomplished both his burgeoise sentimental idea in the case of his wife and his ideals in the case of his son, & now being himself only a shell to which nothing matters but survival as long as possible with the old order.

<Characters
    We have
a. The hero treated 1st entirely from without and then entirely from within.
Technique
    One part retrospective to ten-fifteen parts narrative>

5

(Further Sketch) *Approach*

The Drunkard's Holiday will be a novel of our time showing the break up of a fine personality. Unlike *The Beautiful and Damned* the break-up will be caused not by flabbiness but really tragic forces such as the inner conflicts of the idealist and the compromises forced upon him by circumstances.

The novel will be a little over a hundred thousand words long, composed of fourteen chapters, each 7,500 words long, five chapters each in the first and second part, four in the third—one chapter or its equivalent to be composed of retrospect.

A graph of the novel's action and "A Summary of Part III" are included here with section #49. These were obviously prepared when Fitzgerald was working on Book III, and they will be discussed below at that point in the novel's composition.

Characters & Names

Dick

[ ]

The hero was born in 1891. He is a well-formed rather athletic and fine looking fellow. Also he is very intelligent, widely read—in fact he has all the talents, including especially great personal charm. This is all planted in the beginning. He is a superman in possibilities, that is, he appears to be at first sight from a burgeoise point of view. However he lacks that tensile strength—none of the ruggedness of Brancusi, Leger, Picasso. For his external qualities use anything of Gerald, Ernest, Ben Finny, Archie Mcliesh, Charley McArthur or myself. He looks, though, like me.

The faults—the weakness such as the social-climbing, the drinking, the desparate clinging to one woman, finally the neurosis, only come out gradually.

We follow him from age 34 to age 39.

Actual Age of

[ ]
DICK
September	1891	Born
"	1908	Entered Yale
June	1912	Graduated Yale aged 20
June	1916	Graduated Hopkins. Left for Vienna (8 mo. there)
June	1917	Was in Zurich after 1 year and other work. Age 26
June	1918	Degree at Zurich. Aged 26.
June	1919	Back in Zurich. Aged 27
September	1919	Married—aged 28 (after his refusing fellow-(ship at University in neu-(rology and pathologist to (the clinic. Or does he ac-(cept?
July	1925	After 5 years and 10 months of marriage is aged almost 34. Story starts
July	1929	After 9 years and 10 months of marriage is aged almost 38.

Nicole's Age

[ ]
Always one year younger than century.
Born July 1901
    courtship for two and one half years before that, since she was 13.
Catastrophe June 1917 Age almost 16
Clinic Feb. 1918 Age 17
           To middle October bad period
           After Armistice good period
           He returns in April or May 1919

She discharged June 1, 1919. Almost 18
Married September 1919. Aged 18
Child born August 1920
Child born June 1922
 2nd Pousse almost immediately to October 1922 and thereafter
 Frenchman (or what have you in summer of 1923 after almost 4 years of marriage.
In July 1925 when the story opens she is just 24
 (One child almost 5 (Scotty in Juan les Pins)
 One child 3 (Scotty in Pincio)
In July 1929 when the story ends she is just 28

[ ]

 The heroine was born in 1901. She is beautiful on the order of Marlene Dietrich or better still the Norah Gregor-Kiki Allen girl with those peculiar eyes. She is American with a streak of some foreign blood. At fifteen she was raped by her own father under peculiar circumstances—work out. She collapses, goes to the clinic and there at sixteen meets the young doctor hero who is ten years older. Only her transference to him saves her—when it is not working she reverts to homicidal mania and tries to kill men. She is an innocent, widely read but with no experience and no orientation except what he supplies her. Portrait of Zelda—that is, a part of Zelda.

 We follow her from age 24 to age 29

Method of Dealing with Sickness Material

(1) Read books and decide the general type of case
(2) Prepare a clinical report covering the years 1916-1920
(3) Now examine the different classes of material selecting not too many things for copying.
 (1) From the sort of letter under E
 (2) " " " " " F
  (In this case using no factual stuff)
 (3) From the other headings for atmosphere, accuracy and material being careful not to reveal basic ignorance of psychiatric and medical training yet not being glib. Only suggest from the most remote facts. *Not* like doctor's stories.

Must avoid Faulkner attitude and not end with a novelized Kraft-Ebing—better Ophelia and her flowers.

Classification of the Material on Sickness

A. Accounts
B. Baltimore
C. Clinics and clipping
D. Dancing and 1st Diagnoses
E. Early Prangins—to February 1931
F. From Forel (include Bleuler Consultation)
H. Hollywood
L. Late Prangins
M. My own letters and comments
R. Rosalind and Sayre Family
S. Squires and Schedule
V. Varia

[Here Fitzgerald charted Nicole's and Zelda Fitzgerald's case histories.]

9

The actress was born in 1908. Her career is like Lois or Mary Hay—that is, she differs from most actresses by being a lady, simply reeking of vitality, health, sensuality. Rather gross as compared to the heroine, or rather *will be* gross for at present her youth covers it. Mimi-Lupe Velez

We see her first at the very beginning of her carreer. She's already made one big picture.

We follow her from age 17 to age 22.

10

The Friend was born in 1896. He is a wild man. He looks like Tunte and like that dark communist at the meeting. He is half Italian or French & half American. He is a type who hates all sham & pretense. (See the Lung type who was like Foss Wilson) He is one who would lead tribesmen or communists—utterly aristocratic, unbourgeoise king or nothing. He fought three years in the French foreign legion in the war and then painted a little and then fought the Riff. He's just back from there on his first appearance in the novel and seeking a new outlet. He has money & this French training—otherwise he *would* be a revolutionist. He is a fine type, useful or destructive but his mind is not quite as good as the hero's. Touch of Percy Pyne, Denny Holden also. We see him from age 28 to age 33.

These notes surely demonstrate that his wife's illness was the catalytic agent in Fitzgerald's new approach to the novel. The details of Nicole Diver's case were based on Zelda Fitzgerald's illness, as shown in the table comparing the two cases. The incest factor in Nicole's case was, however, pure invention. But Zelda Fitzgerald's tragedy contributed more than factual background to *Tender is the Night:* it provided the emotional focus of the novel. Dick's response to Nicole's predicament, the very heart of the novel, derives from Fitzgerald's feelings about his own wife.

Indeed, the psychoanalytic branch of criticism would make the relationship between the Divers and the Fitzgeralds still more intimate by reading the novel as a wish fulfillment. On this interpretation, Mrs. Fitzgerald's impossible recovery is achieved through Nicole; Fitzgerald is seen to be punishing himself for his complicity in his wife's breakdown by means of Dick's ignoble end. But it is not really necessary to plunge into the author's subconscious mind, for in the case of Fitzgerald the obvious parallels are sufficiently remarkable. Just as he put his feelings about his courtship into *This Side of Paradise* and *The Great Gatsby,* and his feelings about his marriage into *The Beautiful and Damned,* so he based *Tender is the Night* on his wife's breakdown and his fears for himself.

The only major departures from the "Sketch" in the published novel involve the nature of Nicole's insanity and Dick's political ideas. She does not exhibit a homicidal mania in *Tender is the Night,* nor does she commit a murder which Dick conceals. Far from being a communist, Dick is completely nonpolitical in the novel. Fitzgerald rejected these plot details soon after planning the Dick Diver version, for there is nothing in the manuscripts to indicate that he ever tried to develop the material. Had he retained the idea of Dick's sending his son to Russia, it is not unlikely that those who attacked the frivolity of *Tender is the Night* in 1934 would have received it more cordially. As published, the novel is certainly a scathing denunciation of the corruptions of the very rich, and it is difficult to comprehend how the critics of 1934 failed to appreciate this. Presumably, Fitzgerald committed the blunder of making the life of the leisure class attractive as well as corrupt. Actually, *Tender is the Night* could have been converted into a Marxist tract by means of a few pointed additions; that Fitzgerald did not seize the opportunity at a time when he needed a success is noteworthy.

The most intriguing phrase in the "Sketch" is "spoiled priest," which has been woefully overworked as the master key to all of Fitzgerald's work. "Spoiled priest"—Fitzgerald probably found the expression in *Ulysses,* where it is applied to Stephen Dedalus—is used by Roman Catholics to describe a candidate for the priesthood who has failed to take his final vows. When Fitzgerald applied it to Dick Diver, he appears to have meant that Dick tried to combine his function as doctor of medicine with the role of spiritual doctor to the sick souls around him, but that he lost his idealism and was finally corrupted by his own flock.

In this connection it is useful to consider Fitzgerald's idea in the "Sketch" that Dick would become a quack after his return to America. When the novel was published, Edmund Wilson questioned the final role assigned to Dick, and Fitzgerald replied: ". . . your notion that Dick should have faded out as a shyster alienist was in my original design, but I thot of him, in reconsideration, as an 'homme epuisé,' not only an 'homme manqué.' "[5] This statement, which indicates that Fitzgerald's view of his hero's fate subtly changed as the novel was written, provides a better way to understand Dick than does "spoiled priest." At the end of the novel Dick is both ruined and spent, an emotional bankrupt drifting from small town to smaller town, lacking the energy to be a charlatan. He has been destroyed by defects in his character, and in the process his resources have been so completely drained that there is no hope for him.

In the "Approach" Fitzgerald made what could only have been a guess at the probable bulk of the book, since the book had not been outlined in detail. His estimate was fourteen chapters of 7,500 words each, divided into three parts. In the serial there are two sections of five chapters each and a final section of two long chapters which could have been subdivided. The serial chapters run about 10,000 words long, and the completed novel is half again as long as the 100,000 words Fitzgerald predicted. When the serial was revised for book publication, the twelve chapters were broken into sixty-one chapters.

A criticism that has been made of *Tender is the Night* is that Dick is not a convincing figure as a psychiatrist. It is true that Fitzgerald did not surround Dick with the sort of massive professional documentation that James Gould Cozzens has put into his novels, but Fitzgerald never intended to write a professional novel. His novel is not specifically about a psychiatrist. It is about Dick Diver, who is a psychiatrist. Fitzgerald's note under "Method of Dealing with Sickness Material" shows that the absence of medical details from the novel was planned: "Only suggest from the most remote facts. *Not like doctor's stories.*"

As listed in section #46, the stories Fitzgerald "stripped" for *Tender is the Night* were "The Love Boat," "The Rough Crossing," "Jacob's Ladder," "A Penny Spent," "Majesty," "A New Leaf," "Crazy Sunday," "At Your Age," and "A Night at the Fair." To this should be added "The Swimmers," "Indecision," and "One Trip Abroad."

Two interesting notes in section #47 show the effect Fitzgerald was aiming for in each of the three sections of the novel. The first note is:

Part I   From outside mostly
    II   Nicole from Dick
    III Dick

Book I shows the Divers through Rosemary's adoring eyes as they appear to the world. It is almost all brilliant surface, with only hints of the corruption beneath the facade Dick has erected. In Book II the reader is taken behind the portals of charm to learn the facts about Nicole as Dick did. The third book is concerned with Dick's attempt to work out his fate, to break the bond with Nicole, to cure her, and to save himself.

This, of course, is the rationale behind the long introductory flashback which Fitzgerald later came to reject under critical fire, although the notes and the manuscripts clearly show that at no time during the composition of the novel did Fitzgerald alter the basic structure.

Fitzgerald's conception of the purpose of each book of the novel is further emphasized in the second note:

To call him
- I   Dick
- II   Dr. Diver
- III Diver

That he rejected this scheme is regrettable, for it would have been a splendid device. With great economy this would have underlined the shifting aspects of the hero's career: Rosemary's Dick, the gentleman of leisure; Dr. Diver, husband and physician to a mental patient; and Diver, the emotional bankrupt and spoiled doctor.

In addition to the plans which have a direct bearing on the preparation of the published novel, there are fragmentary notes for the earlier versions which Fitzgerald seems to have considered in planning *Tender is the Night*. While this material is in itself not important, it supports the conclusion that *Tender is the Night* does not represent just the work Fitzgerald began in 1932. Rather, the published novel is the product of a cumulative process which included all the seemingly wasted work Fitzgerald put into the early drafts. The central theme—the collapse of a personality under the frivolity of expatriate life in its most brilliant form—endured throughout, but in the published version this theme is deepened by the special pressures on Dick Diver. The treatment of this theme grew more penetrating as Fitzgerald worked his way from the matricide plot to the Nicole–Dick Diver plot into which he could put his feelings about his own predicament.

The working title, *The Drunkard's Holiday*, which is supplied in the "Approach," is certainly curious. It is thematically linked with *The World's Fair* in that both titles suggest a time of relaxation. Both titles are ironic, but *The Drunkard's Holiday* carries a strong implication of contempt for the hero, who is a sympathetic—even an admirable—figure.

Although the plans for *Tender is the Night* indicate that Fitzgerald finally had his material under control, other information reveals that when he reached the planning stage in 1932 he was so unsure of his ability to organize the material that he found it necessary to seek discipline by imitating another author's planning system. This is significant, for Fitzgerald was not a neophyte; and his use of such a crutch shows how much his confidence had been undermined by his failures with the earlier versions.

Fitzgerald carefully modeled his plans and sketches for *Tender is the Night* on Zola's notes for *L'Assommoir* as described in Matthew Josephson's *Zola and His Time* (1928). Soon after the novel was published, Fitzgerald sent Josephson (whom he had never met) a copy with this inscription:

Dear Matthew Josephson
Save for the swell organization of "Zola" & your reproduction of it, this would never had reached the stalls—I'll skip the obvious remarks & high hopes for you.
Scott Fitzgerald [6]

There are two sections of *Zola and His Time* which Fitzgerald would have found helpful—Chapter VII, "Conception and Gestation of an Epic," which deals generally with the twenty-novel series, *Les Rougon-Macquart*; and the appendix, "Zola's Technique: The Methods and Plans." An examination of the latter, which discusses in detail Zola's planning system and reproduces sections of his notes for *L'Assommoir*, shows that Fitzgerald carefully copied Zola's system.[7]

L'Assommoir tells how a laundress's attempt to rise from the Paris slums is frustrated by her husband's alcoholism. Zola's "portfolio" for the novel had nine parts, cast in the form of a discussion between the author and himself:

1. The preliminary sketch, which includes a statement of purpose.
2. Brief biographical sketches of the characters.
3. An outline.
4. A chapter-by-chapter plan.
5. Notes on alcoholism.
6. Notes on Poulot's Le Sublime (for alcoholism).
7. Notes on the neighborhood.
8. Notes on laundress, workers, etc.
9. Newspaper clippings, slang, etc.

Notes which roughly correspond to seven of these can be found in Fitzgerald's preparatory work on *Tender is the Night*. Only an outline and a chapter-by-chapter plan are wholly lacking. The preliminary sketch, the brief biographies, and the notes on alcoholism (insanity in the case of *Tender is the Night*) can be readily recognized in section #49 of the manuscripts. Fitzgerald's reading in the literature of psychiatry in connection with his wife's case corresponds to Zola's study of Poulot; and the stripping of phrases and descriptions from Fitzgerald's stories corresponds to Zola's documentation.

The echoes of Zola's language and organization are too clear in Fitzgerald to be the result of anything but careful imitation, as is obvious from a comparison of the two preliminary sketches.

The novel should do this: show the poor people's quarter and explain through their milieu the customs of the poor, as for example, drunkenness, the breakdown of the family, fights, submission to all the shame and misery arising from the very conditions of the workman's existence, hard work, promiscuity, indifference, etc. . . . Don't fall into the *Manual*. A frightful picture will carry its own moral lesson. [Zola then summarizes Gervaise's story.] [8]

Fitzgerald's "Sketch," pp. 1-3: "The novel should do this. Show a man who is a natural idealist. . . ." Zola's memo about the moral is reflected in Fitzgerald's warning to himself about avoiding the "Faulkner attitude." The biographies of the protagonists of the novels have the same organization, moving from physical details to character analysis.

Zola's portfolio runs to 239 pages, for he was a compulsively methodical man. Fitzgerald, who had neither the temperament nor the time for this sort of labor, prepared only forty pages of notes. But Zola was starting from scratch, whereas Fitzgerald was working with material which had occupied him for nearly seven years; there was no need for him to make notes on Abe Grant or the Riviera.

Chapter VI

Seventh Draft—*The Drunkard's Holiday*.
First holograph draft of the Dick Diver version.

Description & Pagination	Corresponds to TITN	Remarks	Location	Key
RT: 8½″ x 11″. Pica. H: 8½″ x 13″. [1], insert 1, 2, <16>, 3-5, 7, 8 <4>-13 <9>, 14, 15 <10>-21<16>; 22-27, 28 <19>-33 <24>, 34-36, 36½, 37<36, 25>-40 <39, 28>, insert 40 <41, 37, 38>, 41-45, 46 <47>-47 <48>, <47>, 49 <1>-50 <2>, 2 pp. insert, 51 <3>-55 <7>, 50-53.	I, 1-5. Pp. 1-31.	Chapter I. Francis [Rosemary. Seth Piper [Dick Diver. Early; transitional level. See also under 2nd draft and 6th draft.	Box 4	15
RT: 8½″ x 11″. Pica. H: 8½″ x 13″. 54 <73, [1]>-60 <79, 7>, insert 61, 61 <80>, 62, 63 <64>-65 <66>, 66-73, 74 <83, 11>, 75 <a>-78 <d>, 79 <e, 86, 14>, 80 <a, 87, 15>, 81 <b>-91 <1>.	I, 6-8 Pp. 32-50.	Chapter II (originally III). Dinah [Noel. Seth [Dick. Includes material from narrator version. See also under 4th draft and 6th draft.	Box 4	27
H: 8½″ x 13″. 1 p.	....	Note.	Box 4	51

Description & Pagination	Corresponds to TITN	Remarks	Location	Key
RT: 8½″ x 11″. Pica. H: 8½″ x 13″. 92-124, insert 124, 125-127. Also numbered <a-h, a-j, a-j>. Three other sets of pagination crossed out. <33, 23, 29, 35-38; 90, 92, 95, 87-89; 102, 104-107>.	I, 8-11. Pp. 50-66.	Originally from Francis version. Seth [Dick. Noel Diver. See also under 2nd draft and 6th draft.	Box 1	16
RT: 8½″ x 11″. Pica. H: 8½″ x 13″. <127 [128]> 1-5, <6>, 6, [7].	I, 12. Pp. 67-70.	Includes material from narrator version. Dinah, Noel, and Nicole. Dick Diver.	Box 1	34
RT: 8½″ x 11″. Pica. H: 8½″ x 13″. 1-4, 5 <10>, 6 <5>, 7-9.	I, 12. Pp. 70-73.	P. 5, RT, is from Francis version. Dick and Nicole.	Box 1	35
RT: 8½″ x 11″. Pica. H: 8½″ x 13″. 1-18, 18½, 19-57, 57½, 58-74, 74½, 74¾, 75-78, insert 78, 79-85.	I, 13-18. Pp. 74-104.	5 pp., RT, from Francis version. Remainder is new work.	Box 1	36
T: 8½″ x 11″. Pica. 1 p.	I, 8. P. 49.	Discarded from #16?	Box 1	52
H: 8½″ x 11″. T: 8½″ x 11″. Pica. 1-7, 7½, 8, 8½, 9, 9-15, 15½, insert 15½, 16½, 16, 17, 17½, 18, 18½, 19-21, insert 21, 22, insert 22, 23-39, inserts 39 a-c, 40, insert 40,	I, 19-22. Pp. 105-129.	Chapter IV. Dick and Nicole Diver. Inserts 39 a-c, T, are from Francis version.	Box 1	39

Description & Pagination	Corresponds to TITN	Remarks	Location	Key
41-42, insert 42, 43-46, insert 46, 47-50, 50½, 51-55.				
H: 8½″ x 13″. 56-67, 70-80.	I, 22, 24. Pp. 129-131, 136-141.	Continues #39.	Box 1	53
H: 8½″ x 13″. 81-96.	I, 24-25. Pp. 141-148.	Continues #53.	Box 1	54
H: 8½″ x 13″. [1], [ ], 2-20, [21-23], a-e.	II, 1-2. Pp. 151-161, 164.	Chapter V.	Box 1	55
H: 8½″ x 13″. a-o.	II, 2-3. Pp. 164-171.	Continues #55.	Box 1	56
H: 8½″ x 13″. 26-35.	II, 4, Pp. 172-176.	Chapter V continued.	Box 1	57
H: 8½″ x 13″. (36 or 1)-10.	II, 5-6. Pp. 177-181.	Continues #57.	Box 1	58
H: 8½″ x 13″. 41-54, 54½, 55-70, 51-57, 78-85, 85½, 86-106, 106½, 107-121. 54½, 55-63 also numbered <1-10>; 62-70 also numbered <42-50>.	II, 6-10. Pp. 181-212.	Concludes Chapter V.	Box 1	59
H: 8½″ x 13″. [1], 2-5, 5½, 6, 6½, 7-8.	II, 11. Pp. 213-215.	Chapter VII.	Box 1	60
H: 8½″ x 13″. RT: 8½″ x 11″. Pica. 389, 389½, 390, 393-405, 405½, 406, 406½, 407-412.	II, 11-12. Pp. 213-223.	Chapter VII [VI. RT pp. 389, 390, 393 based on #60.	Box 1	61
H: 8½″ x 11″. 1 p.	. . . .	Notes for an unwritten scene in II, 11.	Box 1	62

Description & Pagination	Corresponds to TITN	Remarks	Location	Key
H: 8½″ x 13″. 410-413, 413, 414-433, 433½, 434, 433-435, 436-449, 500, plus 437 RT.	II, 15. Pp. 245-252. II, 12-13. Pp. 223-232.	Ferris wheel scene occurs here on the Riviera.	Box 1	63
H: 8½″ x 13″. 438- (503 or 50), 51-59.	II, 13-14, 17. Pp. 232-243, 259-261. III, 3. Pp. 326-330.	Includes the first form of the announcement of Abe's death. Morris scene here in place of II, 15. "Chapter VII" at p. 465.	Box 1	64
H: 8½″ x 13″. 60.	II, 16. P. 253.		Box 4	65
H: 8½″ x 13″. 61-62.	III, 3. Pp. 329-330. II, 16. P. 253.		Box 2	66
T: 8½″ x 7″. Pica. 481.	III, 3. Pp. 329-330. II, 16. P. 253.	Typescript of #66. End of Chapter VII.	Box 2	67
H: 8½″ x 13″. [1], 2-8.	II, 16. Pp. 253-255.	Chapter VII (?). Early draft, train trip. Cf. #69.	Box 1	68
H: 8½″ x 13″. 6-11.	II, 16. Pp. 253-255.	Chapter VIII Continued. Later draft, plane trip. Continues #68.	Box 1	69
H: 8½″ x 13″. 1-2, insert 2, 3-6.	II, 17. P. 156.	Cancelled material about Dick and Tommy.	Box 1	70

Description & Pagination	Corresponds to TITN	Remarks	Location	Key
H: 8½″ x 13″. 426-430, 430½, 431, 431½, 432-441.	II, 17. Pp. 256-261.	The Munich episode, but without announcement of Abe's death.	Box 1	71
H: 8½″ x 13″. RT: 8½″ x 11″. Pica. 439, 439½, 440-441, 441½, 442, 441-446, 446-491.	II, 18-19. Pp. 262-269.	Includes cancelled material about Dick's father and about Dick's voyage. RT 481-483, 485-490 based on Kelly version.	Box 1	72
H: 8½″ x 13″. 491-496.	II, 19. Pp. 269.	Continues #72. Includes cancelled material about voyage.	Box 1	73
H: 8½″ x 13″. 1-11.	II, 19. Pp. 270-272.	Sequence A.	Box 1	74
H: 8½″ x 13″. [1], 2-15, 17-55.	II, 20-21. Pp. 273-286.	Follows sequence A. A more detailed account of Dick's affair with Rosemary than appears in published novel.	Box 1	75
H: 8½″ x 13″. <68-69>.	II, 20. P. 275.	Chapter VIII.	Box 1	76
CC: 8½″ x 11″. Pica. short form pagination: 45-72½.	II, 22-23. Pp. 287-306.	See under second draft.	Box 2	14
H: 8½″ x 13″. 549-560	III, 1. Pp. 309-313.	Chapter XII.	Box 2	77
H: 8½″ x 13″. 553-601	III, 2, 3. Pp. 313-325, 330-331.	P. 600: "Transpose auto incident from Rivierra to this place."	Box 2	78

Description & Pagination	Corresponds to TITN	Remarks	Location	Key
H: 8½" x 13". 602.	III, 4. Pp. 331-332.		Box 2	79
H: 8½" x 13". 576-577, 577-578, insert 578, 581, 581½, 579-618, 604-632. 576, 581, 604 are RT	III, 4-6. Pp. 330-360.	The Countessa di Cherelli. First version of the chest medication scene.	Box 2	80
H: 8½" x 13". T: 8½" x 11". 1-18. Pica.	III, 7. Pp. 362-368.	Scene 7 Part III.	Box 2	81
T: 8½" x 11". Pica. 1-4.	III, 7. Pp. 361-364.	Scene 8 Part III. Typescript of #81.	Box 2	82
H: 8½" x 13". [1], 2-17, 17½, 18-73, 73½, 74-84. 17½ and 28 are T.	III, 7-8.	Part III Scene 8. Includes Irv.	Box 2	83
H: 8½" x 13". 85-95.	III, 8-9. Pp. 385-388.	Continues #83.	Box 2	84
H: 8½" x 13". 44-100. 48 is RT.	III, 9-13. Pp. 386-408.	Includes jail episode.	Box 2	85

In planning *The Drunkard's Holiday* Fitzgerald tried to salvage as much as possible from the matricide version. This salvaged material consisted chiefly of sections #15 and #16 from the second draft, and section #27 from the fourth draft. These have already been briefly discussed in connection with Fitzgerald's final attempt to complete the original plot, the sixth draft of 1929-30.

BOOK I

Section #15 (sixty-four pages), the long first chapter of this seventh draft, is headed "Chapter I." It corresponds to the first five chapters of the published novel and to Section I of the first serial installment. When he wrote section #15 Fitzgerald began a new chapter after page twenty-two—the point at which Rosemary first talks with Dick—but the revised heading on section #27 shows he later decided to let the whole of section #15 stand as "Chapter I."

Section #15, and indeed all of the seventh draft, shows that once Fitzgerald had decided on the Diver version, he was able to assume control of the material that had been so recalcitrant. This section is well organized; the various scenes have proportion; and one is impressed with the feeling that Fitzgerald knew what contribution each part of the novel was to make toward the whole work. All the major incidents that appear in the first thirty-one pages of the published novel are present in section #15. There is one unimportant structural difference: Rosemary's trip to the studio at Monte Carlo occurs in the draft after her first day on the beach, whereas in the book it is postponed until after she meets the Divers. Typed revisions which shift the studio visit to its final position appear in section #114 of the ninth draft.

Section #15 is made up of twenty-five pages of revised typescript from the second draft and thirty-nine new holograph pages. In the typescript revisions Francis is transmuted into Rosemary, and the expository material which deals with the conflict between Francis and his mother is cut. The new holograph material mainly develops Rosemary's character and her relationship with her mother. Rosemary's role as the starry-eyed witness to the charm and glamor of the Divers is fully realized. Despite her somewhat limited intelligence, Rosemary is an ideal person to authenticate the attractiveness of the Divers' life; she is herself a celebrity and has been unimpressed by the gaudy glamor of Hollywood.

It is remarkable that this conversion of a violent male character into a rather passive female character is satisfactorily achieved. Nothing of Francis' personality clings to Rosemary. One ingenious explanation for this has been offered by Leslie Fiedler:

> In Fitzgerald's world the distinction between the sexes is fluid and shifting, precisely because he has transposed the mythic roles and values of male and female, remaking Clarissa in Lovelace's image, Lovelace in Clarissa's. With no difficulty at all and only a minimum of rewriting, the boy Francis, who was to be the center of vision in *The World's Fair*, becomes the girl Rosemary as that proposed novel turned into *Tender is the Night*. Thematically, archetypally even such chief male protagonists as Gatsby and Dick Diver are females. . . . It is they who embody innocence and the American dream, taking up the role the flapper had contemptuously abandoned. . . .[1]

Intriguing as this analysis may be, it is undercut by the fact that Rosemary's function in the novel is to serve as a contrast to the hardness of Nicole's character. Rosemary is a completely feminine creature. Fiedler also ignores the fact that some of Francis' qualities went into Dick.

In the revised typescript pages of section #15 the names Seth and Dinah Piper are changed to Dick and Noel Diver. Brugerol becomes Campion, the first step in the process of bisecting Brugerol into two dissimilar figures—the effeminate Campion, whose name is a pun on the slang term for homosexual behavior, *camping*, and the professionally masculine Tommy Costello (later Barban).

Since Fitzgerald was so careful about the names of his characters, the name changes in section #15 merit some comment. Seth Roreback (or Rorebeck), the earliest name of the Dick Diver figure, does not seem to have any significance—even in the phonetic sense of raw-back; but the next stage of the name evolution in the matricide version, Seth Piper, is meaningful. He is the piper who provides the music for the pleasure seekers around him; he is even the Pied Piper who leads Francis to destruction. The name Dick Diver, which first appears in the seventh draft, well suits a character who dives from professional and social prominence into obscurity. Abraham H. Steinberg has suggested that the scurrilous meaning of the phrase *dick diver* indicates the fear and loathing Fitzgerald felt for the type of person he thought he might become.[2]

The change from Dinah to Noel is unimportant, but the name Nicole, which first appears later in this draft, is meaningful. Both Noel and Nicole are Christmas names, Nicole being based on Saint Nicholas of Russia or Santa Claus; but Nicole resembles nickle in sound, suggesting both hardness and money.

Apart from the one instance very early in the matricide version when he is called Walter Naamen, Abe retains the same given name while his surname changes from Caswell (early) to Herkimer to Grant to North. Fitzgerald thought of him as a characteristically American figure: Abraham suggests Lincoln, and Herkimer and Grant recall other patriots. In the final typescript of the novel Grant is changed to North, perhaps because Abe Grant seemed redundant to Fitzgerald.

There is no significance in the change of Rosemary's surname from Prince to Hoyt. Fitzgerald may have changed the name Prince because he had used it for the actress in "Jacob's Ladder." Rosemary, of course, is for remembrance. This suits her, for she clings to the memory of her first meeting with Dick. The name Albert McKisco was probably intended as a reference to Robert McAlmon, with whom Fitzgerald quarrelled in 1925.

Like the preceding section, section #27 (thirty-nine pages) is made up of revised typescript from the matricide version and holograph material newly written for the Dick Diver plot. The ratio—twelve pages of salvaged typescript to twenty-seven pages of holograph—indicates that Fitzgerald was working away from the old material. Thirteen pages of the interpolated holograph material (pp. 76-78, 81-89, 91) are on Johns Hopkins Hospital patient history sheets, for after Fitzgerald settled at La Paix he was in Hopkins several times. This provides additional evidence to dispute Mizener's assertion that Fitzgerald began writing the Dick Diver version in Europe.

The salvaged typescript has been mentioned in connection with the fourth and sixth drafts; and these pages have three sets of paginations. In the typescript the names Dinah and Seth Piper are altered to Noel and Dick Piper; but the holograph pages have the names Noel and Dick Diver.

Section #27, headed "Chapter II"—but originally headed "Chapter III"—continues section #15. Section #27 corresponds to Chapters 6-8 of Book I of the published novel, which describe the dinner party at the Divers' villa. Since almost all the action in this sequence is filtered through Rosemary's eyes, her role is built up in the holograph pages. The crucial event in this section is Violet McKisco's cryptic report that she observed something extraordinary in the villa, which is later revealed to have been one of Nicole's relapses into hysteria. There is no suggestion in the earlier drafts that Dinah Piper suffers from a mental disturbance, and section #27 marks the first appearance in the manuscripts of this crucial element in the plot. It is interesting that here Tommy does not attempt to silence Violet, as he does in subsequent drafts.

With section #27 belongs section #51, a single-page note Fitzgerald made about the Divers' dinner party: "Chap II Dick remarks specifically once or twice that Rosemary has a very romanticized idea of the Divers—to point that this is the set up thru her eyes only." This was probably made while Fitzgerald was writing section #27, as a reminder to emphasize the idea that Rosemary provides the reader with a very partial view of Dick and Nicole. The remarks Fitzgerald included for this purpose may be those on page fifty of the novel when Dick tells Rosemary, "You don't know what you want. You go and ask your mother what you want" and counters her compliments with "You have romantic eyes."

The next section, #16 (thirty-seven pages), corresponds to the last paragraph of Chapter 8 and Chapters 9-11 of the first book of the published novel. Together, sections #27 and #16 correspond to the second section of the first serial installment.

The name Seth appears once in section #16; elsewhere he is called Dick.

Section #16 deals with the events leading up to the duel and with the duel itself. Tommy's attempt to silence Violet McKisco in the car after the dinner party replaces Brugerol's attentions to Violet as the cause of the duel. There are only seven pages of salvaged typescript in section #16. These pages were shifted about before finding their final placement here, for they bear three other sets of paginations in addition to 113-114, 116, 124-127. In these pages Francis (who was McKisco's second) is replaced by Abe (who was Brugerol's second in the first version) and Rosemary.

There are thirty pages of new holograph material in section #16, and it is at this point that it became necessary for Fitzgerald to start blocking out scenes as he reached them, for he did not have anything like a detailed outline to work from—or any outline at all that has survived. His rate of progress was probably about ten pages of new work per writing session. This is shown by the fact that pages 93-100 were originally marked a-h; pages 101-110 were a-j; and pages 118-127 were a-j. In essentials the new holograph material is extremely close to the published novel. Fitzgerald painstakingly revised the holograph material and the typescript prepared from it, but the revisions are predominantly stylistic. Though he endlessly searched for *le mot juste* and recast sentences, the proportions of the episodes and the moods of the scenes were not altered significantly. Obviously, Fitzgerald knew from the start of this draft which effects he desired; there is nothing hit-or-miss about the revisions.

Chapter 12, Book I, which begins the third section of the first installment, was assembled from sections #34 (eight pages) and #35 (nine pages). Section #34 describes the luncheon party at Voisins; and section #35 describes Rosemary's shopping tour with Nicole, who is here so named for the first time. Both sections are based on similar material in the matricide version, but they include only three pages of revised typescript from the fourth draft. In section #35 Nicole tells the anecdote about attending a court ball while suffering from an attack of appendicitis, but this act is assigned to Baby Warren in a later draft. At this stage Fitzgerald had probably not yet fully visualized Baby's role in the novel.

In a few places Dick and Nicole Diver are called Seth and Noel. Rosemary's mother is still called Mrs. Kelly in section #36.

Section #36 (ninety pages) forms the bulk of the third section of the first installment. The longest section in this draft, its physical appearance is neater than any sequence Fitzgerald had written up to this point. Deletions and insertions abound; but there are no fragments, and there are only five interpolated pages which interrupt the numbering. This section carries the story forward from the visit to the trenches through the party that preceded Abe's departure from Paris. Only five pages of salvaged typescript were included in this section, although all the episodes—except the private showing of Rosemary's film and her attempt to seduce Dick—are based on material in the matricide version. Thus the love-play between Dick and Rosemary is a revision of a similar sequence involving Francis and Dinah, and the scene of the couple kissing their way up the hotel stairs also appeared in the matricide version. The visit of Francis and Dinah to Miss Retchmore's salon is taken over by Dick and Rosemary in this draft, and here Fitzgerald included some incidents from the discarded Wanda Breasted episode: Rosemary overhears the cobra-like women disparaging the Divers; and the American Lesbian who tries to date Rosemary is reminiscent of Wanda Breasted. The description of a group of homosexuals which Fitzgerald had used in the nightclub scene of the fourth draft has been shifted to the salon (pp. 62-63); he later moved it to Book III of the novel before finally dropping it.

As it appears here for the first time in section #36, Rosemary's attempt to seduce Dick in the hotel includes a reference to menstruation when Dick is trying to convince her that it would be wrong for them to become lovers: "Isn't it just about your—time to be sick." This may have been cut because Fitzgerald decided that it was out of character for Dick, but it is more likely that he dropped it because he wanted to refer to menstruation during the Rome interlude in Book II. Ironically, Rosemary's remark, "—those things are rythmic," serves to halt Dick's desperate attempt to seduce her in Rome (p. 275). Nevertheless, Fitzgerald sacrificed the irony and omitted the earlier reference, which was the more expendable.

Section #36 shows that even while Fitzgerald was still working with scenes removed from the matricide version, the new version had partly assumed an independent existence. Moreover, the size and degree of finish of this section indicates that Fitzgerald was working from a well-thought-out plan, and that he had developed confidence in the worked-over expatriate material. There is nothing in this section drastically different from the fragmentary drafts he had written during 1926-30, but in the seventh draft it coheres.

Section #39 (seventy-two pages) is headed "Chapter IV" and corresponds to Book I, Chapters 19-21 and most of Chapter 22 of the published novel; it includes only three pages of typescript salvaged from the fourth draft. The section begins with Abe's departure from the Gare Saint Lazare, which is the last scene Fitzgerald wrote for the matricide version. Except for Book II, Chapters 22-23, which covers Dick's brawl in Rome, the rest of *The Drunkard's Holiday* is all true first draft.

In section #39 the station scene has been augmented by the murder which Abe's friends witness. This is a significant incident, prefiguring the tragic result of Abe's trip to America. The murder is also part of the structural scheme of marking the major sections of the novel by acts of violence, especially by gunshots. Thus, the end of the Riviera idyl is marked by the duel; and Abe's embittered departure from Paris and the Divers, ending a warm relationship, is underscored by a murder. This device is associated with the reminders or echoes of the war, which abound in the novel. It has been largely ignored that *Tender is the Night* specifically comments on a post-war civilization; although Dick's statements at the battlefield make it difficult to disregard the interpretation that the world of the novel has not been able to recover from the war, that the characters are war casualties (in the "author's final version" Fitzgerald entitled Book III "Casualties"), and that the war is being continued by senseless acts of violence and self-destruction: " 'This took religion and years of plenty and tremendous sureties and the exact relation that existed between the classes. . . . All my beautiful lovely safe world blew itself up here with a great gust of high explosive love,' Dick mourned persistently" (p. 75). The war was much on Fitzgerald's mind during the years he worked on the novel. He had visited the battlefields in France, and in Paris he spent considerable time studying war photos at Brentano's and discussing the war with Hemingway.

Section #53 (twenty-three pages), which continues the pagination of section #39, completes Book I, Chapter 22 and has most of Book I, Chapter 24. The missing chapter, I, 23, which chronicles Abe's day in the Ritz Bar, was added to the typescript prepared from this draft. The missing pages 68-69 in section #53 correspond to pages 137-138 of the published novel. This is the scene between Rosemary and Dick in her hotel room just before Abe's arrival. It was written, but has been lost. Page 70 and section #96—which is the typescript based on section #53—indicate that the scene as originally written was probably more passionate than in the published novel.

Section #54 (sixteen pages) corresponds to the remaining part of Book I, Chapter 24 and to all of Chapter 25. It continues the pagination of section #53 and completes the fourth section of the installment; this is the end of Book I. Section #54 includes the murder of the Negro, Peterson—which grew out of an anecdote told by Abe in the matricide version. Fitzgerald's interest in the names of his characters can be seen in the case of the hotel manager, a minor figure. In this draft he is named Mac Ready, McReady, Macready, and M^{ac}ready, probably as a word play on his serviceability. But Nicole's reaction to the murder of Peterson causes a temporary derangement in which she tries to wash the bloodied bedspread. That—and the fact that William C. Macready was playing Macbeth the night of the Astor Place Riot—suggested to Fitzgerald the sleepwalking scene in *Macbeth*, and MacReady became McBeth in the revised typescript. The oblique reference to *Macbeth* was also strengthened in the typescript by showing Nicole actually washing the spread, whereas in section #54 only her ravings are heard.

The physical condition of the holograph manuscript for Book I indicates that these twenty-five chapters gave Fitzgerald no real trouble: 127 consecutively numbered pages, two short sections, and then sequences of eighty-five and ninety-six pages. But in Book II Fitzgerald began to find his work more difficult, for these manuscripts have various pagination systems and many inserted sections.

BOOK II

The first chapter of Book II begins at section #55 (twenty-eight pages). It is headed "Chapter V" and corresponds to Section Five which begins the second installment of the serial. Book II opens with the flashback to Dick's first meeting with Nicole in 1917. The criticisms of this aspect of the novel's structure caused Fitzgerald to substitute a straight chronological structure in the "author's final version." It is, therefore, noteworthy that the flashback structure is the only scheme represented in the manuscripts. If Fitzgerald ever worked on a different structural scheme during the composition of *Tender is the Night*, no trace of it has survived.

Section #55 includes fewer of Nicole's letters than appear in the published novel; these are on pages 162-163 of the book. Also, the section ends short of the final three paragraphs of Book II, Chapter 2 of the book (pp. 164-165) which introduce

Gus Struppen's (later Franz Gregorovious) narrative of Nicole's case history. The paginations of section #57 and section #56 show that Book II, Chapter 3—the case history—was an afterthought and was not written until after Chapter 4. It is extremely unlikely, though, that Fitzgerald had ever planned to omit the details of Nicole's illness altogether. The preliminary notes include this information, and nothing would have been gained by keeping Nicole's background mysterious. Chapter 3 (section #56; fifteen pages), along with the end of Chapter 2, was inserted while this draft was in progress. Chapter 4 (section #57; ten pages) lacks the final paragraph of its published form, which was added in the typescript. Section #58 (ten pages), which corresponds to the fifth chapter and part of the sixth, breaks off during the luncheon in Zurich. It is continued by section #59 (eighty-four pages), which carries the story through Book II, Chapter 10. Although the pagination of section #59 (pp. 41-54, 54½, 55-70, 51-57, 78-85, 85½, 86-106, 106½, 107-121) at first seems to indicate that a good deal of cutting and reordering has occurred, this section was written as it stands. The fifteen-page gap between sections #57 and #59 is occupied by section #56 (paged a-o); and the breaks in the pagination of section #59 are explained by the fact that Fitzgerald misread his own numbering (pp. 62-70 were originally numbered 42-50).

On page 51 of section #59 the lines, "But devote half my life to being doctor nurse and company—never. I know what these cases are. One time in twenty this is all. No! No never. I'd rather not see her again" are spoken by Dick during the conference with Dr. Krammer (later Dohmler) at what corresponds to page 185 of the book. In the typescript this warning is given to Dick by Struppen. This was a sound revision; since the rest of the scene emphasizes Dick's indecision, the point is better made by the practical Swiss doctor.

Section #59 carries the flashback to the point when Rosemary appears on the beach in the opening of the novel. Fitzgerald's transition out of the flashback is accomplished with considerable skill. The flashback sequence ends with a free-association passage (Book II, Chapter 10) in which Nicole reviews her honeymoon, the births of her children, her relapse, and Dick's gradual surrender to the scale of living which her wealth permits. The holograph draft for this passage is longer than the published text, and comparison of the two reveals how Fitzgerald revised a brilliant piece of improvisation into a more economical technical device.

114
Will I be well this time for good. I've been too dependant on you, Dick.
∧ I want to be a fine person like you—I'd study medicine except it would be too late. At least we can spend my money and live well—I'm tired of appartments and waiting for you. If we had a house now and I could study something. <and you could spend two> We've been two years here and you <have more notes and> say you're bored and cant find time for writing. I want to see people too—the Grant <s if he's not> and his new wife if he's not drinking, and Tommy Costello, and <and the Bakers> and some young people.
    Abe

    We're
<Not doctors any more now Dick> getting very stodgy and just like Zurich. Why don't we go to Monte Carlo and see what (movie

211
. . . When I get well I want to be a fine person like you, Dick—I would study medicine except it's too late. We must spend my money and have a house—I'm tired of apartments and waiting for you. You're bored with Zurich and you can't find time for writing here and you say that it's a confession of weakness for a scientist not to write. And I'll look over the whole field of knowledge and pick out something and really know about it, so I'll have it to hang on to if I go to pieces again. You'll help me, Dick, so I won't feel so guilty. We'll live near a warm beach where we can be brown and young together.

115

man) means by a psychological movie. It might be fun and a change and you say yourself the pamphlets ought to be collected in English—you say always that <s> its a confession of weakness for a scientist not to write. You're the smartest of any of them, Dick, Gus Struppens told me a dozen times. You ought to now really—you increased your wine ration while I was sick, oh yes you did. I <wa> only wish I could join you—it looks so good.

And I'll survey the whole field of knowledge and pick out something and really know something about it, <in> so I'll have it to hang on to in case I go to pieces again. You'll help me, Dick.

    I adore him and I must show
<conquer> him I am worth something, as good as he is. He says I must not go to extremes but

116

think of him as a <hole wi> whole with all his faults. But sometimes he has none and sometimes he is all faults and bitches me. He is more true to
        <My enemy>
his friends than to me. He is

unhappy, but I will take him to a warm beach where we can be brown and young together . . .

. . . Isn't it terrible. We simply go around holding our breath. Look Mary—the view from back here—for all this I'm counting on amaranth ect (look up in notes). We wont be <m> able to ⟨move in⟩ ∧ before next year but they're keeping the hotel open this summer. Oh, that cess-pool. I simply hope the memory of it wont poison all the time we're here.

The revisions show again how good a critic of his work Fitzgerald was. The temptation in a tour-de-force passage like this is to include too much—thereby weakening the effectiveness of the device, which is essentially a device of economy. In this particular case the function of the reverie is not only to supply background details about the early years of the marriage, but to suggest the pressures that eventually destroy Dick. The chief pressure is Nicole's attack on Dick's independence through her wealth and through her need for him as a psychiatrist. It is enough, then, to indicate the money issue in connection with the larger apartment without bringing in the compromise arrangement whereby Dick paid only for the part of the apartment he used. These financial compromises through which Dick loses his integrity bit by bit are directly connected with the collapse of his career; but here it is sufficient to indicate the problem without mentioning specific details. The financial arrangement for the Villa Diana—described in Book II, Chapter 12 at a time when Dick's morale is low—makes the point more emphatically.

The reference to Dick's increased wine consumption at section #59, page 115 is important, but Fitzgerald probably felt that this was too early for Dick's alcohol problem to manifest itself. One excision that can be challenged is that of the paragraph on pages 115-116 which exposes Nicole's desire to tighten her grasp on Dick and her jealousy of the energy he gives to his friends. The excised passage makes an important point about the marriage: that Nicole as wife and patient requires all of Dick's energy. Her double claim literally wears Dick out; then she sloughs him off. The only explanation for the omission of this paragraph would seem to be that Fitzgerald decided this important point was better made dramatically through the scenes in which Nicole's needs drain Dick's resources.

This draft of Book II is the only place in the Dick Diver version in which the ordering of the episodes differs markedly from that in the published novel. As originally written, the next block of seven sections—#60, #61, #63-67—corresponds to II, 11-12, 15, 13, 17, 14; III, 3; and II, 16.

Section	Action	Corresponding chapter of book
#60 & #61	Return to the Riviera after Paris.	II, 11-12
#63	Hysteria at carnival; trip to Gstaad.	II, 15, 12-13
#64	Abe's death; the clinic; Morris scene.	II, 13, 17, 14; III, 3
#65, #66, #67	Morris, and Dick's leave of absence.	III, 3; II, 16

These episodes all prepare for Dick's crack-up by showing the strain of his life with Nicole and by revealing that he can no longer manage situations he formerly handled with ease. But here, in the first holograph draft, the rate of Dick's decline is more rapid than in the book. The episodes are not really linked together in a causal way in the holograph draft, whereas in the book they clearly build up to Dick's collapse. For example, in this draft Nicole's hysteria at the carnival and Abe's death are isolated catastrophes; but in the novel Nicole's relapse is the cause for Dick's leave from the clinic, during which he learns of Abe's murder.

In this block of sections we see Fitzgerald trying to solve the problem of making Dick's decline credible. This is a crucial sequence in the novel, for the reader will not be deeply moved by the crack-up of the infinitely promising hero if it appears merely accidental. Even after Fitzgerald had reorganized Book II into its published form, some commentators felt that Dick's fall was insufficiently motivated, that Fitzgerald had cheated by giving the plot an arbitrary twist and had thereby achieved only a bogus effect of tragedy. What these critics probably objected to, ultimately, is not the manner of Dick's crack-up, but the opening portrait of him. Having accepted him as an admirable person, they found it hard to accept his degrading collapse. But this is the very heart of the novel. If the book has power, it is because Dick is initially so promising and does turn out so miserably. His crack-up is deeply rooted in his character—in his desire to please, in his egotism, and in his romantic view of life. To say that the reader is not prepared for Dick's crack-up is absurd. *Tender is the Night* does not resemble an unmotivated operetta in which the prince suddenly dies on the eve of his elopement with the commoner. The purpose of Book II is to expose the weaknesses of character which contribute to Dick's failure; and then to show how his failing morale gradually brings about a self-alienation from the society in which he lives.

After the flashback is concluded, the consequences of the Paris trip are exposed when Dick admits his love for Rosemary to her mother. In the first version of this scene in section #60 (ten pages), Dick is made to appear almost incapacitated by self-pity at page 8: "He would come into Cannes alone many afternoons and evenings, park his car up by the Croisette and walk along toward the Cafe as if he were going to meet her there. . . . but he never failed to have a desolating sense of loss when he came to his destination." This scene was entirely rewritten in section #61, in which the interview between Dick and Mrs. Prince (Speers) closely resembles the printed version. Fitzgerald made an error in the chapter heading of section #60, which is actually the sixth chapter of the draft, and not "Chapter VII."

Section #61 (twenty-five pages) corresponds to II, 11-12, and Fitzgerald changed the chapter heading from VII to VI. At first glance, the pagination is puzzling, for the numbering (pp. 389-412, in short form) is much higher than that of any earlier section. Section #59, which precedes this, ends on page 121. The numbering does not indicate that section #61 was originally planned for a later position in the story and then shifted forward. Rather, the explanation is that Fitzgerald's secretary was typing his holograph draft while Fitzgerald was still working on it; and at the beginning of section #61 she caught up with him. Fitzgerald then simply began numbering the pages of section #61 from the end of the typescript. This is clearly shown by typescript section #104—which was prepared from section #61—for its first page was originally 389. This explanation also accounts for the high numbering of sections #63 and #64.

A note on page 412 of section #61 indicates that Fitzgerald had planned to insert a short scene with Dick and his children at Book II, Chapter 11 after his meeting with Rosemary's mother. This note also shows Fitzgerald's concern about keeping the focus of the novel unblurred—or what he called keeping out the sideshows—for he warns himself against allowing the children to usurp the reader's attention. A further note on this unwritten scene is in section #62, where Fitzgerald lists domestic details for it. Section #61 has a few passages which were later cut from the typescript, such as a description of the changes in the life on the Riviera and an account of how Dick and a fellow medical student had once tried taking gin rectally. The only one of these passages that is important is a pretentious attempt in Book II, Chapter 11 to discuss Dick's scientific theories. This passage has a bogus quality, and it is clearly outside the scope of the novel. Fitzgerald wisely pruned it from the typescript.

Section #63 (forty-six pages) is complete; the page numbered 500 is only the result of Fitzgerald's mistaking page 449 for 499. In this holograph section there is a major difference in structure from the finished novel, for the material here corresponds to Book II, Chapter 15 followed by the end of II, 12 and the beginning of Book II, Chapter 13 (pp. 245-252, 223-232). Here Nicole's hysterical behavior at the carnival (which corresponds to II, 15—and occurs in Switzerland in the published novel) takes place while the Divers are still on the Riviera. In the published novel this is made the reason for Dick's leave of absence from the clinic, during which the really conclusive symptoms of his deterioration appear. The position of this important episode in the holograph draft has nothing to recommend it. It is not integrated into Dick's decline; nor does it prepare for any other event. The carnival scene is followed in section #63 by the Divers' trip to Gstaad, which corresponds to II, 13. This episode breaks off and is continued in section #64 (seventy-five pages).

Section #64 was written as it stands; the break in the pagination (pp. 438-503, 51-59) is explained by the fact that Fitzgerald misread 503 for 50. Section #64 corresponds to Book II, Chapters 13, 17, 14, and III, 3 (*Tender is the Night* pp. 232-235, 259-261, 236-243, 326-330). During the Gstaad episode the indications of Dick's flagging morale become increasingly clear. He is attracted to the women he sees; he quarrels with Baby Warren's young Englishman; and he gets tight. Nicole is even made to rebuke Dick for drinking too much. There is one intriguing passage in the holograph draft of II, 13; this is an exchange between Dick and Struppen at the end of the chapter in which Dick asks if he has slept with Baby Warren. Fitzgerald omitted this in typescript. Although the passage indicates that Dick has begun to project his own doubts about society, it is out of character for Dick to misjudge the situation so completely.

The most important structural variant in section #64 is that here the news of the murder of Abe North comes earlier than in the published version. This happens in a scene which describes the Divers' return to the Riviera after Gstaad. Except for the material relating to Abe, no trace of this scene survives in the published novel. Page 452 of section #64 opens with a description of the new wave of Riviera people, which includes an actress who is arranging to rent the Villa Diana while the Divers are in Switzerland. During a party on the terrace of the hotel Dick resists her invitation to begin an affair with her and learns from a director that Rosemary has been having romantic experiences in Hollywood. Then he hears the news about Abe:

(480)

He felt a sharp abdominal pain, "Pull down the blinds ect," but it was gone in a moment.

"She was a nice child," he said lightly, "When are you going to make that picture with me."

"By God, I'll start it tomorrow," ~~~~ if you'll give me the data," said X, and then to the ~~woman~~ short story writer, "I want to do a one reel ~~p~~ movie about psychology, what goes on inside people's minds all visualized. ~~Dick~~ Dr. Diver's a famous psychologist but he can't ~~think any~~ to think of any approach."

People were dancing on the terrace; the name and only the name Black Bottom had reached Europe, and now a stout man whom ~~began~~ Dick had never

(461)

seen began kicking alternately to left and right with a clownish expression announcing "This is the Black Bottom." Gulled by his strong voice the European Americans began to imitate him carefully under the impression that they were correctly performing the dance, and the movie director just returned from the states bent double with laughter "That's no more the Black Bottom than the Lancers!"

"Show us then."
"I can't do it but —" He pointed at the actress, "I'll bet she can."

The latter shook her head.
"Too hard," she said to Dick, "That

tunes from Abe Grant's show, isn't it. Isn't it terrible."

"It's from Abe Grant's show but I think it's pretty good."

"I don't mean that, I mean about him."

"What is it? Is he in some jam?"

"Didn't you read the Herald this morning?"

"No, I didn't."

"He's dead. He was beaten to death in a speakeasy in New York. He just managed to crawl home to the Racquet club to die."

"Abe Grant!"

"Yes, it's all in the paper. They —"

"Abe Grant —" Nicole was

listening too across the table, "I've got to get a paper. Are you sure he's dead?"

Dick stood up. Below him he heard the writer say positively to the actress "But it wasn't the Racquet Club — he crawled to it was the Harvard Club. ~~I know Abe Grant and~~ I'm quite sure he doesn't belong to the Racquet Club—"

"The ~~paper~~ said so."

"It must have been a mistake. I know Mr Grant and I'm quite sure."

"Beaten to death in a speakeasy."

The stout man ~~does~~ still doing his ~~Its~~ bogus Black Bottom to Abe Grant's tune, danced past them chuckling and winked By now the dancers realized from the ~~silly~~ ease of its agreement had begun & realized they had been fooled ~~but they kept on, smiling at each other and~~ ~~...~~ having just as much fun ~~...of children.~~

"I thought he wasn't drinking, I thought he was working hard at last."

"I happen to know most of the members of the raquet club," the short story writer insisted, "It must have been the Harvard—"

All the ~~On his~~ way up to the hotel Dick could hear the dancers feet still hitting the terrace, with in the ~~silly dance~~ the imprecise abandon of children

Tender is the Night is a mood piece, and it is significant that nowhere in this draft does Fitzgerald betray any uncertainty about his mood effects. In both the Munich scene at Book II, Chapter 17 of the published text and the Riviera scene in section #64, the announcement of Abe's murder is surrounded by bitterly ironic details. In the Riviera setting Abe's tragedy is made to seem an almost unimportant intrusion into the frivolous pursuits of expatriate society. In both versions the news about Abe comes against the background of one of his own jazz tunes; and in both, people who did not know him argue about which club he crawled to.

The function of Abe's death is to prepare for Dick's collapse. The world of *Tender is the Night* is, as Nicole remarks at Book I, Chapter 22, a world in which smart men go to pieces. After proud, sensitive, brooding Abe North has gone, Dick is left with Barban and McKisco, Struppen and Baby Warren—and they are too many for him.

There is one thing to be said for the position of the scene in the holograph version. Coming here just before the Divers' departure from the Riviera, it marks the end of the happy time the Divers shared with Abe on the beach, a time of peace the Divers will not be able to recapture. But the final placement of the scene is far more effective because there the blow of Abe's death is made part of a sequence of events which culminates in Dick's dreadful behavior in Rome. In the published text the news about Abe is followed by the description of a parade of veterans going to place wreaths on the graves of their comrades. They are symbolically burying Abe—who in a sense is a war casualty—but they are also mourning the death of the old, ordered, pre-war world. This is followed by the death of Dick's father—Dick's first moral guide—which deprives him of another connection with his former values.

At page 465 of section #64 "Chapter VII" begins. This corresponds to Book II, Chapter 14 of the book and to Section Seven of the serial version. After Dick's dream of war and disaster, there is an account of his day at the clinic. In the holograph draft this sequence includes the scene between Dick and Morris, the Australian kleptomaniac. In the published text Nicole's hysteria at the carnival comes at this point; and the Morris scene appears at III, 3, where it results in Dick's leave of absence. At page 52 of section #64 when Dick and Struppen are discussing the problem of Dick's drinking, Fitzgerald inserted a warning to himself: "Beware Ernest in this scene." This probably meant that Fitzgerald was tempted to write the scene in a style of clipped understatement; however, the scene bears no resemblance to Hemingway's technique. Section #64 breaks off while Struppen and Dick are discussing his situation, and it is concluded in sections #65 (one page), #66 (two pages), and #67 (one page). In the first of these, Dick mentions his anxiety about Nicole's tippling. This is not mentioned again in any draft, and Fitzgerald probably intended it as an alibi Dick had made up. Dick allows Struppen to persuade him to take a trip in section #66. As in the published version, the break with Struppen is forestalled. Section #67, a typescript of #66, is marked "End Chapter VII."

The next block of material consists of sections #68-#76; this completes Book II. Several scenes which were later cancelled are included in this sequence.

The material corresponding to Book II, Chapter 16 is present in two sections—#68 (eight pages) and #69 (six pages). Like II, 10, this chapter is a free-association reverie. It is transitional, and its function is to suggest Dick's disenchantment as he leaves the clinic on his way to what will be a series of disasters. While preparing this draft, Fitzgerald wrote only #68 (headed "Chapter VII?"), which depicts Dick's mood during a train trip from the clinic to Zurich. This occupied five pages of the first typescript draft in section #106. Only after the typescript had been prepared did Fitzgerald write holograph section #69 (numbered pp. 6-11 and headed "Chapter VIII continued"), which describes the plane trip from Zurich to Munich. This was simply added to the typescript. In a later typescript the two scenes were conflated into the published version, which takes place during the plane trip.

At the end of section #69 Fitzgerald added this note: "Now

cheerful cafe scene but remember to avoid Hemmingway." Fitzgerald's awareness of Hemingway—as a competitor and as a critic—has been noted before in this study. Fitzgerald later described the problem in "Handle with Care," one of the *Crack-Up* essays:

> . . . a third contemporary had been an artistic conscience to me —I had not imitated his infectious style, because my own style, such as it is, was formed before he published anything, but there was an awful pull toward him when I was on a spot.[3]

Fitzgerald probably found it easy to visualize the Munich meeting between Tommy and Dick in terms of Hemingway's technique—the clipped sentences, the ironic understatement, the inventories of drinks. At the same time, Fitzgerald recognized the danger of Hemingway's influence in terms of his artistic pride and in terms of corrupting his own style. He was obviously determined to avoid this snare, even at the cost of writing what were probably painful warnings to himself. The popular image of the Fitzgerald who wrote *Tender is the Night* as a broken man desperately grinding out a novel is neither fair nor accurate. As the references to Hemingway indicate, Fitzgerald was worried about his work, but he was also determined to keep his art uncompromised.

The first holograph draft of Book II, Chapter 17, the café scene in Munich, differs markedly from the published version. Here it begins in section #70 (seven pages) with a flashback to the original meeting between Tommy and Dick when Dick was at Johns Hopkins. From the beginning of their acquaintance there was a tension between them which was caused by Tommy's scarcely concealed scorn for the weakness he detected in Dick. The material in section #70 was discarded soon after it was written, and the café scene was rewritten in section #71 (eighteen pages).

The mood of II, 17—the Munich café scene—here differs from that of the published version because in this draft Abe's murder has been already announced. In the printed text, the news of Abe's death comes in this chapter, which produces a mood of shock and pain. As it stands here, the function of the scene is to indicate that the relationship between Dick and Tommy has changed since their last meeting on the Riviera—they are no longer equals. Tommy, a conqueror, is now waiting for the time when he can take Nicole.

The sections in this draft that correspond to Book II, Chapters 18-19 differ significantly from the printed text and have scenes that were deleted. This material is particularly important because it bears on Fitzgerald's attempts to document Dick's crack-up.

It is interesting to compare the symptoms of Fitzgerald's crack-up with those he invented for Dick.

. . . I began to realize that for two years my life had been a drawing on resources that I did not possess, that I had been mortgaging myself physically and spiritually up to the hilt. What was the small gift of life given back in comparison to that?—when there had once been a pride of direction and a confidence in enduring independence.

I realized that in those two years, in order to preserve something—an inner hush maybe, maybe not—I had weaned myself from all the things I used to love—that every act of life from the morning tooth-brush to the friend at dinner had become an effort. I saw that for a long time I had not liked people and things, but only followed the rickety old pretense of liking. I saw that even my love for those closest to me was become only an attempt to love, that my casual relations—with an editor, a tobacco seller, the child of a friend, were only what I remembered I *should* do, from other days. All in the same month I became bitter about such things as the sound of the radio, the advertisements in the magazines, the screech of tracks, the dead silence of the country —contemptuous at human softness, immediately (if secretively) quarrelsome toward hardness. . . .

There were certain spots, certain faces I could look at. Like most Middle Westerners, I have never had any but the vaguest race prejudices. . . . in these latter days I couldn't stand the sight of Celts, English, Politicians, Strangers, Virginians, Negroes (light or dark), Hunting People, or retail clerks, and middlemen in general, all writers (I avoided writers very carefully because they can perpetuate trouble as no one else can)—and all the classes as classes and most of them as members of their class . . .[4]

Though Fitzgerald's collapse came in 1936, these symptoms had been developing since at least as early as 1930. In addition to drinking (whether as cause or effect), both his case and Dick's display the same symptoms: a weariness of people, an inability to participate in routine human relationships, irrational antipathies, and a mounting bigotry. In *Tender is the Night* Dick's breakdown is foreshadowed most clearly by his drinking, his inability to function in situations he once controlled, and his class hatreds—particularly for Englishmen and Italians. These symptoms had appeared in a sketchier form in Anthony Patch of *The Beautiful and Damned*. Dick and Anthony share another symptom of emotional bankruptcy, indulgence in casual affairs.

At Book II, Chapter 18 the pace of Dick's collapse accelerates, and in the holograph draft his unfaithfulness to Nicole is introduced. Clearly, Dick's interest in other women is both a yielding to desire and a sign of his need for approval. This need to be reassured that he is still attractive is a far cry from his old attitude of accepting adoration without responding. His reciprocation, though limited, of Rosemary's passion in Book I was the first clear sign that his morale was damaged; and in Book II he displays an outright hunger for new women.

In section #72 (fifty-eight pages) Dick becomes involved in a nasty situation at Innsbruck as the result of his attentions to the Morgans' (the name later becomes McKibben) governess, who is actually Morgan's mistress. Dick and the girl are surprised by Morgan, and a quarrel results during which Dick tries to be kind to Mrs. Morgan. It is inconceivable that the Dick Diver of Book I would have lusted for this woman or that he would have allowed himself to be dragged into such a messy situation afterwards. This episode was retained through serial publication but replaced in the book by a brief scene in which Dick is attracted by an unnamed woman.

As in the book, the Innsbruck episode is immediately followed by the news of Dick's father's death. Although the senior Diver does not appear in the novel, he had a profound influence on Dick, who always referred judgments back to his father's principles. When he learns that his father is dead, Dick is compelled to judge himself by the standards his father taught him —and by these standards Dick recognizes his corruption.

Dick's reaction to the loss of his father is moving, probably because the feeling in the scene was based on Fitzgerald's response to the death of his father. Edward Fitzgerald died in 1931, while Zelda Fitzgerald was undergoing treatment in Switzerland. Fitzgerald came to America for the funeral. Like Dick, Fitzgerald loved his father and recognized him as a moral guide—even though he was pained by the knowledge that his father was a failure. Edward Fitzgerald came from Southern stock and tried to teach his son respect for the ante-bellum concepts he himself had been raised by: " 'good instincts,' honor, courtesy, and courage" (p. 266). Though it is difficult to concur completely with Henry Dan Piper's suggestion that *The Great Gatsby* and *Tender is the Night* were efforts on the part of Fitzgerald to "explore and dramatize in fiction the reasons for his father's defeat by life," it is clear that the death of Dick's father is a pivotal scene in the novel.[5]

Shortly after the death of Edward Fitzgerald, his son wrote a brief essay, "The Death of My Father," which remained unpublished until 1951.[6] The pages of the manuscript are torn in half, which was Fitzgerald's way of indicating that the material had been used. Sections #72 and #73 contain material removed from the essay, but most of it was omitted before serialization. It is unlikely that Fitzgerald omitted this for reasons of delicacy, for he was not reticent about converting his most personal feelings into fictional material. The focus in Book II, Chapter 18 is on Dick's recognition of his waywardness; the anecdotes about his father are distracting.

The Death of My Father

Convention would make me preface this with an apology for the lack of taste of discussing an emotion so close to me. But all my criterions of taste disappeared when on the advice of a fairy I read Mrs. Emily Price Post's Book of Etiquete some months ago.[7] Up to that time I had always thought of myself as an American gentleman, somewhat crazy and often desperate and bad but partaking of the sensitivity of my race and class and with a record of many times having injured the strong but never the weak. But now I don't know—the mixture of the obvious and the snobbish in that book—and it's an honest book, a frank piece of worldly wisdom written for the new women of the bull market—has sent me back again to all the things I felt at twenty. I kept wondering all through it how Mrs. Post would have thought of my father.

I loved my father—always deep in my subconscious I have referred judgments back to him, [to] what he would have thought or done. He loved me—and felt a deep responsibility for me—I was born several months after the sudden death of my two elder sisters and he felt what the effect of this would be on my mother, that he would be my only moral guide. He became that to the best of his ability. He came from tired old stock with very little left of vitality and mental energy but he managed to raise a little for me. <We walked downtown in the summer to have our shoes shined, me in my sailor suit and father in his always beautifully cut clothes, and he told me the few things I ever learned about life until a few years later from a Catholic priest, Monsignor Fay. What he knew he had learned from his mother and grandmother, the latter a bore to me—"If your grandmother Scott heard that she would turn over in her grave." What he told me were simple things.

"Once when I went in a room as a young man I was confused, so I went up to the oldest woman there and introduced myself and afterwards the people of that town always thought I had good manners." He did that from a good heart that came from another America—he was much too sure of what he was, much too sure of the deep pride of the two proud women who brought him up, to doubt for a moment that his own instincts were good. It was a horror to find the natural gesture expressed with cynical distortion in Mrs. Price Post's book.>

We walked downtown in Buffalo on Sunday mornings and my white ducks were stiff with starch and he was very proud walking with his handsome little boy. We had our shoes shined and he lit his cigar and we bought the Sunday papers. When I was a little older I did not understand at all why men that I knew were vulgar and not gentlemen made him stand up or give the better chair on our verandah. But I know now. There was new young peasant stock coming up every ten years and he was of the generation of the colonies and the revolution.

Once he hit me. I called him a liar—I was about thirteen, I think, and I said if he called me a liar he was a liar. He hit me—he had spanked me before and always with good reason, but this time there was ill feeling and we were both sorry for years, I think, though we didn't say anything to each other. Later we used to have awful rows on political subjects on which we violently [dis]agreed but we never came to the point of personal animosity about them but if things came to fever heat the one most affected quitted the arena, left the room.

<I don't see how all this could possibly interest anyone but me.>

I ran away when I was seven on the fourth of July—I spent the day with a friend in a pear orchard and the police were informed that I was missing and on my return my father thrashed me according to the custom of the nineties—on the bottom—and then let me come out and watch the night fireworks from the balcony with my pants still down and my behind smarting and knowing in my heart that he was absolutely right. Afterwards, seeing in his face the regret that it had to happen, I asked him to tell me a story. I knew what it would be—he had only a few, the story of the spy, the one about the man hung by his thumbs, the one about Early's march.

Do you want to hear them? I'm so tired of them all that I can't make them interesting. But maybe they are because I used to ask father to repeat and repeat and repeat.

Pages 461-462 and 465-466 of section #72 include Dick's memories of his father, which duplicate Fitzgerald's memories in "The Death of My Father"—the going for the papers together, the "liar" argument, and the Civil War stories.

Chapter 19 here includes a rather long shipboard sequence

which was retained through serial publication; and in this the effect of his father's death is shown through Dick's actions during the voyage back to Europe. He becomes involved with an unpleasant woman; and his old urge to be helpful prompts him to try to aid a young wastrel who had jumped overboard. This includes nine pages of typescript copies from the Kelly version.

Both encounters are unsatisfactory to Dick. Although this material does add to the documentation of Dick's decline, it is weak. Fitzgerald later described these episodes as "irrelevancies." The scene with the woman only repeats the point that was made in the Innsbruck chapter, and it is confusing because no exposition is provided for it.[8] The material about Curly, the boy who jumped overboard—rewritten from the Kelly version—is rather more relevant. It makes the point that this good-for-nothing who does not care about consequences can survive, but that Dick has invested too much in his relations with people and cannot even escape through dissipation.

Pages 491-493 of sections #72-73 give a more elaborate analysis of Dick's feelings of apprehension upon returning to Europe than does the book. Here he admits to himself that he is trapped in his failure:

His heart was gone wrong and he knew it, and it was the only heart he would ever ha<d>ve and as strong a one as he had known.

Chapter 19 is continued in section #73 and here there is a longer account than in the book of Dick's attentions to the bewildered party of American tourists he picks up.

Section #74 (eleven pages) concludes Chapter 19. This is headed "Sequence A" and describes Dick's reactions to meeting Rosemary in Rome. It is a significant scene, for both the novel and Dick's decline began at the time of his initial meeting with Rosemary, and this second meeting provides a gauge for measuring Dick's decline during the three intervening years. In section #74 Dick's feelings about Rosemary are analyzed in greater detail than in the book. Here Dick recognizes both his physical appetite for Rosemary and his egotistical need to conquer her. Some of this analysis has a rather pretentious quality, and it was probably trimmed because Fitzgerald found it more effective to demonstrate the effect of the encounter on Dick through action in the next chapters.

Chapters 20-21 are in section #75 (fifty-four pages) and deal with Dick's seduction of Rosemary and his realization that she really means very little to him because he has lost his capacity to be interested in people. Dick's affair with Rosemary is the strongest symptom so far of his deterioration; stronger than the casual pick-ups at Innsbruck and on the ship, for he takes advantage of Rosemary's old feeling about him. He does not seduce her so much as he accepts her pity in the form of her body. This sequence draws rather heavily on "Jacob's Ladder" for the feelings of an older man about a young actress. In the story—as in *Tender is the Night*—the man had previously failed to reciprocate the girl's passion, and now he is jealous of her young suitor. "Jacob's Ladder" includes a scene in which the man visits a movie location on which the actress is working, where he is annoyed by a would-be Valentino named Raffino. Nicotera, the Latin lover of *Tender is the Night*, is named Raffino in this draft. Several speeches in Chapter 20—for example, Rosemary's comment about having sex appeal in the rushes—are taken from the story. The touch about two technicians quarreling over which one is a dope addict was used in Francis Melarky's visit to Brady's studio.

In section #75 Chapters 20 and 21 are more detailed than in either the serial or the book. Here Dick's affair with Rosemary consumes five days instead of three. The actual seduction occurs on the second day in both the holograph and printed forms. Nothing important occurs during the extra two days in section #75: the fourth day is described in a single sentence, and the quarrel about Raffino is continued on the fifth day. Fitzgerald later cut several passages in which Dick or the author analyzed Dick's feelings about his behavior with Rosemary. The scene in Book II, Chapter 20 during which Dick first tries to make love to Rosemary in her room gave Fitzgerald trouble, for he kept making minor revisions in it all through the drafts. In section #76 there is a two-page holograph rewrite of this scene. One of Fitzgerald's problems was to find a way for Rosemary to tell Dick that she is menstruating. The book has a compound of both descriptions, with the substitution of this final remark: "No, not now—those things are rhythmic" (p. 275).

Chapters 22 and 23, the brawls with the cabmen and police, were not rewritten for this draft. Section #14, a carbon copy from the Francis Melarky version, was inserted at this point. Fitzgerald's instructions to his typist specify that Dick is to be substituted for Francis, and Rosemary for Charlotte Melarky. The idea of having Baby Warren aid Dick came later, and there can be no question that Baby is the better choice for this role. The information she gains about Dick supplies her with a weapon she will save until the Warren sisters decide to dispense with Dr. Diver's services.

BOOK III

The physical evidence in the manuscript for the final book of *The Drunkard's Holiday* indicates that Fitzgerald's work on it progressed rapidly. It is clean copy; and instead of the scene-by-scene construction he had used in the first two books, there are holograph sections of seventy and eighty-five pages. The conclusion that the rate of progress on Book III was the result of Fitzgerald's confidence in his writing is contradicted by his rueful admission that this part of the novel did not receive as much of his careful attention as the first two books. In March of 1935—nearly a year after the publication of the novel—he wrote to Maxwell Perkins:

It has become increasingly plain to me that the very excellent organization of a long book on the finest perceptions and judgment in time of revision do not go well with liquor. A short story can be written on a bottle, but for a novel, you need the mental speed that enables you to keep the whole pattern in your head and ruthlessly sacrifice the sideshows as Ernest did in "A Farewell to Arms." If a mind is slowed up ever so little it lives in the individual part of a book rather than in the book as a whole; memory is dulled. I would give anything if I hadn't had to write Part III of "Tender is the Night" entirely on stimulant. If I had one more crack at it cold sober I believe it might have made a difference. Even Ernest commented on sections that were needlessly included and as an artist he is as near as I know for a final reference.[9]

Since Hemingway's letter to Fitzgerald is not available, one can only guess at the sections he thought were "needlessly included." Fitzgerald planned to omit the Divers' visit to Mary North from the "author's final version"; hence, this episode may have been one of the things Hemingway objected to. The episode is, however, important in revealing Dick's mood after his departure from the clinic; and Cowley's decision to include it was sound. The only other episode in Book III which may be regarded as expendable is Dick's interview with the Chileans. All the other episodes in this book—such as the party on Golding's yacht and Dick's aquaplane stunt—document the despair which underlies Dick's collapse. Even so, some critics have found Dick's collapse the least convincing element in the novel.

Fitzgerald was well pleased with the mood of Book III. In a letter to H. L. Mencken written after Fitzgerald had seen the reviews of the novel, he admits that the first section is too long but insists that everything else in the book was based on a plan that he still feels is sound:

. . . I would like to say in regard to my book that there was a deliberate intention in every part of it except the first. The first part, the romantic introduction, was too long and too elaborated, largely because of the fact that it had been written over a series of years with varying plans, but everything else in the book conformed to a *definite intention* and if I had to start to write it again tomorrow I would adopt the same plan, irrespective of whether I had, in this case, brought it off or not brought it off. That is what most of the critics fail to understand (outside of the fact that they fail to recognize and identify anything in the book) that the motif of the 'dying fall' was absolutely deliberate and did not come from any diminution of vitality, but from a definite plan.

That particular trick is one that Ernest Hemmingway and I worked out—probably from Conrad's preface to 'The Nigger'— and it has been the greatest 'credo' in my life, ever since I decided that I would rather be an artist than a careerist. I would rather impress my image (even though an image the size of a nickel) upon the soul of a people than be known, except in so far as I have my natural obligation to my family—to provide for them. I would as soon be anonymous as Rimbaud, if I could feel that I had accomplished that purpose—and that is no sentimental yapping about being disinterested. It is simply that having once found the intensity of art, nothing else that can happen in life can ever again seem as important as the creative process. . . .[10]

Among the preliminary notes for the novel in section #49 are two pieces which deal with Book III, a graph of the action and a "Summary of Part III." Since the graph is numbered up to page 548, and the holograph draft that corresponds to Book III, Chapter 1 begins at page 549, it is obvious that this graph was prepared when Fitzgerald began work on Part III—not when he prepared the preliminary notes. The "Summary of Part III" cannot be dated, but the content makes it likely that it was prepared with the graph.

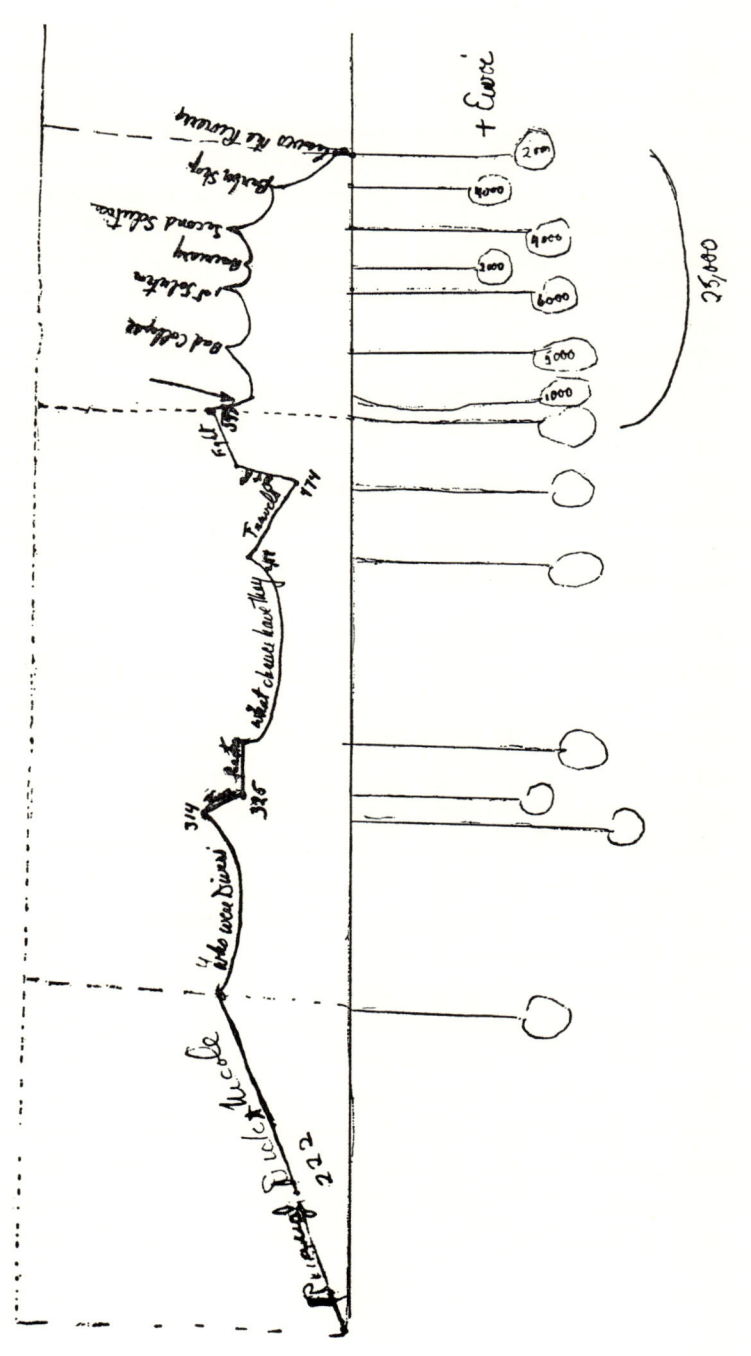

11,000   Summary of Part III (1st half)

The Divers, *as a marriage* are at the end of their resources. Medically Nicole is *nearly* cured but Dick has given out & is sinking toward alcoholism and discouragement. It seems as if the completion of his ruination will be the fact that cures her—almost mystically. However this is merely hinted at. Dick is still in controll of the situation and thinks of the matter practically. They must separate for both their sakes. In wild bitterness he thinks of one tragic idea but controls himself and manages a saner one instead.

His hold is broken, the transference is broken. He goes away. He has been used by the rich family and cast aside.

Part III is as much as possible seen through Nicole's eyes. All Dick's stories such as are *absolutely necessary:* Edwardo, father, auto catastrophe (child's eyes perhaps), Struppen quarrel?, girls on Rivierra must be told without putting in his reactions or feelings. From now on he is mystery man, at least to Nicole with her guessing at the mystery.

The "bad collapse" referred to in the graph is the Ferris wheel and auto-accident episode, which appears in Book III of this draft. It is significant that Fitzgerald originally intended the third book to be about 23,000 words, but that it is about 35,000 words as published. He apparently had hoped for an even sharper decline in Dick than he was able to achieve.

Section #77 (twelve pages) corresponds to Book III, Chapter 1 and to Section Ten of the serial version. It is headed "Chapter XII," which is an obvious error. "Chapter VIII" continues through the seduction of Rosemary; the inserted material about the brawl was probably reckoned as "Chapter IX"; and so section #77 is actually the tenth chapter of *The Drunkard's Holiday*. This material very closely resembles Book III, Chapter 1 of the published text.

In section #78 (forty-eight pages) there are interesting variants. The fact that this section repeats in part the pagination of section #77 is explained by reference to the typescript prepared from this draft. Again, Fitzgerald changed his numbering system when the typist caught up with him. Section #78 corresponds to Book III, Chapter 2 and the end of Book III, Chapter 3. The missing material of Book III, Chapter 3 is the incident at the clinic with Morris; in this draft that scene appears in Book II.

As in the published text, Struppen (Gregorovious) uses Dick's depression about the death of Miss Holt as the first wedge to force Dick out of the partnership. It is interesting that their diagnoses are reversed in the holograph and printed texts. In the book it is in character for Gregorovious to insist that the woman had neurosyphilis, but here it is Dick who makes that diagnosis. In all probability, this was originally intended as an indication of Dick's new bitterness; but in revising, Fitzgerald decided that the diagnosis would be more effectively used to estrange the partners. As it appears in section #78, the material corresponding to Book III, Chapter 2 contains a detailed account of Dick's interview with Francisco, the Chilean homosexual, at Lausanne. This is closer to the book form than to the serial, which was bowdlerized. The second interview with Senor Pardo y Cuidad Real (who is here named Senor Suprema), in which Dick refuses the case, is longer than in either the serial or the book version. This non-essential material was wisely pruned. The entire episode with the Chileans could have been omitted without damaging the novel, for its function is merely to emphasize the corruptness of the society Dick once undertook to heal. It has no direct influence on Dick's crack-up. Fitzgerald tried to integrate the material about the Chileans into the story of Dick's decline by having Lady Caroline insult Dick on the yacht (section #80) with the statement that he was seen associating with homosexuals in Lausanne. The point is that his reputation has fallen so far that a professional interview with a patient can be used to slander him. Dick ironically refers to his reputed homosexuality in this draft during his final interview with Mary at section #85, but Fitzgerald subsequently cut this. Fitzgerald seems to have been intrigued by the idea, for in the cancelled material in section #64 about Dick and the actress who rents the villa, it is mentioned that she starts a rumor about his homosexuality.

The material about the Chileans is followed by the episodes dealing with Nicole's father and the outbreak of hostility between Nicole and Kaethe Struppen (Gregorovious). Dick's reaction to Warren's recovery and Nicole's arrival is stronger here. He appears confused by the series of events, and rather thoughtlessly insists on introducing Nicole to Francisco. There is a note in section #78 indicating that the description of the types of homosexuals Fitzgerald had originally written for the Melarky version was to be inserted in Book III, Chapter 2; but this material was later deleted. The Lausanne sequence ends on page 599 with a repetition of the goodbye motif used at the end of the Gstaad sequence: "Goodbye all you unfortunates, good bye <h> Hotel of <t> Three <w> Worlds, Goodbye Lausanne, Farewell, Goodbye goodbye."

Before the split between Dick and Struppen occurs, Fitzgerald inserted this note on page 600: "(Transpose auto incident from Rivierra to this place.)" This is not the final position of this scene. It was ultimately placed at the beginning of the Divers' residence at the clinic in Book II and used as the reason for Dick's disastrous leave of absence. (See the chart below on sequence of action.) In this draft Dick's depression over Nicole's relapse prompts him to give Struppen the opportunity to dissolve the partnership. Fitzgerald realized that this turn of the plot is weakly motivated, for in revising the typescript he used the Morris episode to precipitate Dick's departure from the clinic.

Sequence of Action

Holograph Draft Chapter VI	*Serial*	*Book*
Return to Riviera	Return to Riviera	Return to Riviera—II, 11-12
Nicole's hysteria at carnival		
Gstaad	Gstaad	Gstaad—II, 13

Holograph Draft	Serial	Book
Chapter VII	*Section VII*	
Riviera—news of Abe's death		
Clinic	Clinic	Clinic—II, 14
Morris case	Nicole's hysteria at carnival	Nicole's hysteria at carnival—II, 15
Chapter VIII	*Section VIII*	
Dick's leave of absence	Dick's leave of absence	Dick's leave of absence—II, 16
Munich	Munich—news of Abe's death	Munich—news of Abe's death—II, 17
Innsbruck and governess	Innsbruck and governess	Innsbruck (governess cut)—II, 18
Death of Dick's father	Death of Dick's father	Death of Dick's father—II, 18
Return to America, memories of father, and Civil War story	Return to America	Return to America—II, 19
Woman on ship and man overboard	Woman on ship and man overboard	
Dick's reaction to return		
Rome and Rosemary	Rome and Rosemary	Rome and Rosemary—II, 19-21
[Chapter IX]	*Section IX*	
Brawl and Rosemary and police	Brawl and Baby and police	Brawl and Baby and police—II, 22-23
Chapter XII [Chapter X]	*Section X*	
Tensions at clinic	Tensions at clinic	Tensions at clinic—III, 1
Nicole's father	Nicole's father	Nicole's father—III, 2
(Insert auto accident)		
	Morris case	Morris case—III, 3
Break with clinic	Break with clinic	Break with clinic—III, 3

Section #79 (one page) continues section #78 and corresponds to the opening of Book III, Chapter 4. This was typed and included in section #80, but was later crossed out and rewritten. Section #80 (seventy-six pages) corresponds to Book III, Chapters 4-6. Despite the two series of paginations in this section, it is complete. Once again, Fitzgerald changed his numbering system when the typist caught up with him. All the scenes of the published chapters are included: the painful visit with Mary after her new marriage (here her husband is named di Cherelli), the argument with the cook, Dick's drunken impulse to commit suicide on the yacht, and the crucial reappearance of Tommy. Emboldened by Tommy's presence, Nicole for the first time asserts her will against Dick when she ignores his request not to give the jar of chest rub to Tommy. That the thing involved is petty does not mitigate the importance of this act, which prefigures her giving of herself to Tommy when next they meet. This is an important point in the plot, for here the graph of Dick's decline crosses Nicole's ascending line. She is able to assert her will against his; but not without suffering a reaction, for she is not yet strong enough to cut herself loose from the man who has been her husband, psychiatrist, and father surrogate. Rather, Dick has not cut her loose. In describing Nicole's reaction to this incident, Fitzgerald was faced with the problem of indicating just how dependent Nicole still is, and the holograph draft presents a significantly different account from that of the printed text. In Book III, Chapter 6 of the book, the episode ends as Nicole flees in a panic, "afraid of what the stricken man above would feed on while she must still continue her dry suckling at his lean chest" (p. 359). It is clear that she is still dependent on him. Pages 629-630 of holograph section #80 present a different assessment of Nicole's situation. After fleeing Dick in fear "of what the stricken man above would do, still nourishing herself on him," Nicole decides to take the children on a picnic, and in giving the necessary orders she finds a new authority:

Then pushing Lanier aside she walked up to Mlle and said with a voice that niether her grandfather nor Lady Sibly Biers would have found wanting

"This is my house. And I said we are going to have a picnic. The doctor is not going

The phrase "a voice that niether her grandfather nor Lady Sibly Biers would have found wanting" makes it clear that Nicole is now capable of the selfishness of an American tycoon or an English noblewoman, both types who have no use for Dick. This is a good touch, but Fitzgerald sacrificed it because it goes further than he wanted. The direction of the third book is to show Nicole's strength developing to the point when she wants to replace Dick with the hedonistic Tommy, but she cannot until Dick decides it is time—until Dr. Diver prescribes the transfer. The holograph version undercuts this important point by announcing Nicole's autonomy too early.

Fitzgerald made three attempts at the next sequence of the novel—sections #81-83. Section #81 (eighteen pages) is headed "Scene 7 Part III" and corresponds to the beginning of Book III, Chapter 7. This is the scene at the beach during which Dick fails to carry off the aquaplane stunt. An interesting item in this scene is Fitzgerald's search for the right comment for Dick to make to relieve the embarrassment the company feels for him. In section #81 he remarks that he could feel his vertebrae cracking; in section #83 he makes a joke about a man who crossed the ocean three times on the same woman; and in the printed text he admits that he couldn't have lifted a paper doll.

Section #82 (four pages) is a typescript of the beginning of section #81. It is headed "Scene 8 Part III," indicating that Fitzgerald had revised his reckoning of the scene division. Section #83 (eighty-six pages), a complete rewrite of section #81, corresponds to Book III, Chapters 7 and 8, and is headed "Part III Scene 8." This draft opens with an analysis of Nicole's feelings about her predicament, which was lacking in section #81. It is an extremely important passage, for it makes clear Nicole's understanding that Dick alone is deciding their fate.

Though this passage was considerably polished in the typescripts, the ideas were all retained in pages 361-362 of the book.

Section #83 includes some of the most important material in Book III: Nicole's impatient reaction to Dick's doubletalk analysis of Rosemary's acting, which results in Nicole's realization that she is *almost* complete; and her affair with Tommy. Steinberg, however, contends that Dick's remarks in this scene are to be taken seriously because they reveal "Dick's own method of facing people, his own emotional structure. . . . Rosemary cannot follow Dick, but Nicole understands only too well. . . ."[11]

As was his practice with crucial scenes, Fitzgerald supported the hotel-room scene with a symbolic commentary. The drunken sailors and their girls indicate the sort of disorder that has destroyed the order Dick tried to impose on Nicole's world. The cannon shot is part of the device of underlining the turning points of the novel with shots. These holograph scenes very closely resemble their printed versions, but section #83 includes a scene which was condensed in typescript and finally omitted from the novel. After they leave the hotel, Tommy takes Nicole swimming on the private beach of an American gangster, Irv. A transcription of a revised version of this scene in typescript section #127 of the ninth draft is appended to the "author's final version." The surviving bits of the scene appear on page 384 of *Tender is the Night*. It is of thematic significance that Tommy takes Nicole to a gangster's hide-out—and Fitzgerald underlined this by comparing Tommy to a barbaric invader—in contrast to Dick's attempts to protect her from disorder. But the third book of the novel is Dick's, and this scene blurs the focus. Effective as it is, the Irv scene was expendable.

Section #84 (eleven pages), which corresponds to the end of Chapter 8 and the beginning of 9, continues section #83. These two sections were originally a single sequence of ninety-five pages. In section #84 the overt break between Dick and Nicole occurs after her night with Tommy. In the book it is a powerful and subtle scene, but the first draft here is clumsy. At the end of the holograph version Fitzgerald made a critical note on the scene, in which the most important criticism is that it is "unfelt"—unfelt by the author and hence would be unfelt by the reader. This was a serious charge for Fitzgerald to bring against his work, for the romantic theory of composition was at the heart of his art. In Fitzgerald's case emotion was not recollected in tranquility; the emotions he worked with were still raw or at least re-experienced in the act of recollection. This is a crude episode by Fitzgerald's standards. The conclusion is unconvincing; the view of the Divers clinging together goes contrary to the rest of the episode, which develops their estrangement. A more serious flaw is that it spells out an idea the reader should grasp for himself—the fact that the fate of the Divers is still in Dick's hands.

Section #85 includes a re-write of section #84. The new version is more highly charged with feeling and more convincing. The new material describing Nicole's struggle to free herself from Dick's influence exposes all the dissimilarities between these two people and reveals the weakness of their marriage. The fact that Nicole is described as pitting her unscrupulousness against Dick's propriety is of signal importance, for it gets to the very core of their predicament. It was Dick's code of conduct, his desire for order, that brought him into his marriage; and it was Nicole's selfishness which made her commandeer Dick as a husband and enables her to discard him when she outgrows her need for him. The comment that by separating from Dick she was severing an umbilical cord is a very apt figure, for she transferred to Dick her love for her father, just as she is now transferring it to a stronger father figure.

The weakest element in the rewrite is the ending with Dick dripping tears of self-pity. His conclusion—"That was a dirty stinking job, but it had to be done"—is also weakened by self-pity. In the published text it reads: "The case was finished. Doctor Diver was at liberty" (p. 390). This sums up the situation perfectly, by substituting irony for pity. Dr. Diver is, after all, just a doctor who was hired by some rich people on a big case.

Section #85 (fifty-seven pages) completes the novel. It clearly contradicts Cowley's statement in his edition of the revised version that, "At almost the last moment before the fourth installment of *Tender* was printed in *Scribner's*, Fitzgerald inserted a new chapter, the arrest of Lady Caroline and Mary Minghetti. . . ."[12] This episode is included in section #85, which is clearly an early draft, for Mary's surname here is still Vallambrosa. Fitzgerald painstakingly revised this episode in typescript, altering the reactions of Dick and of Nicole. The first draft lacks the long paragraph on page 391 of the book which analyzes Dick's first response to the request for help. This passage, which was inserted in the revised serial galleys (section #162), makes the point that Dick is prompted to help these women by the same trait that has brought about his destruction, his "fatal pleasingness." The passage compares his decision to help Mary and Lady Caroline to his decision to marry Nicole. Another interesting variant in this episode is that in the first draft Nicole is rather cross about being awakened when Dick returns; but in the published text they have a return to their old intimacy, her old admiration for his competence, as he tells her about his experiences.

As first prepared, Book III, Chapter 11, the conference with Tommy at which Dick agrees to a divorce, closely resembles the published text. The *Tour de France* material is not included, but there is a note that it is to be added. The newsvendor, that harbinger of disaster who had pestered Dick five years earlier outside the movie studio, is also missing. He was inserted in typescript.[13]

Book III, Chapter 12, Dick's farewell to the beach (see pp. 141-158) was improved in revision. The first draft in section #85—like the first draft of Book III, Chapter 9—is marred by Dick's self-pity.

(83)

The day before ~~he left~~ Dr. Diver left ~~for the Riviera~~ he spent all the time with his children. ~~He and decided not to~~ tell them ~~what was happening only~~ told that this winter they would be with ~~their~~ Aunt in London, and that ~~sometime~~ soon they were going ~~to be~~ come and see him ~~with their father~~ in America.

~~He was very sad at leaving them but to~~ felt they were safe — The Fräulein who looked after them ~~could~~ was not be discharged without ~~the mutual~~ his consent ~~of father and mother~~.

~~He was sorry he had not had more time for them~~ Dick was glad he had given much to the little girl — as for the boy he ~~did not know~~ had never been certain what ~~to teach tell~~ him or teach him. ~~But~~ he seemed a nice boy, ~~and~~ next morning when ~~the~~ doctor said goodbye to them both he

~~of~~ ~~weak with her cry.~~
and
she
cried.   (84)

wanted to kiss their beautiful heads
of their necks and hold them close
for hours.
~~He~~ was sleeping late — he left
a note for her and one for Baby
Warren who ~~was~~ was just back from Corsica and staying in the house.
He embraced the old gardener who had
made ~~with Dicole's first~~ gardens ~~with them ten~~ years and he
kissed the ~~little~~ Provençal girl who
helped with the children. She had been
with them ~~almost~~ for a decade & Nicole

→ Space
here

~~Nicole~~ & ~~Baby~~ ~~Warren~~
~~Rebecca~~ Gauss' Beach ~~had acquired~~
~~the bright silk screen~~ was peopled with
an advance guard of children when Nicole
and her sister arrived. ~~these that~~
A white sun, ~~almost without a~~ deired

of outline against a white sky, boomed over the windless Mediterranean day. An American photographer from A. and P. was working with his equipment in a precarious shade, and looking up quickly at everyone who came down the stone steps; waiters in shirt sleeves were putting extra ice into the bar; up at the hotel his prospective subjects slept late in darkened rooms upon their recent opiate of dawn.

When Nicole started to come out on the beach in her "first costume", she saw Dick suddenly, sitting

(86)

dressed on a rock above looking out toward Cannes. She shrank back quickly and sat down in the shadow of her bath tent where Baby Warren joined her, saying:

"Dick's up there,"

"I saw him." ¶ "I think he ought go."

"This is his place", said Nicole, "He found him a way Gauss always says he owes everything to Doctor Dwer."

Baby looked quickly at her sister; no wiser than ever she remarked:

"We should let him confine himself to his bycycle excursions. When people are taken out of their depths they lose their heads, no matter how charming a bluff they put up."

Nicole stirred angrily

144

(87)

"Dick was a good husband to me for
six years," she said, "All that time I
never suffered a minute's pain through him,
and he always did his best never to let
anything hurt me."
   Baby's lower jaw projected slightly
"That's what he was educated for," she
said.

The two sisters sat in silence. Baby
was considering marrying the latest
candidate for her hand and money, an
authenticated Hapsburg but she wasn't
really thinking about that. Her own affairs
had long had such a sameness like
diminishing fifths, that as she dried
out they became more important for
their conversational value than
in their essence. The only true existence
her emotions had was in the telling
about them.

Nicole was wondering about cook's eyes

(88)

"Is he gone," Nicole said after awhile, "I think his train leaves at noon."

Baby looked.

"No. But he's moved up on the terrace and he's talking to some women. Anyhow there's so many people on the beach now that he doesn't have to see us."

He did see them, though, as they went out to the beach and followed them with his eyes until they disappeared under the domestic beach parasol. He ~~was s~~ sat with Mary Grant, drinking a double sherry. ~~He had come up to ~~ ~~was not not sure the his~~

"You were like you used to be that night, Dick," she said, "Except at the end when you were horrid to Anne (name) ~~Mary~~. Why aren't you nice like that always you can be."

146

"I suppose so," he said vaguely.

"Your friends still like you, Dick. But you say such awful things to people when you've been drinking. And you do such awful things. I spend most of my time defending you this summer."

He laughed.

"That remark is one of the world's classics," ~~he said~~

"But it's true. Nobody cares whether you drunk or not ~~But~~ but you're so mean." She hesitated, "Even Abe when he ~~was~~ drunk hardest never made as many enemies as you do. Do you think those men like to be called fairies to their face?"

"But I understand now. I'm a fairy."

"Oh, I have heard that but of course it's nonsense. Still if people get off you you they believe everything they want to believe. After that party on Chadbourne's yacht you made aloud in a car a whole speech about him, very contemptuous and superior. Don't you think he heard about it — and don't you think everybody in the car wondered what you thought of them and decided to fight shy of you—"

Dick laughed again but thoughtfully.

"I'm not key any more, I think you're a dull bunch."

"But we're all there is!" cried Mary Grant Vallambrosa whose father had mended pipe, "if you don't like nice people just try the ones who aren't nice and see how you like that! All people want is to have a good time and if you make them unhappy — well you just cut yourself off from nourishment."

"Who nourished me?"

148

(91)

She considered

"Probably you gave more than you got. But you enjoyed yourself."

"We were just figures in a ballet,"

"But it was such a beautiful ballet."

She was having a good time and though she had sat down with him out of duty and fear, having come in her new world to think of him as an *homme manqué*, & really and professionally. She refused another sherry and said

"Drink is back of it. And of course after Abe you can imagine how I feel about drink, drink to excess. It's simply a horror to me, a horror. Just once

"I watch the progress of a charming man toward alcoholism"

"Abe thought he was not an alcoholic in a different way from the

149

way I think I'm not an alcoholic."

"Well, you can see how I feel." Down the steps came Lady XX, tripping with old theatricality on the heels of a neat speck Lesbian with a starched blue shirt and a lovely boy's face. "Nothing is as bad as drunk, nothing, nothing."

Dr. Diver felt fine — he was already comfortably well in advance of the day, he was where a man could comfortably be at the end of a dinner, and he showed nothing of it; only the fine considered yet restrained ulicentritude he directed on Mary. His eyes clear as a child's wooed her, he felt it come on, only momentarily, the necessity and the power of convincing her that he was the last man in the world and she was the last woman.

(93)

"You liked me didn't you," he said, like a man drawing a sword.

"Liked you — I loved you," she said, as if she were doing it, "Everybody loved you. You could have had who you wanted for the asking, but you always got a little tired & passed them on to Nicole."

"~~Unseen~~ Junk. You think that, because there was always a very peculiar something between you and me."

She believed him:
"Was there?"

"Always. I always knew your sadnesses and what they were about and how brave you were ~~about~~ with them."

The inner laughter had begun far inside him and he knew he could not keep it up much longer.

"I thought you knew a lot," she said, "then

about me than anyone has ever known. Perhaps that's why I was so afraid of you when we didn't get along so well."

Their eyes met and he held it a moment longer, his glance falling soft and kind with under it a burning flame of emotion upon her glance; then glances marrying suddenly, and bedding and straining together. Then he their laughter inside ~~it~~ became so loud that it seemed as if Mary must hear it, and he switched ~~off~~ the amber light ~~off~~ ~~and they threw on the blue white so~~ and ~~they~~ ~~were going back~~ were back in the Riviera ~~sun of~~ sun.

"I'm going back to work again." I've known most of the celebrated people of my time, and ~~enjoyed~~ ~~made up~~ ~~of such~~ in a material paradise ~~of~~ and parked my bottom in it, now I'm going back to work, and he added after a minute, "If

(95)

I still can." Mary persisted

"Of course you can." "You must work. Why haven't you."

"You see I was hired on a big case—" he began and stopped. He stood up, his voice jumbling and Mary looked up at him in sudden surprise.

Down below Nicole coming in from a first dip saw him collapse. Gauss's nephew was on the beach and she ran to him and saying "Dr Dver's sick—up there!" But by that time a waiter had sloshed water on his face and with the help of another waiter the doctor had clamored upright, his face very pale. A few people came toward the steps—faces turned upward from under many umbrellas. Mary came down the steps quickly and told ~~Must somebody take him to the station~~ Nicole, "He simply passed out. He

153

had not drunken right there. I never dreamed."

"Get him to the station!" Nicole begged young Gauss.

"I can't go myself, I will send a waiter."

On the high terrace Dick swayed in the arms of a waiter raised his right hand and making a papal cross blessed the beach "semper eternam (quote from the last of mass or benediction). Then under the the impression that he was still talking to Mary he mumbled in a loud voice —

"Final message of Sairy Gamp, the drunken nurse; Power measured in women How many women is power Women are the real gold standard.

By that time two waiters had him and were helping him toward a cab still waving ~~benedictions~~ blessings and consecrating with his hand the ~~earthly~~ maternal paradise he had casually created for a certain group at a certain time as he explained to the waiters. Meanwhile everyone ~~who~~ knew Nicole was so sorry for her that she became really happy and ~~it looked as if her new world~~ to everything turned inside out disclosing such a new lining that it seemed as if her future life would have such a logical background as never was.

⟶

98

Space: ⟶
here

Nicole kept in touch with Dick after her new marriage ~~by means of to Tommy Costello next ro ator~~, through ~~business various~~ letters on business matters and through the recurrent problems that faced them about the children — ~~which~~ who tended to gravitate toward her as she grew better and stronger.

He opened an office in Buffalo, but without much success. ~~he could not find something seemed to be the matter there~~, out what the matter was but a few months later he was in ~~Bufo~~ a little town called Batavia practicing general medicine and later in Lockport doing the same thing. ~~By~~ by accident heard ~~definitely~~ more about his life there than anywhere: that he bycycled a lot, ~~and ~~coming to Buffalo it~~~~ was very much admired and always had a great stack of papers on his desk that were known to be an important treatise on something, almost in process of completion. He told someone he was going to ~~Buffalo~~ to see Rosemary Prince who was playing in a stage play there, and arrived home quite drunk. He was considered to have fine manners and ~~was they~~ made a very vehement speech ~~and made a speech~~ once on the question of drugs; but he became entangled with a ~~little girl~~ sixteen year old girl in a grocery store at the same time that he was involved in a suit about a medical question, so he left Lockport, N.Y. After that he didn't ask for the children to be sent to America but he ~~wrote~~ answered with a sharp letter when Nicole wrote asking him if he needed money. On

> (100) n.y.
>
> the last letter she had from him he was practising *general* medicine in Geneva, ~~New York~~, and Nicole got the impression that he had really settled ~~down~~ and a woman to keep house for him, ~~She~~ *ed. Nicole* looked up Geneva N.y. in an atlas and found it was in the heart of the Finger Lakes section and considered a pleasant town. Perhaps he stayed there like Grant at Galena again, but his ~~latest~~ *note* ~~letter~~ was postmarked from Hornell, which ~~some~~ is some distance from there; ~~so he is~~ in ~~probably in one place or the other~~ any case he is certainly in that section of the country, in one town or another.

That Dick is at this point an *homme manqué* was Fitzgerald's first analysis of the situation, but he finally came to think of Dick as an *homme epuisé*. However, the comment was dropped from the published form. The picture in section #85 of Dick passing out dead drunk, being revived with water dashed in his face, and then being half-carried away by waiters makes his departure embarrassing—which is not the effect Fitzgerald intended. As presented here, Dick's gesture of blessing the beach is robbed of its force by having it accompanied by his drunken mumblings. The blessing is, of course, wholly characteristic of Fitzgerald's sensibility, and it is appropriate to the story. Dick had once been the pope of the beach, and it is fitting that he give his corrupted flock a last blessing. The view of Nicole enjoying the sympathy of her friends is replaced in the published text by a description of Tommy's restraining her from going to Dick. These two events present different evaluations of Nicole, and both are effective. The published version is probably more suitable to her, for Nicole is not just a rich bitch. She had good years with Dick, and it is in character for her to feel sympathy for Dick—just as it is in character for her to allow herself to be restrained by Tommy.

The final chapter, which is the great set piece of writing in the work, is a perfect conclusion to the story of Dr. Diver's holiday. As has been noted, Fitzgerald at one time considered having Dick "fade out as a shyster alienist," but there is no surviving manuscript for this. The first draft of Book III, Chapter 13 is remarkably close to the published text in detail and in tone. Fitzgerald's stock-in-trade was his control over tonal effects, but the use of understatement in this chapter represents the apex of his achievement. The tone is one of infinite regret conveyed through a seemingly dispassionate factual account of Dick's failures in America. All the information about him has a second-hand, picked-up quality, which reinforces the impression of Dick's migration from failure to failure. Comparison of the first draft with the book shows that Fitzgerald was sure from the start of the effect of quiet understatement he wanted.

The published text involved two small, but important, revisions. The added comments about Dick by Nicole and Tommy show that his reputation quickly faded in his old kingdom. Nicole patronizes him, and Tommy is not even jealous of Dick's memory. The other important revision is the deletion of Dick's visit to Rosemary. It is unlikely that Dick would attempt to see her again; Rosemary, Nicole, and Europe are all behind him.

Both texts include the reference to Grant at Galena, which echoes the description of Dick at Book II, Chapter 1 when Dick returned to Zurich in 1919. But now Dick is the post-presidential, ruined Grant. As Fitzgerald remarked, "There are no second acts in American lives." [14]

Chapter VII

Eighth Draft—*Doctor Diver's Holiday*
First typescript of the Dick Diver version

Description & Pagination	Corresponds to TITN	Remarks	Location	Key
H: 8½″ x 11″. 1 p.		Title page, *Doctor Diver's Holiday A Romance.*	Box 3	86
RT: 8½″ x 11″. Pica. 1-18.	I, 1-2. Pp. 3-14.	Chapter I. Grant [North. Prince [Hoyt.	Box 3	87
RT: 8½″ x 11″. Pica. 18-43.	I, 3, 5, 4. Pp. 15-19, 28-31, 20-27.	Noel [Nicole. Seth [Dick.	Box 3	88
RT: 8½″ x 11″. Pica. 44-57, 57½H, 58-96.	I, 6-11. Pp. 32-66.	Chapter II.	Box 3	89
CC: 8½″ x 11″. Pica. 51.	I, 6. P. 37.	Discarded CC of #89?	Box 4	90
CC: 8½″ x 11″. Pica. 95.	I, 11. P. 65.	Discarded CC of #89?	Box 4	91
RT: 8½″ x 11″. Pica. 97-129, insert 129, 130-155.	I, 12-18. Pp. 67-104.	Chapter III.	Box 3	92
T: 8½″ x 11″. Pica. 106.	I, 12. P. 73.	Discarded typescript from #92?	Box 1	93
RT: 8½″ x 11″. Pica. 156-159.	I, 19. Pp. 105-107.	Continued in #96.	Box 3	94

Description & Pagination	Corresponds to TITN	Remarks	Location	Key
CC: 8½″ x 11″. Pica. 181.	I, 20. P. 119.	Discarded CC of #96?	Box 1	95
RT: 8½″ x 11″. Pica. 160-195, 195½H, 196, 196½H, 197-201, 201A-201F, 202, 202-205, insert 205H, 206–213, 213A-213C, 214-221, holograph 222A-222C.	I, 19-25. Pp. 105-148.	Chapter IV. Includes full account of Abe in Ritz bar. Struppen [Gregorovious. See #94.	Box 3	96
T & H: 8½″ x 11″. Pica. 1 p.	I, 25. P. 146.	Discarded from #96?	Box 1	97
H: 8½″ x 13″. 202a-202j.	I, 23. Pp. 132-135.	Insert for #96. Abe in Ritz bar.	Box 1	98
H: 8½″ x 13″. 214a-214d, 215e, 216f.	....	Insert for #96. Abe's return to Ritz bar.	Box 1	99
RT: 8½″ x 11″. Pica. 223-252, insert 252H, 253-261, 262H, 262aH, 263-289, 289½, 290-325. Originally numbered <3-95>.	II, 1-10. Pp. 151-212.	Chapter V. Original of #117.	Box 3	100
CC: 8½″ x 11″. Pica. 235-236 <14-15>.	II, 2. P. 159.	Discarded CC of #100?	Box 4	101
CC: 8½″ x 11″. Pica. 292 <64>.	II, 8. P. 196.	Discarded CC of #100.	Box 4	102

Description & Pagination	Corresponds to TITN	Remarks	Location	Key
CC: 8½" x 11". 285 <55>.	II, 7. P. 190.	Discarded CC of #100?	Box 4	103
RT: 8½" x 11". Pica. 326-335, 337-345, (346-359), 360-390. Originally numbered <389-409, 423-453>.	II, 11-13. Pp. 213-235.	Chapter VI. Ferris wheel scene removed from Riviera; see #108. Abe's death still announced at party. Original of #118 & 119.	Box 3	104
RT: 8½" x 11". Pica. 391-418, 418CC. Originally numbered <455-481>.	II, 14; III, 3. Pp. 236-243, 326-330.	Chapter VII. This includes the Morris episode during account of Dick's day at the clinic. Original of #120.	Box 3	105
RT: 8½" x 11". Pica. 419-494, insert 494, 495-514. Originally numbered <2-5, 481½, 484, 427-475, sequence A 1-16, 490-513>.	II, 16-21. Pp. 253-286.	Chapter VII? [VIII. Includes material about governess, recollections about father, woman on ship, and man overboard. Original of #121 & #122.	Box 3	106
RT: 8½" x 11". Pica. 515-549. Originally numbered <1-35>.	II, 22-23. Pp. 287-300.	Chapter VII [IX. Intermediate stage of Rome brawl. Original of #123. Rosemary Prince [Baby Warren in police episode.	Box 3	107

Description & Pagination	Corresponds to TITN	Remarks	Location	Key
RT: 8½" x 11". Pica. 550-578, [ ], 577-578, 579a-b, (c-d), 412, 579e-o. CC: [ ], 577-578. Originally numbered <549-55, 553-574, [ ], 575-576, [ ], 347-348, 412, 349-359>. Other cancelled paginations illegible.	III, 1-2; II, 15 Pp. 309-330, 244-252.	Chapter XII [X. Ferris wheel scene here removed from #104. "The automobile scene from original copy—For reference only." Original of #124.	Box 3	108
RT: 8½" x 11". Pica. 580½, 581-593, insert 593H, 594-614, insert 614H, 615-623, 623½H. Originally numbered <577-619>.	III, 4-6. Pp. 331-360.	Chapter XI. Includes Nicole's picnic after chest rub incident.	Box 3	109
RT: 8½" x 11". Pica. 624-688, insert 688, 689-697, 697½H, 698-700. Originally numbered <1-77>.	III, 7-13. Pp. 361-408.	Part III Scene 8 [7[Chapter XII. Includes Irv and jail scene.	Box 3	110
T: 8½" x 11". Pica. 6-9.	III, 7. Pp. 365-368.	Discarded typescript from #110?	Box 1	111
CC: 8½" x 11". Pica. 699 <76>.	III, 12-13. Pp. 406-407.	Final Chapter. Discarded CC of #110?	Box 1	112
CC: 8½" x 11". Pica. 700 <77>.	III, 13. Pp. 407-408.	Discarded CC of #110.	Box 6	113

The dummy title page for this typescript has the first appearance of the title *Doctor Diver's Holiday,* and is the first indication that Fitzgerald thought of his book as *A Romance.* This title is clearly an improvement over the title of the holograph draft, *The Drunkard's Holiday,* but Fitzgerald regarded *Doctor Diver's Holiday* as only a working title, for he worried that the public would be indifferent to what it would think was another doctor story.

Fitzgerald has left no note of what he understood by the term "romance" or why he placed this book in that category. He certainly did not mean to indicate that the book was a fantasy or that it was intentionally nonrealistic. Whatever Fitzgerald's private theory about the romance form may have been, his practice conforms to Hawthorne's use of the term in the "Preface" to *The House of the Seven Gables* as a form which permits itself:

> . . . a right to present that truth [of the human heart] under circumstances, to a great extent, of the writer's own choosing or creation. If he think fit, also, he may so manage his atmospherical medium as to bring out or mellow the lights and deepen and enrich the shadows of the picture.[1]

Doctor Diver's Holiday or *Tender is the Night* qualifies as a romance not because of its setting or story—which are both realistic—but because of its atmosphere. The book offers a sustained evocation of a romantic mood, of an evanescent glamor which is replaced by a sense of pain and despair.

Since a late, revised typescript for the serial version of *Tender is the Night* was being set in type by October 27, 1933, Fitzgerald probably completed the holograph draft in August or September at the latest. His typist was working closely behind him—even catching up to him several times—and so the first typescript draft was ready for revision at about the same time. An original and one carbon copy were prepared. Fitzgerald began by revising the original typescript in pencil. In four sections (#96, #100, #109, #110) the revisions were so numerous that a fresh typescript was prepared. Though there are numerous revisions, no extensive rewriting was involved. This is an important distinction. At this stage, Fitzgerald was satisfied with his content and organization, but he was concerned about polishing the style to the hard brilliance that was the stamp of his best work.

In revising, Fitzgerald was chiefly interested in the movement of his sentences and in the accuracy or vividness of his descriptive phrases. Only rarely did he alter the organization of a paragraph—and almost never did he revise for meaning. But he was endlessly patient about trying to make a sentence more graceful or striking.

Fitzgerald's comments about the purely technical aspects of writing are scarce, but a note he wrote to his daughter indicates something about his theory of style:

> About *adjectives:* all fine prose is based on the verbs carrying the sentences. They make sentences move. Probably the finest technical poem in English is Keats' *Eve of Saint Agnes.* A line like:
> The hare limped trembling through the frozen grass,
> is so alive that you race through it, scarcely noticing it, yet it has colored the whole poem with its movement—the limping, trembling, and freezing is going on before your own eyes.[2]

This was Fitzgerald's aim in his own writing and revising—to give his sentences movement and to make things happen before the reader.

The first page of this typescript will serve as a sample of Fitzgerald's revision technique. The second sentence of the novel originally read: "The style is Second Empire, with a beam of the crescent; deferential palms cool its flushed facade, and before it, like a prayer rug, stretches a short dazzling beach." In this draft Fitzgerald removed the phrase "like a prayer rug." It is an excellent figure, but he probably wanted to use it more prominently, as will be seen below. By the time the novel was published in book form Fitzgerald had also deleted everything up to the semicolon.

The next sentence originally read: "Lately it has been much in the rotogravures because of the notables who go there in summer, but once it was almost deserted from April, when its middle-class English clientele went North, to December when they returned." This was a rather wordy and fussy sentence for Fitzgerald. The revised form—"Lately it has become a summer resort of notable and fashionable people; a decade ago it was almost deserted after its middle-class English clientele went North in April"—is more economical and reads faster. The revised sentence drops two subordinate clauses, but it is unlikely that Fitzgerald considered the revision from the point of grammar. He relied on his ear, and the reduction from four double-bar junctures to two was the effect he was interested in. The published form omits the adjective "middle-class."

Fitzgerald found a setting to show off his "prayer rug" figure in the opening sentence of the second paragraph, which he changed from "The hotel opened out to the beach where the sun thundered down in summer and sea-planes bound for Corsica roared overhead" to "The hotel and its bright tan prayer rug of a beach were one." The latter is more concise, concrete, and vivid. Two subordinate clauses were dropped, and the revised sentence does not have a double-bar juncture.

This typescript has some duplicate pagination and a few lacunae and inserts, but the final pagination is 1-700. The names of the characters in the typescript are the same as in the holograph draft, but Fitzgerald revised these in pencil: Grant is changed to North; Prince to Hoyt; and, in early sections, Noel to Nicole. Gus Struppen is renamed Franz Gregorovious, which Fitzgerald may have borrowed from Ferdinand Gregorovius, a nineteenth-century German historian and writer of travel books. It sounds more imposing—even pompous—than Struppen, which is probably why it was introduced. Fitzgerald characteristically misspelled the name; the *ious* name ending is unlikely in German.

The organization here is the same as that of the preceding holograph draft, except that Nicole's hysteria at the carnival has been moved to its final position. The material is divided into twelve long chapters which correspond to the twelve sections of the serial (except that as published in *Scribner's Magazine* Sections V and VI differ by one chapter each from the organization in this typescript). Using the chapter divisions of the printed book as a reference, the chapter order of the first typescript is Book I, Chapters 1-3, 5, 4, 6-25; Book II, Chapters 1-15; Book III, Chapter 3; Book II, Chapters 16-23; Book

III, Chapters 1-2 and 4-13. The account of the quarrel between Dick and Morris, the Australian patient, is still part of the second book. It was not put in its final position at Book III, Chapter 3 until the next draft. The announcement of Abe's death in this typescript still comes midway in Book II while the Divers are resident on the Riviera. Both the scene at Irv's hide-out and Dick's successful attempt to get Mary and Lady Caroline released from jail are included here (supplying further proof that the latter was not a last-minute insertion).

Holograph sections #98 (ten pages) and #99 (six pages) chronicle Abe's day in the Ritz bar after his return to Paris. The first describes his morning before going to see Dick, and the second describes his return to the bar. These were typed and included in section #96. Both appear in the serial version. Section #98 was included in the book in abridged form as I, 23; but section #99 was omitted.

Structurally, these two sections form a single block, unified by the presence of Abe and by the setting. This impressionistic study of the Ritz bar is a set piece in which Fitzgerald showed off the kind of writing he excelled at—the evocation of shifting moods during a social occasion. There are brilliant things in this; but it distracts attention from Dick. Fitzgerald recognized it as an intrusion, but he kept the first half of it anyhow.

After revision, this typescript falls between the holograph draft and the serial or book versions. It includes the full form of Dick's involvement with the governess at Innsbruck, the woman on the ship, and the man-overboard material—all of which are in the serial. But it also has the full form of Dick's recollections about his father at the funeral, the extra days with Rosemary in Rome, and Nicole's decision to have a picnic after the chest-rub incident—which are in neither the serial nor the book.

The final paragraph of II, 4—the analysis of Dick's feelings after he learns the details of Nicole's case—was not in holograph section #57. It first appears in a crude form as a holograph insert in section #100 of this typescript, and was then rewritten in section #116 of the next draft. The rewritten version closely approximates the published form of this revealing passage in which Fitzgerald indicates the desires which lead to Dick's emotional bankruptcy. The new phrases in section #116 about wanting to be "brave and wise" and "loved too" resemble Francis' anxieties about himself in section #26.

Fitzgerald did not bother to put Book II, Chapters 22-23—the Rome brawl—in final form. Section #107 is simply a slightly revised typescript of holograph section #14 from the Francis version. In section #107 Dick refers to his experiences in Hollywood and West Point, which are appropriate only to Francis. Although the name of the woman who obtains Dick's release has been revised from Rosemary to Baby Warren, she still resembles Charlotte Melarky.

In section #110, the revised typescript of Dick's farewell to the Riviera, one can see how Fitzgerald went about making Dick's departure less embarrassing. Although Dick still passes out and is doused with water, he is fairly sober as he blesses the beach. His incoherent remarks to the waiters have been cut, and he is not shown as he is helped away by the waiters. At this stage, though, Fitzgerald still describes Dick as an *homme manqué*.

Ninth Draft
Revised Second Typescript of *Doctor Diver's Holiday*

Description & Pagination	Corresponds to TITN	Remarks	Location	Key
R CC: 8½″ x 11″. Pica. 27-28, 31-32, 15, 16H, 17, insert 13H.	I, 4-5. Pp. 27-31.	Fragmentary.	Box 4	114
RT: 8½″ x 11″. Pica. 99-165.	I, 19-25. Pp. 105-148.	Chapter V. Based on #96.	Box 4	115
RT: 8½″ x 11″. Pica. 165-185, 185a, 186-191, 191a, 192, 193H, 194-222, insert 222, 223-246.	II, 1-9. Pp. 151-206.	Chapter V. Based on #100.	Box 4	116

Description & Pagination	Corresponds to TITN	Remarks	Location	Key
R CC: 8½" x 11". Pica. 195-196, 196½, 197-206. Originally numbered <83-95>.	II, 10. Pp. 207-212.	Chapter VI. Revised CC of #100.	Box 4	117
R CC: 8½" x 11". Pica. First page headed (207-389), 390-394, (395-396), 397-408, 409H, (410-423), 424-444.	II, 11-13. Pp. 213-235.	Chapter VI. Revised CC of #104.	Box 4	118
R CC: 8½" x 11". Pica. 445-453.	II, 17.	Early position of news of Abe's death. Revised CC of #104.	Box 4	119
R CC: 8½" x 11". Pica. 454-467.	II, 14.	Chapter VII. Revised CC of #105.	Box 4	120
R CC: 8½" x 11". Pica. 1H, 2-page insert for 2, 2-7, 8H, 9-34. Originally numbered <426-452 and 486-521>.	II, 16-18. Pp. 253-266.	Chapter VIII. Revised CC of #106. Announcement of Abe's death not included in Munich scene. Includes full version of episode with governess at Innsbruck.	Box 4	121
R CC: 8½" x 11". Pica. 35-66, (67-68), 69-93. Also numbered <453-473, 1-16, 490-513; and 522-584>.	II, 18-21. Pp. 266-286.	Continues #121. Revised CC of #106. Includes woman on ship and man overboard, but has shortened version of Dick's affair with Rosemary in Rome.	Box 4	122

Description & Pagination	Corresponds to TITN	Remarks	Location	Key
R CC: 8½″ x 11″. Pica. 94-127. Also numbered <585-619>.	II, 22-23. Pp. 287-306.	Chapter VII [IX. Revised CC of #107. Rosemary Prince [Baby Warren in police episode.	Box 4	123
R CC: 8½″ x 11″. Pica. 549-555, 553-574, 575T, 576T, 577-579, 579b-579c, 579e-579h, insert 579h, 579iT, 580T. <"Number 313 et seq">. Also partly numbered <470-479>.	III, 1-3. Pp. 309-330.	"Section IV of *Tender is the Night*." Chapter XII. Revised CC of #108. Copy for final typescript of serial; Cf. #148 & #146.	Box 4	124
RT: 8½″ x 11″. Pica. [581], 582, 582½, 583-623.	III, 4-6. Pp. 331-360.	Chapter XI (?). Later draft than #109. Cf. #148 & #146.	Box 4	125
CC: 8½″ x 11″. Pica. 580-623.	III, 4-6.	CC of #125. Unrevised.	Box 4	126
RT: 8½″ x 11″. Pica. 624, 624½H, 625-682, insert 682H, 683, insert 683H, 683½, 684, insert 384H, (685-686), 687-697, 698CC. The following pages may be CC: 662-675, 694-697.	III, 7-13. Pp. 361-408.	Chapter XII. Later draft than #110. Cf. #148 & #146.	Box 4	127
CC: 8½″ x 11″. Pica. 624-697.	III, 7-13.	CC of #127. Unrevised.	Box 4	128

Revised Carbon Copy of *Doctor Diver's Holiday*
[*Tender is the Night*

After revising the originals of the first typescript of *Doctor Diver's Holiday,* Fitzgerald assembled a second typescript draft, partly from carbon copies of the previous draft. Book I, Chapters 19-25; Book II, Chapters 1-9; and almost all of Book III are new typescript which is clearly later than the carbon-copy sections, for the new typescript incorporates manuscript revisions present in the original typescript (eighth draft). The names of the characters also establish the sequence of these typescripts. Grant and Prince appear in the carbon-copy sections, but in the new typescripts they are North and Hoyt.

Structurally, this is in almost final form. Section #114, though fragmentary, shows that Chapters 4 and 5 of the first book have been put in their final order. In section #124 the material about Morris has been moved from Book II to its final position in Book III where it supplies Franz with an excuse to squeeze Dick out of the clinic.

The Ferris-wheel scene, II, 15, is lacking here, but it is unlikely that Fitzgerald planned to omit it. It is quite possible that it was lost in the shuffle of assembling this draft, which has four main pagination systems and some minor ones. The announcement of Abe's death still comes early in Book II, on the Riviera (section #119).

Both the scene at Irv's hide-out and the jail episode are included in Book III (section #127). At this stage Fitzgerald inexplicably inserted in section #127 an analysis of Dick's relations with his barber. Coming right after the café scene at which the divorce is agreed on, the barber material is a needless intrusion. Fitzgerald sensibly omitted it from the next draft. The account of Dick's farewell to the beach, also in section #127, revises Mary's evaluation of Dick from *homme manqué* to *homme raté* (i.e., *raté*). The term does not fit Dick, for it means a person who has had a succession of failures through life, and it was cut from the next typescript. In this draft of Dick's departure it is Baby who restrains Nicole from going to Dick. Baby sends a waiter to help Dick, and the scene ends with Nicole enjoying the sympathy of her friends.

This ninth draft has the shortened account of Dick's affair with Rosemary in Rome (section #127); and the newsvendor is inserted in Book III (section #127). See Table A for a comparison of the eighth and ninth drafts.

Table A

8th draft	9th draft
Doctor Diver's Holiday, A Romance	
Original Typescript	*Revised Carbon Copy*
#87—I, 1-2	
#88—I, 3, 5, 4.	#114—I, 4-5. Re-ordered CC of #88.
#89—I, 6-11.	
#92—I, 12-18.	
#98—H Draft of I, 23 in #96.	
#99—H Draft of insert in #96.	
#96—I, 19-25.	#115—I, 19-25. Revised T draft of #96, not CC.
#100—II, 1-10.	#116—II, 1-9. Revised T draft of #100, not CC.
	#117—II, 10. CC of #100.
#104—II, 11-13. News of Abe's death here.	#118—II, 11-13. CC of #104.
	#119—News of Abe's death here. CC of #104.
#105—II, 14; III, 3.	#120—II, 14. CC of #105.
#106—II, 16-21.	#121—II, 16-18. CC of #106.
	#122—II, 18-21. CC of #106.
#107—II, 22-23.	#123—II, 22-23. CC of #107.
#108—III, 1-2; II, 15.	#124—III, 1-3. Partly CC of #108.
#109—III, 4-6.	#125—III, 4-6. Revised T draft of #109, not CC.
#110—III, 7-13. Includes Irv and women in jail.	#127—III, 7-13. Revised T draft of #110, not CC. Includes Irv and women in jail. N. B. II, 15 is lacking here.

The ninth draft, then, bridges the first rough typescript and the typescript serial version. It is transitional in another way, too, for at the beginning of Book III the title *Tender is the Night* appears for the first time.

Fitzgerald was pleased with the new title, but he had to persuade Maxwell Perkins that it was appropriate to the novel. Others have been puzzled by the apparent irrelevance of the title, but it fits the mood of the book. The title is not descriptive; it is evocative. The words from "Ode to a Nightingale" do not, by themselves, have any specific application to the book. "Tender is the Night" refers the reader back to the whole poem, which shares a spirit of disenchantment with *Tender is the Night*.

Keats was Fitzgerald's favorite poet. He thought he had read "Ode on a Grecian Urn" a hundred times and he wrote to his daughter that he could never read "Ode to a Nightingale" "without tears in my eyes." [3] His reference to the poem in *Tender is the Night* was clearly not careless.

Albert Guerard has said that the "Ode to a Nightingale" expresses a desire for the submersion of consciousness.[4] In the fourth stanza the poet resolves to flee painful, harsh reality and announces his escape:

> Already with thee! tender is the night,
> And haply the Queen-Moon is on her throne,
> Cluster'd around by all her starry fays;
> But here there is no light,
> Save what from heaven is with the breezes blown
> Through verdurous glooms and winding mossy ways.
> (35-40)

The escape proves illusory, and the poet is called back to the despair of his situation. Dick suffers the same experience as the poet. The final lines of the ode, in which the poet questions the actuality of his escape, apply equally to Dick as he migrates from town to smaller town in his private hell of upstate New York.

> Was it a vision, or a waking dream?
> Fled is that music:—Do I wake or sleep?
> (79-80)

Tenth Draft. Carbon Copy for Serial

Description & Pagination	Corresponds to TITN	Remarks	Location	Key
T: 8½" x 11". Pica. 5 unnumbered pages.		Preliminary matter for book; includes two title pages: (1) Doctor Diver's Holiday [TENDER IS THE NIGHT / A Romance / by . . . "*Already with thee! tender is the night / And haply the Queen-Moon is on her throne*" (2) Tender is the Night by . . . "*Already with thee! tender is the night . . . / . . . But here there is no light, / Save what from heaven is with the breezes blown / Through verdurous glooms and winding mossy ways.*" / "Ode to a Nightingale"	Box 6	129

Description & Pagination	Corresponds to TITN	Remarks	Location	Key
T: 8½" x 11". Pica. 1-12, 13CC, 13T, 13½, 14-15, (16-18), 19-27, 27A-17C. 27A-C originally numbered <16, 17, 30>.	I, 1-5. Pp. 3-31.	Chapter I. Original of #140.	Box 6	130
CC: 8½" x 11". Pica. 27C-27D T, 28-60.	I, 6-11. Pp. 32-66.	Chapter II. CC of #140. Fitzgerald changed from T to CC in this section.	Box 6	131
CC: 8½" x 11". Pica. 60-98.	I, 12-18. Pp. 67-104.	Chapter III. CC of #140.	Box 6	132
CC: 8½" x 11". Pica. 99-101, 103-142. Two copies of 141-142.	I, 19-25. Pp. 105-148.	Chapter IV. CC of #141.	Box 6	133
CC: 8½" x 11". Pica. 143-162, insert A-insert D, 163-194. Two copies of each page, except inserts.	II, 1-19. Pp. 151-206.	Chapter V. CC of #141.	Box 6	134
CC: 8½" x 11". Pica. 195-207, 207½, 208-228.	II, 10-13. Pp. 207-235.	CC of #148. Section III Chapter VI. Announcement of Abe's death still occurs on the Riviera.	Box 6	135
CC: 8½" x 11". Pica. 228-246.	II, 14-15. Pp. 236-252.	Chapter VII. CC of #143.	Box 6	136

Description & Pagination	Corresponds to TITN	Remarks	Location	Key
CC: 8½" x 11". Pica. 246-293, (294-295), 295. Two copies of 292-293, (294-295).	II, 16-21. Pp. 253-286.	Chapter VIII. CC of #143. Includes full version of Innsbruck and return voyage to Europe.	Box 6	137
RT: 8½" x 11". Pica. 296-315. RT & CC for each page. New T for 315. Originally numbered <1-20>.	II, 22-23. Pp. 287-306.	Chapter IX.	Box 6	138
RT: 8½" x 11". Pica. 275.	II, 19. P. 271.	Discarded revision of #137?	Box 1	139

Incomplete Typescript (Carbon Copy) for Serial

After Fitzgerald had revised and reorganized the ninth draft, he still did not have anything that would do for printer's copy. A devoted compositor might have been able to set type from it; but the real difficulty is that the ninth draft is complete but not finished. The style was not yet uniformly polished, and Fitzgerald was probably not altogether satisfied with Book III.

A fresh typescript—an original and a carbon copy—was prepared from the ninth draft. As he had done with the first typescript, Fitzgerald began by revising the original copy of the new typescript, but—perhaps recalling the problems this procedure had involved that time—he changed to the carbon copy after revising the opening of the first serial installment (Book I, Chapters 1-5). The chapter divisions marked on this draft are those of the serial version.

Since Fitzgerald abandoned this draft at the end of Book II, it does not merit much attention. The revisions included here were also included in the eleventh draft. It is worth noting, though, that the announcement of Abe's death still comes early in Book II. Nicole's hysteria at the carnival (Book II, Chapter 15)—which is lacking in the ninth draft—appears here in its final position (section #136).

The relation between this draft and the next draft is summarized below in Table B.

Eleventh Draft. Typescript Printer's Copy for Serial

Description & Pagination	Corresponds to TITN	Remarks	Location	Key
R CC: 8½″ x 11″. Pica. 1-13, 13½, 14-15, (16-18), 19-26, 27A-27E. RT: 8½″ x 11″. Pica. 28-98.	I, 1-18. Pp. 3-104.	Printer's copy for 1st installment of serial. Richard Diver [Tender is the Night. "Oct 27 Rec'd." Marked for galleys 1-33. Identification number: 7132, CC of #130 and original of #131 & #132.	Box 5	140
RT: 8½″ x 11″. Pica. 99-194.	I, 19-25; II, 1-9. Pp. 105-206.	Printer's copy for 2nd installment. Marked for galleys 35-68. Identification number: 7400. For galley proof see #149, which was rewritten in #150 and reset. Original of #133 & #134.	Box 5	141
RT: 8½″ x 11″. Pica. 225-226.	. . . .	Draft for pp. 225-226 in #143.	Box 1	142

Description & Pagination	Corresponds to TITN	Remarks	Location	Key
RT: 8½″ x 11″. Pica. 195-207, 207½, 208- 291.	II, 10-21. Pp. 207-238.	Printer's copy for 3rd installment. Marked for galleys 1-29. Identification number: 7648. Set in #152. Original of #135-#137. II, 22-23 lacking.	Box 5	143
RT: 8½″ x 11″. Pica. 313-319, insert 319H, 320-323.	III, 1-2. Pp. 309-318.	4th installment, but not printer's copy. Earlier than #146, #148.	Box 5	144
RT: 8½″ x 11″. Pica. 320-336.	III, 2-3. Pp. 315-330.	Continues #144.	Box 5	145
R CC: 8½″ x 11″. Pica. 313-333, 338-359, 369, 361-411.	III, 1-13. Pp. 309-408.	4th installment, but not printer's copy. CC of #148. Includes Irv. Jail scene and Dick's last appearance on beach intended for book only.	Box 5	146
CC: 8½″ x 11″. Pica. 334-335, 337.	III, 3-4. Pp. 329-332.	Discarded from #146?	Box 6	147
RT: 8½″ x 11″. Pica. 313-319, 322-328, 331-335, 337-361, 361, 362-393, [ ], 400-406, 410-411.	III, 1-13. Pp. 309-408.	Printer's copy for 4th installment. This is a new typescript. Marked for galleys 1-29. Identification number: 7755. Includes Irv, but jail and beach scenes cut. For galley proof see #155.	Box 5	148

Typescript Printer's Copy for Serial

After breaking off work on the carbon copy in the tenth draft, Fitzgerald prepared printer's copy from the original copy of the typescript. The eleventh draft is not a new version and does not involve structural changes. It is basically a fair copy, which includes the revisions made in the typescript ninth draft. Only in the last installment (Book III of the novel) are there content revisions, and this installment is present in three layers.

This draft was printer's copy for the first set of serial galley proof, but the galleys were so extensively revised that installments two and four were entirely reset. The galleys are discussed under the twelfth draft. The tenth (carbon copy) and eleventh (original copy) drafts are compared in Table B. The relationship between the eleventh draft and the galleys is indicated in Table C.

In section #140, which was received by the printer on October 27, 1933, there is a revised title page. The change from *Richard Diver* to *Tender is the Night* indicates that at this stage Fitzgerald finally overcame Perkins' objections to *Tender is the Night*. This is the only appearance of *Richard Diver*, which is flat and commonplace when compared to Fitzgerald's other titles. Its chief virtue in Fitzgerald's eyes would have been that it did away with the word *doctor*, which troubled him.

Table B

10th Draft. CC	*11th Draft. T*
#130—I, 1-5. T. Original of #140.	#140—I, 1-18. CC. Printer's copy for 1st installment.
#131—I, 6-11. CC of #140.	
#132—I, 12-18. CC of #140.	#141—I, 19-25; II, 1-9. T. Printer's copy for 2nd installment.
#133—I, 19-25. CC of #141.	
#134—II, 1-9. CC of #141.	
#135—II, 10-13. CC of #143.	#143—II 10-21. T. Incomplete printer's copy for 3rd serial installment; II, 22-23 lacking.
#136—II, 14-15. CC of #143.	
#137—II, 16-21. CC of #143.	
#138—II, 22-23. T & CC.	

10th Draft. CC	11th Draft. T
	#144—III, 1-2. T.
	#145—III, 2-3. T.
	#146—III, 1-3. CC of #148.
	#148—III, 1-3. T. Printer's copy for 4th serial installment.

The first installment (Book I, Chapters 1-18), section #140, gave Fitzgerald less trouble than any of the others. Although the galleys set from it have not survived—and this is the only missing block of serial galley proof—comparison of section #140 with *Scribner's Magazine* shows that only minor revisions were made in the galleys.

The printer's copy for the second installment (Book I, Chapters 19-25; Book II, Chapters 1-9), section #141, was set in galleys twice before it appeared in *Scribner's Magazine*. After section #141 was set in galleys (section #149), Fitzgerald reworked them so thoroughly (section #150) that new galleys had to be set (section #151).

The third installment (Book II, Chapters 10-21), section #143, here lacks Chapters 22-23, the account of Dick's drunken brawl and his beating at the hands of the Rome police. It is certain that these chapters were lost from the *Tender is the Night* material before it came to Princeton, for they are in section #152, the galleys set from this typescript. This installment was revised in galley, but not so heavily as to necessitate complete resetting. With section #143 belongs typescript #142, which is a revised account of the scene on the Riviera at which Dick learns that Abe has been beaten to death in New York. The galleys were revised and reset, at which point the announcement of Abe's death was moved to its final position.

The typescript printer's copy for the fourth installment (Book III) has a complicated history and exists in three layers. The earliest layer is an original typescript corresponding to Book III, Chapters 1-3 (sections #144 & #145). It was probably never continued beyond Chapter 3. This was followed by two complete drafts of the installment—an original typescript (section #148) and its carbon copy (section #146). Only section #148 was set in galleys. The carbon copy, section #146, was revised for the book version, but was never set in type. It includes the description of the homosexuals at Lausanne, the full scene at Irv's hide-out, the scene in which Dick obtains the release of Mary and Lady Caroline from the police, and Dick's conversation with Mary on the terrace before he leaves the Riviera. The latter two scenes are marked "For book only" and were omitted from section #148.

It is not easy to understand why Fitzgerald made these two cuts. The material omitted from the serial usually deals with sexual matters. The jail scene, it is true, hints at Lesbian symptoms in the prank Mary and Lady Caroline played on the French girls; but the idea is treated delicately enough to permit publication in *Scribner's Magazine.* Another factor involved in Fitzgerald's uncertainty about including the jail scene is revealed by a draft for a telegram to Gerald Murphy which is with some personal papers in section #190. In this telegram, Fitzgerald requests permission to include in the novel a scene based on Murphy's rescue of two women from the French police. Fitzgerald says that the scene was already written, but that it can still be deleted "today or tomorrow." The conversation between Dick and Mary on the terrace is unobjectionable on moral grounds. The only possible literary explanation for these excisions is that Fitzgerald wanted the last serial installment to have a more rapid pace, and that he cut these two scenes which delay the resolution of the story.

As set in the galley, section #148 includes some important revisions which point toward the final form of Book III: Franz, not Dick, insists on the diagnosis of neurosyphilis for the American artist; Nicole does not arrange a picnic after the chest-rub incident; and the newsvendor appears for the first time during the conference at which Dick agrees to a divorce. Of greater import is the fact that at this stage Dick's reaction to the break with Nicole at Book III, Chapter 9 first appears in the final form. This is the scene that Fitzgerald had labelled "unfelt" in section #85 of the holograph draft. Instead of Dick's tears of self-pity, the scene now ends with the author's observation that "The case was finished. Doctor Diver was at liberty." The non-functional analysis of Dick's relations with his barber is cut in this section. The arrest of Mary and Lady Caroline and the terrace conversation between Dick and Mary are both lacking in section #148; however, Dick still exits drunk, supported by a waiter. Here it is still Baby who restrains Nicole, and the scene ends with Nicole enjoying her friends' sympathy.

The fourth installment was revised in galley and reset. It is easy to see why Book III gave Fitzgerald so much trouble—or why he took so much trouble with it—for it is the most delicate part of the book. In it Fitzgerald depicts the ignominious collapse of an admirable man who has been ruined by the very traits which made him admirable. This is where Fitzgerald sought the greatest emotional reaction from the reader, in response to what he called the "dying fall" technique.

Chapter VIII

Twelfth Draft. Galleys for serial and typescript revisions

Description & Pagination	Corresponds to TITN	Remarks	Location	Key
No. 7400. Galleys 34-68. Uncorrected duplicate.	I, 19-25; II, 1-9. Pp. 105-206.	2nd installment. Set from #141. Revised in #150.	Box 6	149
T & revised galleys mounted on 8½" x 11" sheets. Pica. Pp. 1-4, 4A, 5-65. 23-26, 28-31, 36-39, 41-42, 46, 48, 50, 52, 54-64 are elite.	I, 19-25; II, 1-9. Pp. 105-206.	2nd installment. Special Rush Alt. This is a revision of #149. Printer's copy for #151.	Box 5	150
No. 7400. Galleys 36-67. Uncorrected duplicate.	I, 19-25; II, 1-9. Pp. 111-206.	2nd installment. Set from #150.	Box 6	151
No. 7648. Galleys 1-37. Uncorrected duplicate. Also a corrected second copy of galley 10 and a section of galley 9.	II, 10-23. Pp. 207-306.	3rd installment. Set from #143. Revised in #153 & #154.	Box 6	152
T & corrected galleys. 8½" x 11". Elite. Pp. 1-19 <10-28>. Galleys 14-21.	II, 15-18. Pp. 245-264.	Revision of #152. Abe's death moved to the Munich scene.	Box 6	153
T & galleys. 8½" x 11". Elite. Pp. 1-20. No. 7648. Galleys 22-28.	II, 18-21. Pp. 264-284.	Continues #153. Revision of #152.	Box 6	154

Description & Pagination	Corresponds to TITN	Remarks	Location	Key
No. 7755 also No. 7555. 2 Gal 1-2 Gal 29.	III, 1-13. Pp. 309-408.	4th installment. Uncorrected. Revised in #162. This includes Irv, but omits jail, and final meeting between Dick and Mary.	Box 6	155
T & H: 8½″ x 11″. Pica. A, holograph insert A, [ ] holograph, 395-399.	III, 10. Pp. 391-396.	Revision of the jail scene.	Box 6	156
CC: 8½″ x 11″. Pica. A-C.	III, 10. Pp. 391-396.	Another revision of the jail scene.	Box 6	157
H & galley, 8½″ x 13″. 1 p.	III, 8. P. 384.	Draft of Nicole & Tommy swimming, which replaces Irv. See #162.	Box 6	158
RT: 8½″ x 11″. Pica. A-F.	III, 10. Pp. 391-396.	Jail scene. This is insert for 2 galley 26.	Box 6	159
CC: 8½″ x 11″. Pica. A-F.	III, 10. Pp. 391-396.	Jail scene. Later version than #159. Insert for 2 galley 26. Not CC of #189.	Box 6	160
CC: 8½″ x 11″. Pica. A-B.	III, 12. Pp. 404-406.	Mary and Dick on the terrace. Insert for 2 galley 28.	Box 6	161
T & revised galley. 8½″ x 11″. 1-16 (elite), 17-46 (pica), 47-67 (elite), 68-69 (pica & elite), 70-71 (elite), 72-84 (pica), 85-86 (elite), unnum-	III, 1-13. Pp. 309-408.	4th installment, revised. Rec'd Feb. 23. Reset in #164. Irv cut. Jail and final meeting with Mary in-	Box 6	162

Description & Pagination	Corresponds to TITN	Remarks	Location	Key
bered section of galley, 87-88 (pica), 89 (elite). 74-79 also labeled insert A-F; 87-88 also labeled insert A-B.		serted. Identification number: 7755. Marked for galleys 1-30.		
Galley No. 7755. 2 Gal 15-2 Gal 30.	III, 6-13. Pp. 358-408.	Setting of #162. Uncorrected. See #164. 27 Feb. 1934.	Box 6	163
Galley No. 7755. Galleys 1-7. 2 Gal 8-2 Gal 30.	III, 1-13. Pp. 309-408.	4th installment. Final galley proof. Uncorrected.	Box 6	164

Table C—Pedigree of Serial Installments

1st Installment (I, 1-18)
#140—CC
Galleys lacking

2nd Installment (I, 19-25; II, 1-9)
#141—T printer's copy for #149
#149—first galleys
#150—T & galleys of #149 ("Special Rush Alt")
#151—reset galleys

3rd Installment (II, 10-23)
#143—T, incomplete, lacks 22-23. Printer's copy for #152
#152—first galleys
#153—T & galleys of #152 (15-18)
#154—T & galleys of #152 (18-21)
Final galleys lacking

4th Installment (III, 1-13)
#148—T Printer's copy for #155
#155—first galleys
#156—T & H ⎫
#157—CC   ⎪
#158—H & galley ⎬ revisions of #155
#159—TR   ⎪ for #162
#160—CC   ⎪
#161—CC ⎭
#162—T & galley
#164—reset galleys
#163—incomplete reset galleys

Galleys for Serial and typescript revises.

Of the four serial installments, only the first escaped complete resetting in galley. Although there is no surviving galley for the first serial installment, comparison of typescript section #140 and *Scribner's Magazine* shows that only minor revisions were made in the serial galley.

For the second installment galleys were set from typescript (section #141). Section #149 is an untouched duplicate set of galleys which Fitzgerald saved. The working galleys were heavily revised and pasted on sheets of 8½" x 11" paper; some scenes were almost completely retyped—the station scene, Abe's experiences in the Ritz bar, and the events leading up to Dick's marriage. This produced section #150, which is a thoroughgoing revision of section #149. Section #150 is headed "Special Rush Alt." The revisions themselves are all stylistic; there is no change in content or organization. The versions of the opening of the installment show the nature of this revision.

#149. Galley 34-7400	#150. Typescript
IV	IV
Abe left from the Gare St. Lazare at eleven—alone under the fouled glass dome, relic of the seventies and from the Crystal Palace, hands within his coat pockets to conceal trembling fingers, the contours of his face drawn into an expression at once impish and ashamed; with his hat removed, it was plain that only the top layer of his hair was brushed back—lower layers were pointed sidewise resolutely. Thus he stood, his hands were of the vague gray color that only sev-	Abe left from the Gare St. Lazare at eleven—he stood alone under the fouled glass dome, relic of the seventies, imitated from the Crystal Palace; his hands, of that vague grey color that only twenty-four hours can produce, were in his coat pockets to conceal the trembling fingers. With his hat removed it was plain that only the top layer of his hair was brushed back—the lower levels were pointed resolutely sidewise. He was scarcely recognizable as the man who had swum

eral consecutive days can produce; he was scarcely recognizable as the man who had swum upon Gausse's Beach a fortnight ago.

Abe was early; he looked from left to right with his head only; it would have taken nervous forces out of his control to use any other part of his body; new-looking baggage went past him; presently prospective passengers, with dark little bodies, were calling: "Jew-uls-*Hoo*-oo!" in dark piercing voices.

At the minute when he wondered whether or not he had time for a glass of beer at the buffet, and began fumbling at the soggy mass of thousand-franc notes in his pocket, one end of his pendulous glance came to rest upon the apparition of Nicole at the stairhead; she was self-revelatory in her little expressions as people seems to some one they are meeting but whom they have not yet seen themselves. She was frowning, less gloating over them, humble and vain, then merely animally counting them—a cat checking her cubs with a paw.

upon Gausse's Beach a fortnight ago.

He was early; he looked from left to right with his eyes only; it would have taken nervous forces out of his control to use any other part of his body. New-looking baggage went past him; presently prospective passengers, with dark little bodies, were calling: "Jew-uls-*Hoo*-oo!" in dark piercing voices.

At the minute when he wondered whether or not he had time for a drink at the buffet, and began clutching the soggy wad of thousand-franc notes in his pocket, one end of his pendulous glance came to rest upon the apparition of Nicole at the stairhead. He watched her— she was self-revelatory in her little expressions as people seem to someone waiting for them who as yet is himself unobserved. She was frowning, thinking of her children, less gloating over them than merely animally counting them—a cat checking her cubs with a paw.

It was impractical to revise the standing type of the galleys this extensively, and so the second installment was completely reset. Section #151 is an untouched duplicate set of the reset galleys. The working set was corrected and returned. This kind of extensive revision, of course, was charged to the author.

The third installment had the same revision history as the second. Galleys were set from typescript section #143. Section #152 is an untouched duplicate set of these galleys. The working set was revised and retyped in sections #153 and #154 in the same way that the second installment was treated. The retyped passages do not alter the content or organization of the original galley—except in section #153, where the announcement of Abe's death is transferred from the Riviera to Munich. New galleys were almost certainly set for the third installment, but these have not survived.

The fourth installment has the most intricate history. Fitzgerald probably did most of the work on Book III during a period of heavy drinking; but his judgment was unimpaired, and the galley revisions improve the third book. The first serial galleys were set from typescript section #148. An untouched duplicate set for this is section #155. It is numbered "2 Gal 1"-"2 Gal 29," but it is not a revise or a resetting. The designation "2" is a printer's error, and it is not difficult to see how Fitzgerald's copy had the printers confused. Section #155 includes a full account of the visit to Irv, but omits both the jail scene and the final conversation between Dick and Mary—Fitzgerald had intended these two scenes for the book version only. Fitzgerald then drafted two versions of the jail scene (sections #156 and #157) for insertion into this installment. This is probably what led Cowley to conclude that the jail scene was a last-minute idea. Section #158, a single page of holograph and galley proof, has the description of Nicole and Tommy swimming which was inserted in place of the description of Irv. Sections #159 and #160, drafts of the jail scene, are marked as an insert for 2 galley 26. Dick's conversation with Mary on the terrace is drafted in section #161 and is marked as an insert for 2 galley 28. These revisions and inserts were incorporated in section #162 which revises the galleys. Section #162 is predominantly new typescript; only seventeen pages have pieces of galley pasted on them. It was received by the printer on February 23, 1934, and was entirely reset by February 27. Section #164 is an unmarked duplicate of the new galleys; the corrected set was returned to the printer.

Thirteen. Page Proof for *Scribner's Magazine*.

Description & Pagination	Corresponds to TITN	Remarks	Location	Key
168-174, 207-229. 2 sets of each.	II, 10-23. Pp. 207-306.	3rd installment. Slightly revised.	Box 5	165

Of the page proof for *Scribner's Magazine*, only two sets of the third installment survive. These have only a few inconsequential markings: two word changes, one spelling query, and some dozen underlinings for italics. None of these revisions appears in the actual serial, and only the spelling change (bruskly [brusquely) appears in the book; however, a few punctuation changes (periods changed to question marks, and added commas) not marked on this page proof do appear in the serial. It is likely that the changes were made by an editor or a copy reader, for Fitzgerald would probably have revised more extensively. If the revisions which appear in the third installment were made by Fitzgerald, these two sets are duplicates which he saved after returning the working set to the printer. There is no way to determine anything about authorial page-proof revision for the other installments.

Fourteen. *Scribner's Magazine*

First Installment. January 1934.
Pp. [1]-8, [60]-80.

Serial section	corresponds to	book
I		I, 1-5
II		I, 6-11
III		I, 12-18

Second Installment. February 1934.
Pp. [88]-95, 139-160.

Serial section	corresponds to	book
IV		I, 19-25
V		II, 1-9

Third Installment. March 1934.
  Pp. [169]-174, 207-229.

Serial section	corresponds to	book
VI		II, 10-13
VII		II, 14-15
VIII		II, 16-21
IX		II, 22-23

Fourth Installment. April 1934.
  Pp. [252]-258, [292]-310.

Serial section	corresponds to	book
X		III, 1-3
XI		III, 4-6
XII		III, 7-13

Although it is reasonable to assume that Fitzgerald would have made notes in his copies of the serial, no marked set has survived.

The characteristics of the serial version have been discussed in its typescript and galley stages, and can be summarized here. Tommy Barban is named Tommy Costello in the serial; this is the only important name change between the serial and book.[1] The serial has an account of Abe's return to the Ritz bar, the episode at Innsbruck with the governess, Dick's involvement with the woman on the ship, and the boy who jumps overboard —all of which were omitted or cut down in the book for structural reasons. The book, however, has material that was omitted from the serial for reasons that had nothing to do with craftsmanship: Warren's confessions of his incestuous relations with Nicole, and Dick's interview with the Chilean homosexual. Except for these, the serial is essentially the same as the book. The painstaking revision of *Tender is the Night* between serial and book publication only polished the style and pointed up scenes. The book is an improvement over the serial, to be sure; but there is no great difference between the emotional and thematic content of the two versions.

The decision to serialize *Tender is the Night* was probably prompted by the fact that Fitzgerald had gone into debt to complete it and had borrowed money against his royalties. In addition to supplying him with ready money—or at least ready credit—the idea of serialization probably appealed to Fitzgerald because it would provide him with a chance to preview the novel. He had used this scheme with *The Beautiful and Damned*, which he overhauled after it appeared in *The Metropolitan Magazine*. Nonetheless, the indifferent popular and critical reception of the serial of *Tender is the Night* almost certainly hurt the sale and reception of the book. The mood of the story could not survive the month-long interruptions between installments, and the flashback structure probably seemed disjointed to readers of the serial.

Fifteen. Tearsheets from *Scribner's Magazine*.

Description & Pagination	Corresponds to TITN	Remarks	Location	Key
5-6, 61-64, 69-70, 73-74.	I, 2-3, 5-7, 10-12, 13-15. Pp. 12-18, 28-44, 59-68, 76-84.	1st installment. Unrevised and incomplete.	Box 5	166
91-92, 95, 141-142, 147-156, 159-160.	I, 19-20. 21-24; II, 1-8, 9. Pp. 111-117, 122-125, 130-138, 159-195, 202-206.	2nd installment. Unrevised and incomplete.	Box 5	167

Tearsheets from *Scribner's Magazine* survive for most of the first two installments. Except for underlinings, this material is untouched. It is clear that Fitzgerald did not carefully revise a set of tearsheets, for the book galleys were set from the serial version without changes.

It is difficult to understand why the book version was not prepared by revising serial tearsheets, since both author and publisher knew that the serial version would be revised for book publication. The explanation that suggests itself is the time factor. To get the book out as soon as possible after serialization, book galleys had to be set while the serial was being run. But not improbably Fitzgerald was then too busy working upon the future serial installments to have time for revising the printed ones; and so the book galleys were necessarily set from unrevised tearsheets.

Sixteen. Book Galleys.

Description	Corresponds to TITN	Remarks	Location	Key
Fragment of one galley	II, 14-15. Pp. 243-246.	Revised to published form.	Box 6	168
Galley 68	II, 18. Pp. 262-264.	Revised to published form.	Box 6	169
Galley 69	II, 18. Pp. 264-265.	Revised to published form; full form of governess incident at Innsbruck set in type.	Box 6	170
Galleys 70-72	II, 18-20. Pp. 265-274.	Revised to published form.	Box 6	171
Galley 73	II, 20. Pp. 274-278.	Revised to published form.	Box 6	172
Galley 74	II, 20-21. Pp. 278-281.	Revised to published form.	Box 6	173
Galleys 75-76	II, 21-22. Pp. 282-289.	Revised to published form.	Box 6	174
Galley 83	III, 1-2. Pp. 312-318.	Revised to published form.	Box 6	175
Galley 85	III, 2-3. Pp. 321-326.	Unrevised. Not published form. See #177.	Box 6	176

Description	Corresponds to TITN	Remarks	Location	Key
2 fragments of galley 85 and a T fragment	III, 2-3. Pp. 321-326.	Revised to published form.	Box 6	177
Galley 90	III, 4-5. Pp. 341-343.	Revised to published form.	Box 6	178
Galley 91	III, 5. Pp. 345-346, 348-349.	Revised to published form.	Box 6	179
Galley 93	III, 5-6. Pp. 353-357.	Unrevised. Not published form.	Box 6	180
Galley 94	III, 6. Pp. 357-359.	Unrevised. Not published form.	Box 6	181
3 fragments of galleys 93-95	III, 5-7. Pp. 353-357, 362-364.	Revised to published form.	Box 6	182
Galleys 95-106	III, 6-13. Pp. 359-408.	Unrevised. Not published form.	Box 6	183
CC: 8½″ x 11″. Pica. Unnumbered. 65 pages.	II, 18-22; III, 2-7. Pp. 243-246, 262-289, 321-322, 324-327, 341-343, 345-346, 348-349, 353-357, 361-364.	Based on revised galleys 65-69, 70-76, 85, 90-91, 93-95.	Box 6	184

Galley proof for the last third of Book II and all of Book III has survived. It is heavily revised, except for untouched duplicates retained by Fitzgerald. This proof was set directly from the serial version without any intermediate revision; even the shipboard material about Dick's involvement with the woman on the ship and the boy who jumped overboard was set. Extensive galley revision is costly, and the additional expense was almost certainly charged to the author. The revised galleys are literally covered with revisions. As was his habit, Fitzgerald cut up most of the galleys and patched them together.

The first installment was the most heavily revised, probably because it was the installment least revised in the stage of serial galley. (See the textual collation of the serial and book versions, which is appended to this study.)

With the book galleys belongs section #184, sixty-five pages of unnumbered carbons which are all that survive of the typed printer's copy based on the revised galleys. Fitzgerald's revisions in these galleys were so heavy that it was impossible to correct the standing type, and since new type had to be set, it was simpler to work from typescript than to try to set from the revised galleys. The original typed pages have been lost, but Fitzgerald saved the carbons.

Although there are no surviving pieces of later revised proof, it is demonstrable that the revision of the original book galleys was followed by further revision of the reset galleys and/or page proof. The book includes new readings which are not in the surviving revised galleys. These second-level revisions bulk much smaller than the first level of book galley revisions. Samples of these final revisions are:

	revised galley		*book*
section #168	manic	p. 245	maniac
section #168	the flood of	p. 245	short floods of
section #171	are we	p. 270	are; we
section #171	lobby her beauty groomed now as he had never thought of it, shocked	p. 270	lobby, her beauty all groomed like a young horse dosed with Black-seed oil, and hoops varnished, shocked
section #182	hook	p. 363	nook [an obvious typo]

Since the book was published in April, and the serial appeared during January-April, Fitzgerald had little opportunity for leisurely preparation of the book version. Probably he did not have the opportunity to study the complete serial version before undertaking to revise it. Since he was still working on the fourth installment at the end of February, it is probable that there were times when he was revising both the serial galleys and book galleys—though not of the same part of the novel.

As a stylist who depended heavily upon his ear, Fitzgerald could not help revising his prose as long as it was still in his hands. It is surprising, though, that in *Tender is the Night* this revising is not purely nervous, for his work on the book galleys did polish the style. John Hall Wheelock, who was then an editor at Scribners, remembers Fitzgerald waiting for the office to open in the morning, anxious to revise the book galleys of *Tender is the Night.* Though Fitzgerald usually appeared to have been drinking, Wheelock testifies that his editorial judgment was unimpaired. Indeed, Wheelock gives Fitzgerald the distinction of being the only author he worked with who could reliably revise copy while obviously tight.[2]

Fitzgerald's own estimate of the value of these revisions appears in a letter he wrote to Edmund Wilson in March 1934 —before the book was issued. This letter is quoted below. In it Fitzgerald claims that the omissions and stylistic revisions have given the book a smoother surface. (See p. 200.)

"You never cut anything out of a book that you regret later," Fitzgerald told Thomas Wolfe in 1934 to console him for the amputations that were then being performed on *Of Time and the River;* and in 1937 Fitzgerald tried to explain his theory of "the novel of selected incidents" to Wolfe, who took umbrage at this professional interference. It does not matter, though, how Wolfe reacted, for Fitzgerald was really writing to himself about *Tender is the Night:*

The novel of selected incidents has this to be said that the great writer like Flaubert has consciously left out the stuff that Bill or Joe (in his case Zola) will come along and say presently. He will say only the things that he alone sees. So Mme. Bovary becomes eternal while Zola already rocks with age. . . .³

Seventeen. Book Page-Proof.

There is no surviving page proof for the book. As a matter of standard publishing practice, page proof was prepared; and Fitzgerald may have revised it. See the preceding discussion of the galley proofs for a comment on this possibility (p. 195).

Chapter IX

The Book

Fitzgerald had discussed the serial version with Dean Christian Gauss of Princeton University, whose comments on the book version must have gratified the author, even though it is apparent that Gauss went out of his way to write an ego-boosting letter.

I cannot tell you how delighted I was to have the inscribed copy of *Tender is the Night*. I had read it with increasing satisfaction as it came out in *Scribner's*. Your effect was very decidedly crescendo and if I had any reservations it was about the low key and rather slow tempo in which you started. Going through the volume I noticed that you have done wonders in rewriting and I think you have now finished the most magnificent job you have yet done.

I was delighted to see the note from T. S. Eliot on the jacket. My opinion of him as a critic is already high but I shall raise it a notch on the strength of his bracketing you with Hemingway as the most important interpreters of contemporary life. You two take your places at the opposite ends of the modern spectrum. Without any disrespect to him I put Hemingway down at the infrared side and you on the ultraviolet. His rhythm is like the beating of an African tom-tom—primitive, simple, but it gets you in the end.

You are on the other end. You have a feeling for musical intervals and the tone-color of words which makes your prose the finest instrument for rendering all the varied shades of our complex emotional states. There are passages that I read over and over to myself as I would read a poem. I need not tell you, therefore, how proud I am of you and of your book.

You remember that I had a feeling in the third part that Dick went haywire too fast and I was afraid that you'd have him try to make a comeback. I'm glad you didn't.[1]

Because Fitzgerald made hundreds of revisions between the serial and the book, it would be impractical to present a full collation here. Instead, only a specimen collation of the most heavily revised portion is appended to this study.

The revisions which a writer makes in a published work have a special interest because they usually represent his most considered judgment. This generalization cannot be strictly applied to *Tender is the Night* because, as has been noted, Fitzgerald had precious little leisure for pondering fine stylistic distinctions during January-March 1934. Nevertheless, his revisions are concerned primarily with style and emphasis, and merit attention because so much of the novel's effect depends upon the color and texture of the prose.

Cowley's comment on the revision of the serial, though substantially accurate, is misleading: ". . . he omitted half a dozen scenes, shortened many others, and inserted page after page of typescript into the galley proofs." [2] In point of fact, Fitzgerald did omit six scenes (three of which are connected), but he added only a few pages of new material. This does not mean that the revisions are negligible. They are not. But the importance of the revisions is not just in the large-scale deletions and additions Fitzgerald made, but rather in the cumulative effect of all the revisions on the texture of the book.

Although Fitzgerald was careless about many things in his career—and notoriously indifferent to the principles of orthography—he was keenly sensitive to the effect of the slightest word change in a novel. In 1936, when *Tender is the Night* was being considered for inclusion in the Modern Library, he asked Bennett Cerf for permission to make revisions in the text: "I don't want to change anything in the book but sometimes by a single word change one can throw a new emphasis or give a new value to the exact same scene or setting." [3] This may be taken as a statement of the purpose of his stylistic serial-to-book revisions in 1934.

Soon after he completed the revision of the serial, Fitzgerald wrote about it to Edmund Wilson (the letter is characteristically undated, but the envelope is postmarked March 12, 1934):

Any attempt by an author to explain away a partial failure in a work is of course doomed to absurdity—yet I could wish that you, and others, had read the book version rather than the mag. version which in spots was hastily put together. The last half for example has a *much* more polished facade now. Oddly enough several people have felt that the surface of the first chapters was *too* ornate. One man even advised me to "coarsen the texture," as being remote from the speed of the main narrative!

In any case when it appears I hope you'll find time to look it over again. Such irrelevancies as ****'s nosedive [the alcoholic who jumps overboard in Book II] and Dick's affair in Ohnsbruck are out, together with the scene of calling on the retired bootlegger at Beaulieu, [this was omitted *before* serial publication] & innumerable minor details. I have driven the Scribner proofreaders half nuts but I think I've made it incomparably smoother.[4]

As an explanation of the author's purpose in revising the serial, this is helpful, but curiously inaccurate. The most densely revised section of the novel is Book I; and within it the first eighteen chapters, which correspond to the first serial installment, have an even greater concentration of revisions. The first installment had been the one least revised in serial galley proof; Fitzgerald, apparently feeling that it had not achieved the same state of finish as the others, took the opportunity to work over it exhaustively at book-galley stage. The author's claim that "the last-half . . . has a *much* more polished facade now" is clearly contradicted by collation of the two texts; Fitzgerald did comparatively little polishing in the later sections of the book. He did omit four scenes from Book II, but this is not the same thing at all. It may be, as his reference to the Beaulieu scene indicates, that Fitzgerald forgot he had done his heavy revisions of the last half before serial publication. He had no reason to lie to Wilson about this, but he may have been betrayed by his anxiety to have Wilson reread *Tender is the Night.*

As can be seen from the specimen collation, the revisions in the early chapters are mainly stylistic, although some descriptive phrases are added. In the opening description of the beach, for example, "the horns of motors began to sound on the winding road" is changed to the more vivid "the horns of motors began to blow down from the winding road." The initial description of Rosemary is augmented by two sentences transferred from the third chapter. In Chapter 2 a description of the terrace at the hotel has been omitted. The most interesting revision in the opening sequence is the addition to the book of the stage direction—"To resume Rosemary's point of view" —at the beginning of the Divers' dinner party. Fiedler and others have branded this direction as amateurish: "All his life, point-of-view baffled him, and he was forced to make his transitions with such awkward links as: 'To resume Rosemary's point of view, it should be said . . .' or 'This is Cecilia taking up the story. . . .'"[5]

At the end of Chapter 8 McKisco's drunken singing was cut and an important sentence was added: "Again she wondered what Mrs. McKisco had seen in the bathroom." This, of course, reminds the reader that something very important has been adumbrated in the chapter.

In the Paris sequence, Dick's admission to Rosemary that he loves her is moved from Chapter 16 to 17. The effect is to retard the pace of Dick's loss of control; it is a decided improvement.

The first notable omission of material from the book comes in the account of Abe's activities in the Ritz bar. Though this had already been trimmed before serialization, Fitzgerald reluctantly recognized that—remarkable as the writing here is— it distracts too much attention from Dick. In Chapter 23 the description of the bar room, the recipes for Abe's drinks, the activities of the barmen, and the description of the patrons were all deleted; and in Chapter 24 the long description of the Ritz bar in full swing was deleted.

In 1934 there was a clearer line of demarcation than exists today between what could appear in a magazine and what could appear in a book. In the serial Fitzgerald could only suggest that Nicole had been raped by her father, but in Chapter 3 of the second book, he added nearly a page to Warren's confession (pp. 170-171).

As has been noted, Fitzgerald worked hard over the Gstaad chapter in Book II, for he was faced with the problem of indicating Dick's restlessness without at the same time making his deterioration too apparent. Near the end of the chapter Fitzgerald deleted Nicole's admonition to Dick that "Some people can drink, but you'd be ridiculous drinking." It is too early in the game for her to assert herself.

The second substantial omission in the book version occurs in the Innsbruck chapter in Book II, when an episode of some thousand words which treats Dick's messy involvement with the governess is omitted. Although this incident underlines the collapse of Dick's code of behavior, it is—as Fitzgerald said—an irrelevancy. Three related incidents that mar the plot line were deleted from the shipboard chapter in Book II. Here some 1200 words describing the McKiscos, the female writer on the ship, Dick's brief entanglement with the blonde, and his interest in the young alcoholic who jumped overboard have been omitted. Although this material focuses on Dick, it slows down the pace of the story and anticipates some of the Rome material.

Dick's encounter with Rosemary in Rome was more heavily revised than were the other chapters in Book II, and this almost certainly indicates that Fitzgerald was dissatisfied with the serial form of these chapters. In connection with these episodes, it is useful to consider a comment on writing that Fitzgerald wrote to John Peale Bishop: "I could tell you plenty of books in which the main episode, around which swings the entire drama, is over and accomplished in 4 or 5 sentences."⁶ Clearly the scenes with Rosemary in Rome are crucial in *Tender is the Night* and Fitzgerald undoubtedly gave special care to revising them. Dick's behavior with Rosemary —his clumsy seduction to which she yields at least partly out of pity—emphasizes the change in him since their initial meeting. It is immediately followed by the beating of Dick, which in effect marks the end of his promise. In revising Book II, Chapter 20—Dick and Rosemary's first afternoon in her suite —Fitzgerald pointed up Dick's need for Rosemary and his peculiar interest in her sexual history. The statement that "He felt himself going out toward her but he was in control of the situation" was deleted because the point of the scene is that Dick cannot control his appetite for Rosemary. The lovemaking in this chapter was made more passionate for the book.

Serial (March, p. 222)	Book (pp. 275-276)
"Don't," she said. "Really you don't **understand**."	When they were still limbs and feet and clothes, struggles of his arms and back, and her throat and breasts, she whispered, "No, not now—those things are rhythmic."
"I understand."	
Her face had changed with his looking down at it; there was the eternal moonlight in it now.	
	Disciplined he crushed his passion into a corner of his mind, but bearing up her fragility on his arm until she was poised half a foot above him, he said lightly:
"That would be poetic justice if it should be you," she said, still resisting . . . "It's impossible now, can't you tell?" She twisted away from him, walked to the mirror, and boxed her disarranged hair with her hands. Presently she drew a chair close to the bed and stroked his cheek.	"Darling—that doesn't matter."
	Her face had changed with his looking up at it; there was the eternal moonlight in it.
"It always seems impossible," he said. "Tell me the truth about you."	"That would be poetic justice if it should be you," she said. She twisted away from him, walked to the mirror, and
"I always have."	

"In a way—but nothing hangs together."

They both laughed but he pursued.

"Looking

boxed her disarranged hair with her hands. Presently she drew a chair close to the bed and stroked his cheek.

"Tell me the truth about you," he demanded.

"I always have."

"In a way—but nothing hangs together."

They both laughed but he pursued.

"Are you actually a virgin?"

"No-o-o!" she sang. "I've slept with six hundred and forty men—if that's the answer you want."

"It's none of my business."

"Do you want me for a case in psychology?"

"Looking

The new material about Dick's interest in Rosemary's virginity indicates rather more than an attempt to restore their relationship to its former intimacy. It shows Dick's inability to drop the idea of sleeping with her; and it may also be interpreted as an amateurish attempt to continue the seduction by getting her to talk about sexual matters. It is interesting, though, that Fitzgerald made no changes in the actual seduction. In Book II, Chapter 21 Dick continues his line of questioning about Rosemary's sexual history, but Fitzgerald deleted the question, "When did you first fall off the—golden chariot?" The close of this chapter, which describes the parting between **Dick and Rosemary**, was augmented with the following lines:

"Oh, such a shame, such a shame. Oh, such a shame. What's it all about anyhow?"

"I've wondered for a long time."

"But why bring it to me?"

"I guess I'm the Black Death," he said slowly. "I don't seem to bring people happiness any more."

(p. 286)

This is a key addition, for it had been Dick's ambition to bring people happiness, both socially and professionally. Here he admits that his grand plan, his scheme of a good life, has utterly failed.

In Chapter 2 of Book III Fitzgerald added two pages about the Chilean homosexual Dick interviews in Lausanne. This material was in the typescript and had been omitted from the serial because of possible censorship problems. But it is interesting that Fitzgerald also deleted from this chapter a description of the homosexual colony at the hotel—thus removing the last vestige of the detailed description of a group of homosexuals that had been whittled down through the history of the novel. The end of this chapter, which describes the effect on Nicole of her father's reappearance in her life, was augmented in the book to strengthen the point that Dick can no longer minister to Nicole and protect her from dangerous stresses—which is his last remaining function:

They sat silent. From Nicole flowed a vast tragic apathy.

"It was instinct," Dick said, finally. "He was really dying, but he tried to get a resumption of rhythm—he's not the first person that ever walked off his death-bed—like an old clock—you know, you shake it and somehow from sheer habit it gets going again. Now your father—"

"Oh, don't tell me," she said.

"His principal fuel was fear," he continued. "He got afraid, and off he went. He'll probably live till ninety—"

"Please don't tell me any more," she said. "Please don't—I couldn't stand any more."

"All right. The little devil I came down to see is hopeless. We may as well go back to-morrow."

"I don't see why you have to—come in contact with all this," she burst forth.

"Oh, don't you? Sometimes I don't either."

She put her hand on his.

"Oh, I'm sorry I said that, Dick."

Some one had brought a phonograph into the bar and they sat listening to The Wedding of the Painted Doll.

(pp. 324-325)

One more revision is worth mentioning: the sole revision in the brilliant final chapter of the novel. The grocery clerk Dick became involved with in Lockport was described in the serial as an "eighteen-year-old girl," but in the book her age was deleted. Fitzgerald probably felt that this specific detail conflicted with the second-hand-news quality of the rest of the paragraph.

The Text

For all of Fitzgerald's work on the proofs—or, perhaps, because of it—the first edition of *Tender is the Night* has an appallingly sloppy text. The book is freckled with misspellings, and there are serious errors in chronology. Fitzgerald even confused the name of Nicole's father, calling him Devereux (p. 166) and Charles (p. 320). Cowley places some of the blame for the sloppy text on Maxwell Perkins, who "had an aristocratic disregard for details so long as a book was right in its feeling for life. Since Fitzgerald was regarded as one of his special authors, the manuscript was never copy-edited by others."[7] No attempt was made to clean up the text in the second and third printings of 1934, even though Clifton Fadiman listed thirteen spelling errors in his review of *Tender is the Night*.[8]

Allowing himself considerable editorial license, Cowley made some 800 emendations in his edition of the novel; however, many of his changes strike me as arbitrary. What follows is a list of the emendations I would make in the first printing, with the *C* indicating that Cowley makes the change. I have been very conservative about altering punctuation. Fitzgerald punctuated by ear; and if his pointing is not always strictly correct, it is usually unambiguous.

4.10; 18.25; 19.16; 220.2	Hotel [hotel *C*
12.6	Anthiel [Antheil *C*
12.8; 13.5	Ulysses [*Ulysses* *C*
16.11; 30.11	'Daddy's Girl.' [*Daddy's Girl.* *C*
17.11	The [the *C*
18.11	Nice Carnival Song ["Nice Carnival Song"
18.12	Le Temps [*Le Temps* *C*
18.13	The Saturday Evening Post [*The Saturday Evening Post*
18.30	Czar [czar *C*
19.1	Buddha's [Buddhas' *C*
19.5	Ten [Eleven *C*
20.19	were [was *C*
21.26	swimming, [swimming. *C*
22.18	The New York Herald [the *Paris Herald*
24.23	disinterested [uninterested *C*
24.30	Signor [Señor *C*
42.8	Diver's [Divers' *C*
42.25	irrelative [irrelevant *C*
48.20	Isles des Lerins [les de Lérins *C*
60.4	parties [party *C*
68.16	chair . . . [chair. . . .
70.6	"Daddy's Girl" [*Daddy's Girl* *C*
74.5	Beaumont Hamel [Beaumont-Hamel *C*
75.21	Undine [*Undine* *C*
75.23	Wurtemburg [Württemberg *C*
76.26	six [seven *C*
78.6	Wurtemburgers [Württembergers *C*
78.8	old [Old *C*
79.2	Art [Arts *C*
79.4	Hotel [Hôtel *C*

97.5	Hôtel [hotel *C*
101.9	Odyssey [odyssey *C*
102.5	Hengest [Hengist *C*
104.28; 136.15	Champs Élysées [Champs-Élysées *C*
105.1	Saint Lazare [Saint-Lazare *C*
106.9	on world [on a world *C*
111.19	Diaghileff [Diaghilev *C*
111.21	decor [décor *C*
117.5	friends [friend *C*
119.10, 12	1000 chemises [100,000 Chemises *C*
*119.30	Ferrara [Canossa
120.14	Rue des Saintes-Anges [Rue de Saint-Ange
121.11	through. [through?
122.31	Brizzard [Brizard *C*
122.31	André Fernet Blanco [Fernet-Branca
122.32	Rochet [Rocher *C*
125.4	had awakened [had been awakened *C*
128.23	Evreux [Évreux *C*
*129.26	conversation [conservatism
131.4	Moseby [Mosby *C*
132.10	concessionaire [concessionnaire *C*
132.23	Liberty [*Liberty* *C*
133.4, 8	France [*France* *C*
133.15	of [about *C*
136.2	arrondisement [arrondissement *C*
137.21	Godlike [godlike *C*
139.9	States [states *C*
139.29	French Latin quarter [Latin Quarter *C*
142.13	third [Third *C*

*119.29 I can discover no such incident associated with Ferrara. Henry Dan Piper has suggested to me that F. may have been thinking of the penance performed by the emperor Henry IV before Pope Gregory VII at Canossa in 1077.

*129.26 *Conservatism* is in all drafts through the serial; *conversation* appears only in the book and is a typographical error made in the lost book galleys.

145.32	unexceptionally [unexceptionably
152.18	Damenstiff Strasse [Damenstiftgasse *C*
153.18	in [at *C*
153.27	criteria [criterion *C*
153.31	The Rose and the Ring [*The Rose and the Ring* *C*
156.16	cervical [cortex *C*
157.2; 158.34	Zurichsee [Zürichsee
157.7; 193.31	Krapaelin [Kraepelin *C*
193.10	*Krapœlin* [*Kraepelin* *C*
158.5	private soldiers [privates *C*
162.21	farcicle [farcical
164.3	life . . . [life. . . . *C*
164.4	clouds . . . [clouds. . . . *C*
164.5	war . . . [war. . . . *C*
164.8	me . . . [me. . . . *C*
164.13	weiss . . . [weiss. . . . *C*
167.7	eleven [thirteen
175.9	Clinic [clinic *C*
175.9	Interlacken [Interlaken *C*
177.4	gladiola [gladiolus *C*
178.10	Suppe's [Suppé's *C*
180.10	A ["A *C*
180.12	down . . . [down. . . ."
181.26	Service [service
183.11	Glas-Bier [Glas Bier *C*
187.17	burberry [Burberry
192.12	whom [who *C*
*193.17	Jugenhorn [Dent du Midi *C*
193.22	trained-bands [trainbands *C*
193.31	siz [sie *C*
194.7	down port [down into port *C*

*193.17 I have been unable to locate a *Jugenhorn* in Switzerland. Cowley emends to *Dent du Midi*, which Dick could have seen from Montreux.

195.3	Kursal [Kursaal *C*	
197.19	five [four *C*	
199.23	'Vanity Fair.' [*Vanity Fair.* *C*	
199.24	schizzoid [schizoid *C*	
200.1	guards' [Guards *C*	
205.12	Rochers [Rocher *C*	
209.23	camerière [camérière	
209.30	Grotte [Grotto *C*	
211.28	*Affaires Etrangères* [Affaires Étrangères *C*	
215.10	Nice Carnival Song, ["Nice Carnival Song," *C*	
217.23	MacBeth [McBeth *C*	
219.30	in [into *C*	
221.11	Menagerie [menagerie *C*	
223.28	Hôtel [hotel *C*	
223.29	Casino [casino *C*	
226.5	almost [just over *C*	
226.8	spinsters' [spinster's *C*	
*227.23	Gregorovius [Gregorovious	
230.11	haven't [have *C*	
230.20	Privat docent [Privatdocent	
233.3	Humpty-Dumpty [Humpty Dumpty *C*	
236.5	Prokofieff's "Love of Three Oranges." [Prokofiev's *Love for Three Oranges.* *C*	
236.8	lamp light and [lamp and *C*	
238.1	eight [seven *C*	
239.30	instructed [uninstructed	
240.25	as imprisoned [as if imprisoned	
243.14	with a nail [with nail *C*	
246.22	six [nine *C*	
249.20	apposite [opposite *C*	
250.21	"schizophrêne" [schizophrenic *C*	
252.20	Emile's [Émile's *C*	
252.30	Emile [Émile *C*	

*227.23 This is the only place F. spells the name *Gregorovius*. Cowley changes the spelling to *Gregorovius* in all appearances, on the ground that *Gregorovious* "is highly improbable in German" (Cowley—TITN, p. 349). However, I have retained *Gregorovious*—as I have resisted changing *Chillicheff* to *Chillichev*—because these are not names of real people.

254.7	patient's [patients' *C*
255.10-11	The Century, The Motion Picture, L'Illustration, and the Fliegende Blätter [the *Century,* the *Motion Picture, L'Illustration,* and *Fliegende Blätter C*
256.13	A [a *C*
257.7	nor [or *C*
257.7	their [his
257.32	inordinately meanwhile [inordinately, meanwhile
258.2	grand Tour [grand tour
259.11	departed [stood ready to depart
259.31	The Herald [the *Herald C*
262.7	erbsen-suppe [Erbsensuppe
262.7	würstchen [Würstchen *C*
262.8	helles [steins
262.9	"kaiser-schmarren." [Kaiserschmarren.
266.16	of it [the income *C*
268.17	its [the steamer's *C*
270.11	hoops [hoofs *C*
270.17	'The Grandeur that was Rome' [*The Grandeur that was Rome C*
271.1	Corriere della Sera [*Corriere della Sera C*
271.1	'Wall Street' [*Wall Street C*
271.3	citta [città *C*
271.14	four [three
271.16	twenty-two . . . thirty-eight [twenty-one . . . thirty-seven
274.2	Daddy's Girl [*Daddy's Girl C*
274.17	now . . . [now. . . . *C*
274.21	heaven . . . [heaven. . . .
276.12	twenty-two [twenty-one
288.16	Nationale [Nazionale *C*
290.5	mousseaux [mousseux *C*
294.16, 23	saoûl [soûl
296.7	guards' [Guards
301.10	whereon [on which *C*

211

301.18	*semper* [*sempre C*
301.18	*dritte* [*diretto C*
301.18	*dextra* [*destra C*
301.18	*sinestra* [*sinistra C*
301.22	Piazzo d'Espagna [Piazza di Spagna *C*
309.28	cable [telegram *C*
311.26	Clinic [clinic *C*
313.6	to [with *C*
314.3	Wassermans [Wassermanns
314.15	Chilian [Chilean *C*
316.7, 25; 319.22	Chili [Chile *C*
317.3	forties [late thirties *C*
320.17	Charles [Devereux *C*
320.20	wherein [in which
320.27	*gratis* [*grata C*
323.6	The New York Herald [the *Paris Herald*
325.5	The Wedding of the Painted Doll. ["The Wedding of the Painted Doll." *C*
327.18	'cess [cess *C*
331.6	is [are *C*
331.11	eleven and nine [eight and six
332.4	regimentation [regimen *C*
332.13	nine [six
334.1	Kyble [Kabyle *C*
334.1	Sabaean [Sabæan *C*
336.27	herself [itself *C*
337.11	El [La
342.13	Moutonne [Mouton *C*
344.7	Saland [Salaud *C*
345.8	guess at in [guess in *C*
345.23	Bay [bay *C*
345.32; 346.6; 349.16; 353.30	Margin [*Margin C*

212

347.23	nous héros," he said, "il nous faut [nous autres héros," he said, "il faut *C*
347.24	héroisme [héroïsme
*348.6	Corps d'Afrique du Nord [Légion Étrangère
349.23	Lady Sibly-Biers [Lady Caroline *C*
350.24	enfanterie [enfantillage *C*
351.14	saying: "What [saying, "What
353.16	it [them *C*
354.2	attendant [waiting
354.13	a [à *C*
357.17	Niçoise [Niçois *C*
361.20	personified [expressed *C*
363.30	nook [hook *C*
364.5	five [four
364.8	years [summers
364.14	five [four
368.33	Abram's [Abrams' *C*
369.31	Loos' [Loos *C*
380.18	than [from what *C*
382.6	Korniloff [Kornilov *C*
384.15	finding [to find *C*
*391.28	Sibley [Sibly
399.16	The Herald . . . The Times [the *Herald* . . . the *Times C*
399.20	Ouste [ouste *C*
399.31	Due de Saints Anges [Rue de Saint-Ange
400.31	dupes [victims *C*
401.11	principal [principle *C*
403.5	Beach [beach *C*
403.10	A. and P. [A. P.

*348.6 I have not been able to find a *Corps d'Afrique du Nord*. There was a *Corps Franc d'Afrique*, but it was a penal unit. Cowley emends to *Bataillon d'Afrique*, which was also a penal unit. Since Tommy seems to be referring to the film *Beau Geste*, the general term for the French Foreign Legion seems best here.

*391.28 Cowley changes the spelling to *Sibley* in all appearances.

407.9 N. Y. [New York C
408.7 Section [section C

Another kind of error in the novel is the repetition of phrases as a result of Fitzgerald's practice of saving good phrases from his stories for insertion in his novels. There are three such cases of repetition in *Tender is the Night:* at pages thirty-three and eighty-nine the description of Nicole's hair; at pages thirty-five and sixty-nine the phrase "compromises of how many years"; and at pages 138 and 204 the description of a kiss.

Malcolm Cowley is probably right in suggesting that the errors in *Tender is the Night* "had a cumulative effect on readers and ended by distracting their attention." [9] But a much more crucial effect is that the chronological errors obscure the time-scheme of the novel and seriously undermine the impact of Book III. We know from Fitzgerald's preliminary plan that the time-span of *Tender is the Night* is from June 1925 to July 1929—*five summers, but four years.* But Fitzgerald seems to have been confused by counting 1925 as a full year. Thus, on page 276 Fitzgerald states that the Rome episodes take place during 1928, but he mistakes the ages of Rosemary and Dick. The break-up of Dick's marriage and his final departure from the Riviera occur one year later, or four years after Rosemary's first visit to the Riviera—not five years, as Fitzgerald states on page 364. It is the summer of 1929, and the unexpressed idea that the new breed of new-rich Riviera people have less than four months of paper profits left gives the conclusion a special feeling. Unfortunately, Fitzgerald's carelessness blurred this effect. Indeed, Cowley is convinced that Fitzgerald changed his time-scheme while the novel was in progress, and that *Tender is the Night* really does occupy five years:

We will be told several times that five years have passed since Rosemary's first visit to the Cap d'Antibes in the summer of 1925. Her second visit, then, was in June, 1930. The date reveals a change in Fitzgerald's plans, since his earlier intention had been to end the story in July, 1929, a few months before the Wall Street crash. . . . At this point, however, the author needed more elapsed time to accomplish Dick's ruin—five years instead of four —and actually 1930 was better for the historical background than 1929. It was the year when, in spite of the crash, there were more rich Americans in Europe than ever before and when the summer season on the Riviera was the biggest and maddest.[10]

However, Cowley does not account for the year 1929. A piece of evidence that argues against a five-year time-span is Tommy's remark to Nicole on the *Margin* that his stocks are doing well (p. 353). Surely this remark belongs to 1929, not 1930.

Cowley is right, though, in saying that one year, 1926, is unaccounted for in the first edition.[11] The trip to Gstaad occurs at Christmas 1925, and on page 238 Fitzgerald says that Dick has been at the clinic eighteen months—which would make it June 1927. But we know from the Rome chapters that follow that this is 1928. Cowley's suggestion that the Divers spent 1926 on the Riviera while the clinic was being renovated accounts for the missing year.

Fitzgerald appears to have remained unaware of the concentration of bad readings in his novel, for he did not mention them when, at the time *Tender is the Night* was being considered for the Modern Library in 1936, he asked Bennett Cerf for permission to alter the plates. The changes "would include in several cases sudden stops and part headings which would be to some extent explanatory. . . ."[12] The revisions and notes in Fitzgerald's dummy for the "author's final version" chiefly deal with stylistic matters and do not indicate any concern with the errors in the text. These notes, in Fitzgerald's copy at the Princeton University Library, are listed below. Page references are to the first edition.

3.1	the pleasant shore [the shore
3.2	stands [stood
3.4	stretches [stretched

3.5	Lately [Now
3.6	a decade ago [in 1925
3.7-8	April. Now, many bungalows cluster near it, but when this story begins only [April; in those days only
3.17	came [had come
4.8	one [this
24.19	His [Dick's
24.19-23	His eyes were of a bright, hard blue. His nose was somewhat pointed and there was never any doubt at whom he was looking or talking—and this is a flattering attention, for who looks at us? —glances fall upon us, curious or disinterested, nothing more. [Shift this forward.
75	<At the top of this page Fitzgerald drew a Greek key design.>
120.1-122.6	hour of standing . . . It had become [hour it had become
153.18	in [at (L.)
154.17	yourself—once [yourself. Once
154.24	subject." [subject. No good sense."
154.28	people; illusions [people—they were the illusions
155.7-9	Moreover it is confusing to come across a youthful photograph of some one known in a rounded maturity and gaze with a shock upon a fiery, wiry, eagle-eyed stranger. [*deleted*
157.7	Krapaelin [Kraepelin
157.13-15	You have the same stupid and unaging American face, except I know you're not stupid, Dick." [You are still a carrot-top" Here insert description from page 24 old numbering <It is impossible to be sure what Fitzgerald intended here because he seems to have revised this passage twice. At one point he may have wanted

216

	the passage to read: You have the same unaging American face.">
157.16	war—you [war" Dick said, "You
158.5	private soldiers [privates
158.10	"—toward ["Toward
159.6	eminence [plateau
159.12	Some [Outside, some
159.13	they [one
159.20	room; pushing [room. Pushing
159.24	first one was [first was
159.29	etc., etc. [etc. etc.
160.1	about the time of the [about the
160.16	(2) [[page] 2-Follow this form with the breaks here
160.23	(3) [[page] 3-(ect)
160	*This is my mark to say I have made final corrections up to this point.
178.19-20	path—where in a moment a shadow cut across it. She [path; where, in a moment, a shadow cut across it—she
179.33	By and by [Bye-and-bye (?)
180.22	shoulder. [shoulder—then apart.
180.23	record," she said. "—Have [record,—Have
181.4	table, eyes [table, male eyes
193	<Extra space after 1. 15.>
193	Lester begin here & go to end of Chapter (2 pages)
212.9	Tommy [Abe North
212.23-4	beach with my husband and two children. [beach near my home above the Mediteranean with my husband and two children and our dear friends
362	This is DULL
362	You lay down the book & never pick it up—
369	Tiresome stuff! True but why?

Another note on the text of the novel appears in Fitzgerald's notebooks.[13]

Analysis of Tender:

I	Case History	151-212	61 pps. (change moon) p. 212
II	Rosemary's Angle	3-104	101 pps. P. 3
III	Casualties	104-148, 213-224	55 pps. (−2) (120 & 121)
IV	Escape	225-306	82 pps.
V	The Way Home	306-408	103 pps. (−8) (332-341)

The moon on p. 212—if that is what the note means—has not been located. This page is the end of Nicole's stream-of-consciousness passage which bridges the flashback and the Divers' return to the Riviera in book two; and it is just possible that *moon* is a typing error for *mood*. Fitzgerald's decision to delete the visit to Mary Minghetti was sound, for this chapter retards the pace of book three.

The unavoidable conclusion to be drawn from a scrutiny of the text of *Tender is the Night* is that a scrupulously-edited edition is needed. Cowley made a painstaking attempt to provide an improved text in the "author's final version," but the silent emendations render this edition less useful than it should have been. Both the general reader and the critic of *Tender is the Night* need to know which words are the author's, a need that is especially serious when an editor takes a liberal position on emending. As for the author's original version, it is scandalous that a work held in high esteem should exist only in bad texts—and this applies to the Scribner Library, Bantam, and Viking Portable editions of *Tender is the Night*.

Appendices

Appendix 1: Unlisted Sections of Manuscript

The boxes of the *Tender is the Night* manuscripts include sixteen sections of material that have not been listed or discussed in the course of this study. Although most of them have no bearing on *Tender is the Night*, they are listed here as an aid to other researchers.

Description & Pagination	Corresponds to TITN	Remarks	Location	Key
CCX & H: 8½″ x 11″. Pica. 1 p.	....	Letter marked for copying.	Box 1	185
H: 8½″ x 13″. 1 p.	....	Draft of personal letter.	Box 1	186
H & T: 6 pp.	....	Notes & itineraries for trip to North Africa in 1930.	Box 1	187
H (ink): 5½″ x 8½″. 1 p.	II, 8; p. 193.	German translation of Dick's book for Feb. installment, p. 156.	Box 1	188
H fragment.	II, 14; p. 239.	Note to change Borosk to Lladislau at serial VII.	Box 1	189
CC fragment.	III, 7: p. 361.	"How you remember things! You always did —and always the nice things!"	Box 1	190

Description & Pagination	Corresponds to TITN	Remarks	Location	Key
H & T: 30 pp.	....	Personal papers and a few scraps of work on the novel. Includes telegram to Murphy about jail scene.	Box 1	191
T: 8½″ x 11″. Pica.	....	Beginning of a short story about Palm Beach.	Box 1	192
H: 3″ x 5″. 1 p.	....	Note on contents of Box 4. Not Fitzgerald's.	Box 4	193
H: 3″ x 5″. 2 pp.	....	Note on Contents of Box 4. Not Fitzgerald's.	Box 4	194
H: 8½″ x 11″. 1 p.	....	Note on contents of Box 5. Not Fitzgerald's.	Box 5	195
RT: 8½″ x 11″. Elite.	....	Synopsis for serial.	Box 5	196
H: 8½″ x 11″. 1 p.	....	Note on contents of Box 6. Not Fitzgerald's.	Box 6	197
H: 8½″ x 11″. 1 p.	....	Note on contents of Box 6. Not Fitzgerald's.	Box 6	198
H: fragment. 1 p.	....	Note on Baby Warren. May not be Fitzgerald's.	Box 6	199
RT: 8½″ x 11″. Pica. 1-63.	....	"One Trip Abroad."	Box 6	200

Appendix 2: Textual Collation of Serial and First Six Chapters of the Book

	SERIAL		BOOK
all appearances	Costello	all appearances	Barban
p. [1], column 2		p. 3	
l. 3	The style is Second Empire, with a beam of the crescent; deferential	l. 3	Deferential
l. 7	its middle-class English	l. 7	its English
ll. 7-8	Now, there are many bungalows clustered	ll. 7-8	Now, many bungalows cluster
l. 10	*Gausse's Hôtel des Etrangers*	l. 10	Gausse's Hôtel des Étrangers
l. 14	lay wavering with the ripples	ll. 15-16	lay quavering in the ripples
		p. 4	
l. 21	began to sound on the winding road up on the	ll. 4-5	began to blow down from the winding road along the
l. 24	where the pines	l. 7	where pines
l. 27	faded prettiness patted with broken veins	ll. 10-11	fading prettiness that would soon be patted with broken veins
p. 2, column 1			
ll. 8-9	gold. Her body [see *p. 6, column 2, ll. 3-9*]	ll. 18-21	gold. Her eyes were bright, big, clear, wet, and shining, the color of her cheeks was real, breaking close to the surface from the strong young pump of her heart. Her body [see *p. 17, l. 6*]

221

	SERIAL		BOOK
l. 17	but they were	l. 28 p. 5	but were
l. 30	hotel. There the hot [see *p. 6, column 2, 11. 3-9*]	ll. 5-8	hotel. When she walked she carried herself like a ballet-dancer, not slumped down on her hips but held up in the small of the back. Out there the hot [see *p. 17, 1. 6*]
ll. 36-37	with any activity	l. 13	with activity
l. 41	dozen people	l. 17	dozen persons
l. 48	peignoir	ll. 23-24	bath- / robe
ll. 48-49	face down- / ward	l. 24	face down
l. 50	dragging her slim legs	l. 26	dragging slim legs
ll. 51-53	when it was breast high, she stopped and glanced back toward shore. A	ll. 27-28	when it was about breast high, she glanced back towards shore: a
column 2			
l. 1	evenly returned	l. 30 p. 6	returned
l. 10	it and wallowing	l. 4	it, wallowing
ll. 11-14	tanned pretty woman looked down at her, and suddenly conscious of the raw whiteness of her own body Rosemary turned on her back and drifted toward shore. The hairy man, still holding	ll. 5-8	tanned woman with very white teeth looked down at her, and Rosemary, suddenly conscious of the raw whiteness of her own body, turned on her back and drifted toward shore. The hairy man holding
l. 17	but he spoke	l. 11	but spoke
l. 21	come for	l. 15	come in for

222

	SERIAL		BOOK
l. 23	minced two steps off	l. 17	minced off two steps
ll. 26-27	this brief conversation	l. 20	this conversation
l. 29	umbrella, and besides	ll. 22-23	umbrella; besides
l. 38	bathrobe	l. 30 *p. 7*	peignoir
ll. 52-55	shoulder. She was one of the white-skinned group, and Rosemary forming a vague antipathy to them, turned away. Nearest her on the other side a	ll. 11-13	shoulder. Rosemary, forming a vague antipathy to her and her companions, turned away. Nearest her, on the other side, a
p. 3, column 1		*p. 8*	
l. 34	pearls. From	l. 4	pearls. Perhaps from
l. 45	people looking at her, waiting.	l. 15	people were waiting.
column 2		*p. 9*	
l. 29	Dumphry, towheaded	l. 12	Dumphry, a towheaded
l. 37	but very compact	l. 19- *p. 10* l. 1 *p. 10*	but com- / pact
ll. 41-42	America, newly superimposed	ll. 4-5	America, these latter superimposed
p. 4, column 1			
l. 13	Suddenly realizing his	l. 27 *p. 11*	Suddenly remotely conscious of his
l. 43	body floated motionless	ll. 21-22	body lay motionless
column 2		*p. 12*	
l. 7	my name	l. 5	my man

	SERIAL		BOOK
p. 5, column 1		p. 13	
ll. 26-30	Noon now dominated sea and sky, but in barren victory—even the white line of Cannes, five miles off, had faded to a mirage of what was fresh and cool. Rosemary watched a robin-breasted sailing boat, pulling in	ll. 23-25	Noon dominated sea and sky—even the white line of Cannes, five miles off, had faded to a mirage of what was fresh and cool; a robin-breasted sailing boat pulled in
column 2		p. 14	
l. 7	fell asleep.	l. 3	fell really asleep.
ll. 11-12	lay, still blinking	l. 6	lay blinking
l. 28	They both faced the seascape momentarily.	l. 20	They faced the seascape together momentarily.
ll. 31-33	and his bright blue eyes seemed to her like glittering worlds—for a moment she lived in them, eagerly	ll. 23-24	and for a moment she lived in the bright blue worlds of his eyes, eagerly
l. 35	peignoir,	l. 26	peignoir
p. 6, column 1		p. 15	
l. 3	things—she had twice been	ll. 19-20	life—twice
l. 4	widowed, and	l. 20	widowed, her
l. 7	she got something from them both	ll. 22-23	they both left something to her
l. 12	and which saw	l. 27 p. 16	and saw
ll. 15-16	the trivial, the facile, the vulgar, and the merely common.	l. 3	the trivial, the facile and the vulgar.
l. 34	"No, I want	l. 19	"I want

224

	SERIAL		BOOK
ll. 34-35	way and it	l. 19	way—it
l. 36	"But I'm not going," Rosemary reiterated. "Mother	l. 21	"Mother
l. 38	"Well—" Mrs. Speers considered. "Well, then later."	l. 22	"Oh, well then go later,—but some day before we leave."
		p. 17	
ll. 54-55	to Monsieur Gausse	l. 3	to Gausse
column 2			
ll. 3-9	métier. Rosemary's eyes were bright, big, clear, wet, and shining, the color of her cheeks was real, breaking close to the surface from the strong young pump of her heart. When she had got her information she walked from the lobby carrying herself like a ballet dancer, not slumped down upon her hips, but held up in the small of her back. She [see *p. 2, column 1,* *ll. 8-9*]	l. 6	métier. She [see *p. 4,* *ll. 18-21; p. 5, ll.* *5-8*]
l. 12	on and talk. Enjoy	l. 8	on, talk, enjoy
l. 19	absorbed during their journey in	l. 14	absorbed in
l. 23	leaves, and the	l. 18	leaves, the
l. 26	cabbies were asleep in	l. 21	cabbies slept in

225

	SERIAL		BOOK
ll. 27-28	promenade she found that the	l. 22	promenade the
l. 31	became even a	ll. 25-26	became a

ll. 36-37	by.
	    As
		ll. 30-31	by.
			[space]
			    As

l. 39	Diver, walked past with	l. 32– *p. 18* l. 1	Diver, crossed her path with
l. 41	her and a	*p. 18* l. 3	her, a
l. 52	tunes.	l. 12	tune.
p. 7, column 1			
l. 3	paper. Lately accustomed	ll. 17-18	paper. It was the same feeling that had oppressed her at the hotel—accustomed
ll. 9-10	was after all empty	l. 21	was empty
ll. 11-15	surcharged by watching an American tourist take what would inevitably turn out as small black photographs of scenery, and by listening to the sad tunes reminiscent	ll. 22-23	surcharged by listening to the sad tunes of the orchestra, reminiscent
l. 18	hotel. Her	ll. 25-26	Hotel. Her
ll. 22-23	her notions about money	l. 28	her valuations of money
l. 24	Riviera. The	l. 29 *p. 19*	Riviera, the delta of many rivers. The
l. 31	into long Baltic	l. 2	into Baltic

226

	SERIAL		BOOK
ll. 48-55	aqueducts, and on the terrace of Gausse's Hotel French girls were chattering with naval aviation officers from St. Raphael; later the white uniforms grew dimmer with each veil of darkness until, like the heavy roses and the nightingales, they became an essential part of the beauty of this proud gay land. . . . Somewhere	ll. 18-20	aqueducts. . . . Somewhere

column 2

ll. 11-12	place that part	l. 27	place the part
l. 15	the McKiscos and Mrs. Abrams.	l. 29	the other ones.
		p. 20	
l. 21	blonde one, given	l. 4	blonde man, given
ll. 35-36	possibilities, one after another. He	l. 17	possibilities. He
		p. 21	
ll. 43-45	book, for chicken Maryland, she said, and Rosemary spread the peignoir beside her. She	ll. 5-6	book for chicken Maryland. She

p. 8, column 1

l. 4	low and almost	l. 18	low, almost
l. 15	grippe and	l. 28	grippe and didn't know it, and
		p. 22	
l. 32	"No, we	l. 10	"We
l. 33	"Our theory	l. 11	"The theory

227

	SERIAL		BOOK
l. 45	Medonca, Otto Dunkels, Mme.	ll. 22-23	Medonca, Mme.
l. 52	restlessness and stretched	l. 28	restlessness, stretching
column 2			
l. 2-3	handsome in a dark way—	l. 33	handsome—
		p. 23	
l. 5	afterward when	l. 2	afterward, when
l. 6	the anti-social inability	ll. 2-3	the inability
l. 8	fretful pain	l. 4	fretful and unprofitable pain
l. 13	work very seriously	l. 9	work seriously
l. 15	Mrs. S. Flesh	l. 11	S. Flesh
ll. 20-21	up some sewing	l. 15	up a piece of sewing
l. 23	a rubber	ll. 17-18	a pneumatic rubber
l. 28	beware society people	l. 22	beware such people
l. 30	immobility, as complete	l. 24	immobility, complete
l. 34	other—she	l. 28	other, she
ll. 36-37	inter-relation that she	ll. 29-30	inter-relation, which she
l. 37	they had a	ll. 30-31	they seemed to have a
ll. 40-41	They were all three very personable in different ways, they were	l. 33-*p. 24* l. 1	All three were personable in different ways; all were
		p. 24	
ll. 48-49	heterogeneous and indistinguishable	l. 8	heterogeneous, indistinguishable
l. 52	three men were	l. 11	three were
l. 54	North had	l. 13	North, had

	SERIAL		BOOK
p. 60, column 1			
l. 24	was married.	l. 28	was already possessed.
		p. 25	
l. 43	said:	l. 8	said with a smile that was a rakish gleam:
l. 53	I have	l. 15	I *have*
ll. 56-57	pile." She lowered her	l. 17	pile." She considered, and then lowering her
column 2			
l. 2	English	l. 19	British
ll. 2-3	shouting: 'Isn't	l. 20	shouting about: 'Isn't
		p. 26	
ll. 33-34	suits! Time to go in."	l. 7	suits!"
l. 43	stinging curry	l. 13	tingling curry
ll. 44-45	She did not know that the Divers'	l. 14	The Divers'
l. 49	and that there	ll. 16-17	and she did not know that there
column 3			
l. 2	a general commotion	l. 24	a commotion
ll. 4-5	A moment's inspection	l. 25	Close inspection
ll. 7-8	cloth. "Well,	ll. 26-27	cloth. [space] "Well,
		p. 27	
ll. 23-24	a most desperate	ll. 4-5	a desperate
ll. 30-32	them—the inner truth that all things are in motion, that in reality a qualitative change had already set in was	ll. 9-10	them—in reality a qualitative change had already set in that was

229

	SERIAL		BOOK
ll. 36-37	with his cold blue eyes, his kind, strong mouth, and said	ll. 12-13	with cold blue eyes; his kind, strong mouth said
ll. 41-42	blooming." In	ll. 15-16	blooming." [space] In
		p. 28	
l. 57- *p. 61,* *column 1* l. 1	Carlo as nearly sulky as	l. 1	Carlo nearly as sulkily as
p. 61, column 1			
l. 2	be; she	l. 2	be. She
l. 3	Turbie, an old	l. 3	Turbie, to an old
l. 4	as Rosemary stood	l. 4	as she stood
l. 11	cherries as large	l. 8	cherries large
ll. 13-14	amaranth, the mimosa, the cork	l. 10	amaranth, mimosa, cork
l. 16	two big barnlike	l. 11	two barnlike
		p. 29	
ll. 19-20	a bareheaded young	l. 1	a young
l. 28	the big blank wall of a stage	ll. 7-8	the blank wall of stage
ll. 30-31	into its half	l. 9	into half
ll. 32-22	twilight, figures that turned up	l. 10	twilight, turning
l. 44	with tired dogged	l. 18	with dogged
l. 52-53	above and called	l. 23	above, called
column 2			
l. 3	strenuous as	l. 31	strenuous. As
l. 4	hand. She	l. 31	hand she
		p. 30	
l. 23	Paris and I	l. 11	Paris. I

	SERIAL		BOOK
l. 24	coast immediately to	ll. 11-12	coast right away to
l. 25	signed up."	l. 12	signed."
l. 26	I was sorry."	l. 13	I'm sorry."
l. 39	decides all business	l. 23	decides business
ll. 43-44	liking, it was not	l. 26	liking, not
column 3			
ll. 3-4	with equanimity a surrender	l. 30	a surrender with equanimity
		p. 31	
ll. 11-12	I'd rather	l. 2	Rather
l. 15	way about you. Why	l. 4	way. Why
ll. 26-27	off the conversation and called	l. 12	off, calling
l. 29	California was	l. 13	Los Angeles was
ll. 30-31	moved again through	l. 14	moved once more through
ll. 34-35	finished. She	l. 17	finished and she
ll. 37-38	knew Brady's studio	l. 19	knew the studio
		p. 32	
l. 48	Feeling high from	l. 1	Feeling good from
ll. 49-50	arms so high that the	l. 2	arms high enough for the
l. 51	shoulder almost touched her	l. 3	shoulder to touch her
l. 58- *p. 62, column 1* l. 1	side everything was	l. 8	side all was
p. 62, column 1		*p. 33*	
ll. 22-23	brighter and prettier than	l. 5	brighter than

231

	SERIAL		BOOK
ll. 35-37	though some one had carelessly thrown down a handful of seeds, listening	ll. 14-15	though sprung from a careless handful of seeds, listening
column 2		*p. 34*	
l. 35	nothing she could do	l. 20	nothing to do
l. 37	his little house	ll. 21-22	his one-room house
		p. 35	
l. 59-60	where they're brawls	l. 5	where there's a brawl
column 3			
ll. 25-27	experience and in the shadow of his charm people believed that he	l. 22	experience: people believed he
ll. 31-32	won people quickly	l. 25	won everyone quickly
l. 34	could only be	l. 27	could be
ll. 37-38	amusing and tender world	l. 29	amusing world
l. 42	evaporated, vanished before	l. 32	evaporated before
		p. 36	
l. 54	Still under	ll. 7-8	To resume Rosemary's point of view it should be said that, under
ll. 55-56	air, they looked	l. 9	air, she and her mother looked
p. 63, column 1		*p. 37*	
l. 9	terrace under the open sky.	l. 18	terrace.
l. 14	time. She worries	l. 21	time, worries
l. 19	lightness that seemed to	l. 24	lightness seeming to
l. 24	he began to mix a	ll. 27-28	he poured a

232

	SERIAL		*BOOK*
l. 27	studio, and as	l. 30	studio, as
l. 33	ill-bred, yet once more she	l. 1	ill-bred; once more, though, she
column 2			
ll. 2-4	stage so fortunately lighted, so brilliantly scented from the garden, some	l. 24	stage some
ll. 13-14	mingling of elements.	l. 31	mingling.
ll. 16-17	with a masculine politeness, blended of a proud	l. 32	with a proud
		p. 38	
l. 20	much now that	l. 2	much that
ll. 23-28	along. The newcomers were in a whooped-up mood. They had had cocktails before leaving and their brasher characteristics were in evidence. "I've	ll. 4-5	along. "I've
l. 42	group formed	l. 15	grouping formed
l. 45	this small social	l. 17	this social
ll. 48-49	effort. He wanted a	l. 20	effort, waiting
column 3			
l. 16	all, so	l. 31	all—so
		p. 39	
l. 38	She found herself feeling far	l. 14	She felt far
l. 49	neat, fascinating brightness	l. 21	neat brightness

	SERIAL		BOOK
l. 51	year now, which	l. 22	year, which

p. 64, column 1

ll. 5-6	was in the movies but not at all at them.	ll. 32-33	was In the movies but not at all At them.

p. 40

l. 9	thing," and it	l. 2	thing"; it
ll. 21-24	friends. The point is to recognize the exact time when." With	ll. 10-11	friends." With
l. 34	to Earl Brady	l. 17	to Brady

Appendix 3: Structural Comparison of the First Edition with "The Author's Final Version"

First Edition	Corresponds to	"The Author's Final Version"
Book I: 1		Book II: 2
2		3
3		4
4		5
5		6
6		7
7		8
8		9
9		10
10		11
11		12
12		13
13		Book III: 1
14		2
15		3
16		4
17		5
18		6
19		7
20		8
21		9
22		10
23		11

First Edition	*Corresponds to*	*"The Author's Final Version"*
(Book I): 24		(Book III:) 12
25		13
Book II: 1		Book I: 1
2		2
3		3
4		4
5		5
6		6
7		7
8		8
9		9
10		Book II: 1
11		Book III: 14
12		Book IV: 15 & Book IV:1
13		1
14		2
15		3
16		4
17		5
18		6
19		7
20		8
21		9
22		10
23		11
Book III: 1		Book V: 1
2		2
3		3
4		4
5		5
6		6
7		7
8		8
9		9
10		10
11		11
12		12
13		13

References

The following abbreviations are used in these notes:
Cowley—TITN: *Tender is the Night*, "The Author's Final Version,"
ed. Malcolm Cowley (New York, 1951).
F.: F. Scott Fitzgerald.

The epigraphs are F., "Introduction" to *The Great Gatsby* (New York, 1934), p. x; Maxwell Perkins to Ann Chidester, Jan. 6, 1947, *Editor to Author, The Letters of Maxwell E. Perkins,* ed. John Hall Wheelock (New York, 1950), p. 284; and F. to Maxwell Perkins, n.d. (ca. May 1932). See Arthur Mizener, *The Far Side of Paradise* (Boston, 1950), p. 221.

Introduction

1. F., "One Hunded False Starts, *Saturday Evening Post,* CCV (March 4, 1933), p. 65. Reprinted in F., *Afternoon of an Author* (New York, 1957), pp. 132-136.
2. Malcolm Cowley errs in giving the sequence as Grant [Herkimer[North. Cowley—TITN, p. 337.
3. Cowley—TITN, p. ix.
4. Cowley—TITN, p. x.
5. Cowley—TITN, p. 353.

Chapter One

1. Edward Wagenknecht, *Cavalcade of the American Novel* (New York, 1952), p. 479.
2. Edmund Wilson, "Foreword" to F.'s *The Last Tycoon* (New York, 1941), pp. x-xi.
3. J. B. Priestly, *Literature and Western Man* (New York, 1960), pp. 433-434.
4. Frederick J. Hoffman, *The Modern Novel in America* (Chicago, 1956), pp. 138-140.
5. Louis Untermeyer, *Makers of the Modern World* (New York, 1955), pp. 698-699.
6. Cowley—TITN, p. x.
7. See footnote 8.
8. *American Mercury* (reviewed by Gertrude Diamant), XXXIII (Oct. 1934), pp. 249-251; *Canadian Forum* (reviewed by D'Arcy March), XIV (July 1934), p. 404; *Forum & Century* (reviewed by Mary M. Colum), XCI (April 1934), pp. 219-223; *Modern Monthly* (reviewed by C Hartley Grattan), VIII (July 1934), pp. 375-377, reprinted in Alfred Kazin, *F. Scott Fitzgerald: The Man and His Work* (New York and Cleveland, 1951), pp. 104-107; *The Nation* (reviewed by William Troy), CXXXVIII (May 9, 1934), pp. 539-540; *New Republic* (reviewed by Malcolm Cowley), LXXIX

(June 6, 1934), pp. 105-106; *N.Y. Herald-Tribune* (reviewed by Lewis Gannett), April 13, 1934, p. 15; *N.Y. Herald-Tribune Books* (reviewed by Horace Gregory), April 15, 1934, p. 5; *N.Y. Post* (reviewed by Herschel Brickell), April 14, 1934, p. 13; *N.Y. Times* (reviewed by John Chamberlain), April 13, 1934, p. 17, April 16, p. 15, both reprinted in Kazin, pp. 95-99; *N.Y. Times Book Review* (J.D.A. [J. Donald Adams]), April 15, 1934, p. 7; *New Yorker* (reviewed by Clifton Fadiman), X (April 14, 1934), pp. 96, 98-99; *News-Week* (anon. reviewer), III (April 14, 1934), pp. 39-40; *New Statesman & Nation* (reviewed by Peter Quennell), VII (April 28, 1934), p. 166, (also reviewed by E.B.C. Jones), VIII (Sept. 22, 1934), p. 366; *North American Review* (reviewed by Herschel Brickell), CCXXXVII (June 1934), pp. 569-570; *Saturday Review* (anon. reviewer), CLVIII (Dec. 8, 1934), p. 501; *Saturday Review of Literature* (reviewed by H. S. Canby), X (April 14, 1934), pp. 630-631; *Scrutiny* (reviewed by D. W. Harding), III (Dec. 1934), pp. 316-319, reprinted in Kazin, pp. 100-103; *Spectator*, CLIII (Sept. 21, 1934), p. 410; *Time* (anon. reviewer), XXIII (April 16, 1934), p. 77; *Times Literary Supplement* (anon. reviewer), MDCCIV (Sept. 27, 1934), p. 652.

9. Fadiman's review included a list of spelling errors in the novel.
10. Cowley—TITN, p. xi.
11. This book is in the Clifton Waller Barrett Library at The University of Virginia. See "F. Highlights from the Barrett Library," *Fitzgerald Newsletter*, #11 (Fall 1960), 1-4.
12. F., "Introduction" to *The Great Gatsby* (New York, 1934), pp. viii, x.
13. Cowley—TITN, p. xi.
14. Peter Monro Jack, "The James Branch Cabell Period," *After the Genteel Tradition*, ed. Malcolm Cowley (New York, 1937), pp. 152-153.
15. Alfred Kazin, "Introduction," *F. Scott Fitzgerald: The Man and his Work* (New York and Cleveland, 1951), p. 17.
16. Cowley—TITN, p. xv. This view is shared by Wayne C. Booth, who states that the original version prevents the reader from identifying with Dick: "The achievement of the revision is, in short, to correct a fault of over-distancing, a fault that springs from a method appropriate to other works at other times but not to the tragedy Fitzgerald wanted to write. His true effect could be obtained only by repudiating much of what was being said by important critics of fiction about point of view and developing a clean, direct, old-fashioned presentation of his hero's initial pre-eminence and gradual decline." *The Rhetoric of Fiction* (Chicago, 1961), pp. 190-195.
17. Edwin S. Fussell, "Fitzgerald's Brave New World," *English Literary History*, XIX (Dec. 1952), pp. 291-306.
18. Otto Friedrich, "F. Scott Fitzgerald: Money, Money, Money," *American Scholar*, XXIX (Summer 1960), pp. 392-405.
19. Robert Stanton, " 'Daddy's Girl': Symbol and Theme in *Tender is the Night*," *Modern Fiction Studies*, IV (Summer 1958), pp. 136-142; D. S. Savage, "The Significance of F. Scott Fitzgerald," *Arizona Quarterly*, VIII (Autumn 1952), p. 206; Maxwell Geismar, "A Cycle of Fiction," *Literary History of the United States*, ed. Robert E. Spiller, *et al.*, revised edition (New York, 1953), p. 1299.
20. Leslie Fiedler, *Love and Death in the American Novel* (New York, 1960), pp. 301-302.
21. Friedrich, "F. Scott Fitzgerald: Money, Money, Money," p. 400.

22. Albert J. Lubell, "The Fitzgerald Revival," *South Atlantic Quarterly*, LIV (Jan. 1955), pp. 103-104.
23. Fitzgerald Papers, The Princeton University Library, key #49.
24. F. to H. L. Mencken, April 23, 1934. MS., The Enoch Pratt Free Library. See p. 129-130.
25. Ford Madox Ford, *Joseph Conrad: A Personal Remembrance* (Boston, 1924), pp. 136-137. F.'s reason for using the "dying fall"—or the understated ending rather than the emotional one—is explained in a letter he wrote to John Peale Bishop on April 7, 1934: "I did not want to subject the reader to a series of nervous shocks because it was a novel that was inevitably close to whoever read it in my generation." See John Kuehl, "Scott Fitzgerald's Reading," *The Princeton University Library Chronicle*, XXII (Winter 1961), pp. 58-59.

Chapter Two

1. In the early drafts, F. sometimes spelled the name *Melarkey*.
2. F., "Love in the Night," *Saturday Evening Post*, CXCVII (Mar. 14, 1925), pp. 18-19, 68, 70.
3. See Andrew Turnbull, *Scott Fitzgerald* (New York, 1962), pp. 188-189. Sophie Irene Loeb was a journalist and social crusader of the period.
4. Gerald Murphy in an interview with Matthew J. Bruccoli, Jan. 1950.
5. F., *The Crack-Up*, ed. Edmund Wilson (New York, 1945), p. 79.
6. Ernest Hemingway to F., May 28, 1934. See Mizener, *The Far Side of Paradise*, pp. 238-239.
7. See Turnbull, *Scott Fitzgerald*, p. 184.
After *Tender is the Night* was published, F. wrote to Sara Murphy explaining how he had used her in the novel:

In my theory, utterly opposite to Ernest's, about fiction, i.e. that it takes half a dozen people to make a synthesis strong enough to create a fiction character—in that theory, or rather in despite of it, I used you again and again in *Tender:*
"Her face was hard & lovely & pitiful"
and again
"He had been heavy, belly-frightened with love of her for years"
—in those and in a hundred other places I tried to evoke not *you* but the effect that you produce on men—the echoes and reverberations—a poor return for what you have given by your living presence, but nevertheless an artist's (what a word!) sincere attempt to preserve a true fragment rather than a "portrait" by Mr. Sargent. . . .

This letter is quoted in Calvin Tompkins, "Living Well is the Best Revenge," *The New Yorker*, XXXVIII (July 28, 1962), pp. 64-65. Although it patronizes F., this profile of the Murphys is invaluable for background on the world of *Tender is the Night*.

8. Theodore Chanler in an interview with Matthew J. Bruccoli, Aug. 1959.
9. Gerald Murphy to Matthew J. Bruccoli, Feb. 15, 1960.
10. An account of F.'s behavior in Rome appears in Carmel Meyers, "Scott and Zelda," *Park East* (May 1951), pp. 18, 32-33.
11. F. to Maxwell Perkins, Feb. 20, 1926. The letter was seen in the files of Charles Scribner's Sons. See Mizener, *The Far Side of Paradise*, p. 202.
12. See Turnbull, *Scott Fitzgerald*, p. 151. The first quotation is from a letter to Maxwell Perkins; the second is undocumented, but is probably also from a letter to Perkins.

13. F. to Maxwell Perkins, n.d. (ca. Feb. 1926). The letter was seen in the files of Charles Scribner's Sons. See Mizener, *The Far Side of Paradise,* p. 189.

14. Edmund Wilson to Matthew J. Bruccoli, Mar. 16, 1959.

15. F. to Howard Coxe, April 15, 1934. See Mizener, *The Far Side of Paradise,* pp. 166, 335.

16. F. to Harold Ober, n.d. (received Oct. 3, 1925). The letter was seen in the files of Harold Ober Associates.

17. The article has been published in *Interim,* IV (1954), pp. 6-15.

18. F. to Harold Ober, n.d. (received Jan. 23, 1925). The letter was seen in the files of Harold Ober Associates.

19. In the early drafts F. sometimes spells the name *McKiscoe* or *MacKiscoe.*

20. F.'s respect for Lardner is shown in an obituary essay he wrote about him, "Ring," *New Republic,* LXXCI(Oct. 11, 1933), reprinted in *The Crack-Up,* pp. 34-40.

21. F. to Harold Ober, May 1926. The letter was seen in the files of Harold Ober Associates.

22. Gerald Murphy in an interview with Matthew J. Bruccoli, Jan. 1959.

23. James E. Miller, *The Fictional Technique of F. Scott Fitzgerald* (The Hague, 1957).

24. F., *The Crack-Up,* pp. 312-316.

25. See, for example, Robert W. Stallman, "Conrad and *The Great Gatsby,*" *Twentieth-Century Literature,* I(1955), pp. 5-12; and Kuehl, "Scott Fitzgerald's Reading," pp. 73-74, 86-87.

26. This outline is part of a letter F. wrote on Sept. 29, 1939, to Maxwell Perkins and to an editor of a magazine (possibly *Collier's*) in which he hoped to serialize the novel. The letter appears with the "Notes" to *The Last Tycoon,* pp. 138-141.

27. See Mizener, *The Far Side of Paradise,* pp. 182-183, which seems to print a composite version.

28. F., "The World's Fair," *Kenyon Review* (Autumn 1948). Reprinted in Cowley—TITN, pp. 338-345.

29. Maxwell Perkins to F., Jan. 20, 1927. A copy of the letter was seen in the files of Charles Scribner's Sons.

30. F. to Maxwell Perkins, Feb. 6, 1927. The wire was seen in the files of Charles Scribner's Sons. See Mizener, *The Far Side of Paradise,* p. 206.

30A. During the summer of 1929 F.'s wallet was stolen by a Negro in a Paris night club, and after accusing the wrong Negro, F. spent the rest of the night trying to straighten out the affair with the gendarmes—Morley Callaghan, *That Summer in Paris* (New York, 1963), pp. 190-192. Callaghan's memoir, which appeared after this study was in proof, reveals a good deal about F. at this time.

31. Edmund Wilson, "A Weekend at Ellerslie," *The Shores of Light* (New York, 1952), pp. 373-383.

32. F. to Paul Reynolds, June 4, 1928. The letter was seen in the files of Harold Ober Associates.

33. F. to Harold Ober, n.d. (received Aug. 4, 1928). The letter was seen in the files of Harold Ober Associates.

34. F. to Maxwell Perkins, n.d. (November 1928 ?). The letter was seen in the files of Charles Scribner's Sons.

35. F. to Maxwell Perkins, Nov. 1928. The letter was seen in the files of Charles Scribner's Sons.
36. F. to Maxwell Perkins, Oct. 11, 1933. The letter was seen in the files of Charles Scribner's Sons.
37. F. to Maxwell Perkins, n.d. (ca. Mar. 1, 1929). The note was seen in the files of Charles Scribner's Sons.

Chapter Three

1. F. to Maxwell Perkins, n.d. (ca. June 1929). The letter was seen in the files of Charles Scribner's Sons.
2. Mizener, *The Far Side of Paradise*, p. 213.
3. F. to Harold Ober, n.d. (received June 26, 1929). The letter was seen in the files of Harold Ober Associates.
4. F. to Paul Reynolds, Aug. 29, 1929. The letter was seen in the files of Harold Ober Associates.
5. F. to Harold Ober, n.d. (received Sept. 1, 1929). The letter was seen in the files of Harold Ober Associates.
6. F. to Harold Ober, n.d. (received Oct. 23, 1929). The letter was seen in the files of Harold Ober Associates.
7. The possible connection between Lew Kelly and Rex Ingram was suggested to me by Henry Dan Piper. Ingram's Victorine studios at Nice served as the model for the studio Francis and Rosemary visit. For a brief history of the Victorine studios, see Thomas Quinn Curtiss, "End of Another Chapter in Film-Making," *New York Herald Tribune, Paris*, August 25-26, 1962.
8. Gertrude Stein to F., May 22, 192- [1925]; printed in *The Crack-Up*, p. 308.
9. For example, Robert McAlmon's *Being Geniuses Together* (London, 1938), pp. 115-116:

> I found myself at Bricktop's. Florence Martin, Sylvia Gough, a young man she called California, Nina Hamnett, Man Ray and Kiki were there too. The place was crowded, and with people I knew. . . . I sat for an hour at Beatrice Lillie's table. . . .
> Buddy, the trap-drummer, came in looking cheerfully insinuating. . . . He gurgled down the half-bottle of champagne, and his audience went wild with enthusiasm at his wild and rhythmic drum beating. By seven in the morning most of the other guests had departed, but I lingered. Other negroes came in from orchestras about town: Joe Caulk, of Palermo's, Mitchell, two tap dancers. They stood at the bar drinking whisky or gin, arguing about their various degrees of talent.

10. See Turnbull, *Scott Fitzgerald*, pp. 187-188. The letter is undocumented, but it was probably written late in 1929.

Chapter Four

1. Harold Ober to F., April 8, 1930. A copy of this letter was seen in the files of Harold Ober Associates.
2. F. to Harold Ober, n.d. (received May 13, 1930). The letter was seen in the files of Harold Ober Associates.
3. Although F. usually saw no problem in this procedure, he added a footnote to "A Short Trip Home" when the story was collected in *Taps at Rev-*

eille: "In a moment of hasty misjudgement a whole paragraph of description was lifted out of this tale where it originated . . . and applied to quite a different character in a novel of mine. I have ventured none the less to leave it here, even at the risk of seeming to serve warmed-over fare." *Taps at Reveille* (New York, 1935), p. 323.

4. T. S. Matthews, *New Republic,* LXXXII (April 10, 1935), p. 262.

5. F., "Our April Letter," *The Crack-Up,* p. 165.

6. F., "One Trip Abroad," *Saturday Evening Post,* CCIII (Oct. 11, 1930), pp. 6-7, 48, 51, 53-54, 56. Reprinted in *Afternoon of an Author.*

7. F., *The Crack-Up,* p. 72.

Chapter Five

1. F. to Maxwell Perkins, Jan. 15, 1932. The letter was seen in the files of Charles Scribner's Sons. See Mizener, *The Far Side of Paradise,* p. 225.

2. F. to Dayton Kohler, June 25, 1932. The letter is in the Clifton Waller Barrett Library at The University of Virginia.

3. Sheilah Graham and Gerold Frank, *Beloved Infidel* (New York, 1958), p. 240.

4. Turnbull, *Scott Fitzgerald,* p. 239.

5. F. to Edmund Wilson, n.d. (postmarked Mar. 12, 1934); printed in *The Crack-Up,* p. 278.

6. Matthew Josephson's memo about this, with a copy of the inscription, is in the Yale University Library.

7. Matthew Josephson, *Zola and His Time* (New York, 1928), pp. 523-545.

8. *Ibid.,* p. 528.

Chapter Six

1. Fiedler, *Love and Death in the American Novel,* pp. 301-302.

2. Abraham H. Steinberg, "Hardness, Light, and Psychiatry in *Tender is the Night,*" *Literature and Psychology,* III (Feb. 1953), pp. 3-8. It is unlikely that Fitzgerald knew the Old Testament well enough to have intended any significance in *Seth* (the substitute for Abel), *Dinah* (Jacob's daughter, whom Shechem defiled), and *Abraham* (the father of many nations).

3. F., *The Crack-Up,* p. 79.

4. *Ibid.,* pp. 72-73.

5. Henry Dan Piper, "F. Scott Fitzgerald and the Image of his Father," *The Princeton University Library Chronicle,* XII (Summer 1951), pp. 181-186.

6. F., "The Death of My Father," *The Princeton University Library Chronicle,* XII (Summer 1951), pp. 187-189. The text of the essay as given here follows Piper's transcription in the PULC.

7. F. evened this score by ridiculing Dumphry and Campion for reading an etiquette book in I, 4. This point supports the claim that "The Death of My Father" predates *Tender is the Night.*

8. The girl with the "corn-colored" hair may have been inspired by an interesting blonde F. met on the ship he took to his father's funeral. See Turnbull, *Scott Fitzgerald,* p. 197.

9. F. to Maxwell Perkins, March 11, 1935. The letter was seen in the files of Charles Scribner's Sons. See Mizener, *The Far Side of Paradise,* pp. 231-232.

10. F. to H. L. Mencken, April 23, 1934. MS, The Enoch Pratt Free Library. In point of fact, the preface to *The Nigger of the Narcissus* does not discuss this matter. See also Joseph V. Ridgely, "Mencken, Fitzgerald and *Tender is the Night*," *Menckeniana*, No. 3 (Fall, 1962), pp. 4-5.

11. Steinberg, "Hardness, Light, and Psychiatry in *Tender is the Night*," p. 6. Another critic who finds this conversation thematically relevant is W. F. Hall, who says that Dick is really talking about his relationship with Rosemary and revealing that he is incapable of love. "Dialogue and Theme in *Tender is the Night*," *Modern Language Notes*, LXXVI (Nov. 1961), pp. 616-622.

12. Cowley—TITN, p. 356.

13. Henry Dan Piper has suggested to me that the symbolic appearances of the newsvendor may have been based on the blind beggar in *Madame Bovary*, who also represents disaster.

14. F., *The Last Tycoon*, p. 163. The phrase obviously applies to Monroe Stahr, another exhausted hero.

Chapter Seven

1. *The House of the Seven Gables*, Riverside Edition, III (Boston, 1883), pp. 13-16.

2. F. to Frances Scott Fitzgerald, n.d. Printed in *The Crack-Up*, p. 303.

3. F. to Frances Scott Fitzgerald, Aug. 3, 1940. Printed in *The Crack-Up*, p. 298.

4. Albert Guerard, "Prometheus and the Aeolian Lyre," *Yale Review*, XXXIII (Spring 1944), pp. 482-497.

Chapter Eight

1. The pun on *barbarian* is the most obvious reason for this name change; but *Barban* may also have been intended as an echo of the name of a Frenchman Mrs. Fitzgerald had been attached to, Edouard Josanne. See Turnbull, *Scott Fitzgerald*, pp. 145-146.

2. John Hall Wheelock in an interview with Matthew J. Bruccoli, Dec. 2, 1956.

3. F.'s remark about cutting is reported by Wolfe in a letter to Robert Reynolds, July 8, 1934; *The Letters of Thomas Wolfe*, ed. Elizabeth Nowell (New York, 1956), p. 416. F's letter about the "novel of selected incident" was written July 19, 1937. Wolfe's reply and his comment to Hamilton Basso are on pp. 641-647.

Chapter Nine

1. Christian Gauss to F., April 6, 1934. Printed in *The Papers of Christian Gauss*, ed. Katherine Gauss Jackson and Hiram Haydn (New York, 1957), pp. 217-218.

2. Cowley—TITN, p. 337.

3. Cowley—TITN, p. xi.

4. F. to Edmund Wilson, n.d. (postmarked Mar. 12, 1934). Printed in *The Crack-Up*, p. 278.

5. Leslie Fiedler, "Some Notes on F. Scott Fitzgerald," *An End to Inno-*

cence (Boston, 1955), p. 180. It should be noted that the second stage direction is from the unfinished novel, *The Last Tycoon*.

6. F. to John Peale Bishop, Jan. 30, 1933, MS, Princeton University Library.

7. Cowley—TITN, p. xiii.

8. *Tender is the Night* was reprinted in April and May 1934, but I have been unable to differentiate these two printings. The first printing is readily identified by the A on the copyright page. Two corrections appear in the 1951 reprint from the original plates: Saland [Salaud (p. 344) and Charles [Devereux (p. 320). Charles Marquis Warren, then a young writer F. was interested in, has written me that *Charles Warren* was intended as a friendly gesture, but that F. later changed his mind. Charles Marquis Warren to Matthew J. Bruccoli, August 5, 1959.

For a more detailed examination of the text, see my "Material for a Centenary Edition of *Tender is the Night*," *Studies in Bibliography*, xvii (1964).

9. Cowley—TITN, p. xiii.
10. Cowley—TITN, p. 355.
11. Cowley—TITN, p. 352.
12. Cowley—TITN, p. x. F. also stated that he wanted to delete the "dry loins" remark on p. 401—"There is not more than one complete sentence that I want to eliminate, one that has offended many people and that I admit is out of Dick's character: 'I never did go in for making love to dry loins.' It is a strong line but definitely offensive." (Cowley—TITN, p. 356).

13. This note is inaccurately transcribed on pp. 180-181 of *The Crack-Up*; it is more accurately transcribed on p. xii of Cowley-*TITN*.

List of Works Consulted

Anon. Review of *TITN*, *News-Week,* III(April 14, 1934), pp. 39-40.

———. Review of *TITN, Saturday Review,* CLVIII(Dec. 8, 1934), p. 501.

———. Review of *TITN, Spectator,* CLIII(Sept. 21, 1934), p. 410.

———. Review of *TITN, Time,* XXIII(April 16, 1934), p. 77.

———. Review of *TITN, TLS,* MDCCIV(Sept. 27, 1934), p. 652.

Booth, Wayne C. *The Rhetoric of Fiction.* Chicago, 1961.

Brickell, Herschel. Review of *TITN, N. Y. Post* (April 14, 1934), p. 13.

———. Review of *TITN, North American Review,* CCXXXVII (June 1934), pp. 569-570.

[Bruccoli, Matthew J.] "F. Highlights from the Barrett Library," *Fitzgerald Newsletter* #11(Fall 1960), pp. 1-4.

———. "*Tender is the Night* and the Reviewers," *Modern Fiction Studies,* VII(Spring 1961), pp. 49-54.

Callaghan, Morley. *That Summer in Paris.* New York, 1963.

Canby, H. S. Review of *TITN, Saturday Review of Literature,* X(Apr. 14, 1934), 630-631.

Chamberlain, John. Review of *TITN, N. Y. Times,* April 13, 1934, p. 17, April 16, 1934, p. 15. Both reprinted in Kazin, *Fitzgerald.*

Colum, Mary M. Review of *TITN, Forum & Century,* XCI(April 1934), pp. 219-223.

Cowley, Malcolm, ed. *After the Genteel Tradition.* New York, 1937.

———. Review of *TITN, New Republic,* LXXIX(June 6, 1934), pp. 105-106.

———, ed. *TITN,* "The Author's Final Version." New York, 1951. See under Fitzgerald.

Curtiss, Thomas Quinn. "End of Another Chapter in Film-Making," *New York Herald Tribune, Paris Edition,* 25-26 August, 1962.

Diamant, Gertrude. Review of *TITN, American Mercury,* XXXIII (Oct. 1934), pp. 249-251.

Fadiman, Clifton. Review of *TITN*, *The New Yorker*, X(April 14, 1934), pp. 96, 98-99.
Fiedler, Leslie. *Love and Death in the American Novel*. New York, 1960.
———. "Some Notes on F. Scott Fitzgerald," *An End to Innocence*. Boston, 1955.
Fitzgerald, F. Scott. *Afternoon of an Author*. New York, 1957.
———. *The Crack-Up*. New York, 1945.
———. "The Death of My Father," *Princeton University Library Chronicle*, XII(Summer 1951), pp. 187-189.
———. *Tender is the Night*. New York, 1934.
———. "The High Cost of Macaroni," *Interim*, IV(1954), pp. 6-15.
———. "Introduction," *The Great Gatsby*. New York, 1934.
———. *The Last Tycoon*. New York, 1941.
———. "Love in the Night," *Saturday Evening Post*, CX(March 14, 1925), pp. 18-19, 68, 70.
———. "One Hundred False Starts," *Saturday Evening Post*, CCV (Mar. 4, 1933), pp. 13, 65-66.
———. "Ring," *New Republic*, LXXVI(Oct. 11, 1933), pp. 254-255. Reprinted in *The Crack-Up*.
———. "The World's Fair," *Kenyon Review*, X(Autumn 1948), pp. 567-578. Reprinted in Cowley's edition of *TITN*.
Ford, Ford Madox. *Joseph Conrad: A Personal Remembrance*. Boston, 1924.
Friedrich, Otto. "F. Scott Fitzgerald: Money, Money, Money," *American Scholar*, XXIX(Summer 1960), pp. 392-405.
Fussell, Edwin S. "Fitzgerald's Brave New World," *English Literary History*, XIX(Dec. 1952), pp. 291-306.
Gannett, Lewis. Review of *TITN*, *N. Y. Herald-Tribune* (April 13, 1934), p. 15.
Geismar, Maxwell. "A Cycle of Fiction," *Literary History of the United States*, ed. Robert E. Spiller, *et. al.*, revised edition, New York, 1953.
Graham, Sheilah and Gerold Frank. *Beloved Infidel*. New York, 1958.
Grattan, C. Hartley. Review of *TITN*, *Modern Monthly*, VIII (July 1934), pp. 375-377. Reprinted in Kazin, *Fitzgerald*.
Gregory, Horace. Review of *TITN*, *N. Y. Herald-Tribune Books* (April 15, 1934), p. 5.

Guerard, Albert. "Prometheus and the Aeolian Lyre," *Yale Review*, XXXIII (Spring 1944), pp. 482-497.

Hall, W. F. "Dialogue and Theme in *Tender is the Night*," *Modern Language Notes*, LXXVI (Nov. 1961), pp. 616-622.

Harding, D. W. Review of *TITN*, *Scrutiny*, III (Dec. 1934), pp. 316-319. Reprinted in Kazin, *Fitzgerald*.

Hoffman, Frederick J. *The Modern Novel in America*. Chicago, 1956.

J. D. A. [J. Donald Adams]. Review of *TITN*, *N. Y. Times Book Review* (April 15, 1934), 17.

Jack, Peter Monro. "The James Branch Cabell Period," *After the Genteel Tradition*, ed. Malcolm Cowley, New York, 1937.

Jackson, Katherine Gauss and Hiram Hayden, eds. *The Papers of Christian Gauss*, New York, 1957.

Jones, E. B. C. Review of *TITN*, *New Statesman & Nation*, VIII (Sept. 22, 1934), p. 366.

Josephson, Matthew. *Zola and His Time*. New York, 1928.

Kazin, Alfred, ed. *F. Scott Fitzgerald: The Man and His Work*. Cleveland and New York, 1951.

Kuehl, John. "Scott Fitzgerald's Reading," *The Princeton University Library Chronicle*, XXII (Winter 1961), pp. 58-89.

Lubell, Albert J. "The Fitzgerald Revival," *South Atlantic Quarterly*, LIV (Jan. 1955), pp. 103-104.

March, D'Arcy. Review of *TITN*, *Canadian Forum*, XIV (July 1934), p. 404.

Matthews, T. S. Review of *Taps at Reveille*, *New Republic*, LXXXII (April 10, 1935), p. 262. Reprinted in Kazin, *Fitzgerald*.

McAlmon, Robert. *Being Geniuses Together*. London, 1938.

Meyers, Carmel. "Scott and Zelda," *Park East* (May 1951), pp. 18, 32-33.

Miller, James E. *The Fictional Technique of F. Scott Fitzgerald*. The Hague, 1957.

Mizener, Arthur. *The Far Side of Paradise*. Boston, 1950.

Nowell, Elizabeth, ed. *The Letters of Thomas Wolfe*. New York, 1956.

Piper, Henry Dan. "F. Scott Fitzgerald and the Image of His Father," *Princeton University Library Chronicle*, XII (Summer 1951), pp. 181-186.

Priestly, J. B. *Literature and Western Man.* New York, 1960.
——. "Introduction," *The Bodley Head Scott Fitzgerald.* London, 1958.
Quennell, Peter. Review of *TITN, New Statesman & Nation,* VII (April 28, 1934), p. 166.
Ridgely, Joseph V. "Mencken, Fitzgerald and *Tender is the Night, Menckeniana,* No. 3 (Fall 1962), pp. 4-5.
Savage, D. S. "The Significance of F. Scott Fitzgerald," *Arizona Quarterly,* VIII (Autumn 1952), pp. 197-210.
Stallman, Robert W. "By The Dawn's Early Light *Tender is the Night,*" *The Houses that James Built.* East Lansing, 1961.
——. "Conrad and *The Great Gatsby,*" *Twentieth-Century Literature,* I (1955), pp. 5-12, Reprinted in *The Houses that James Built.*
Stanton, Robert. " 'Daddy's Girl': Symbol and Theme in *Tender is the Night,*" *Modern Fiction Studies,* IV (Summer 1958), pp. 36-142.
Stein, Gertrude. A letter about *The Great Gatsby, The Crack-Up,* p. 308.
Steinberg, Abraham H. "Hardness, Light, and Psychiatry in *Tender is the Night,*" *Literature and Psychology,* III (Feb. 1953), pp. 3-8.
Tompkins, Calvin. "Living Well is the Best Revenge," *The New Yorker,* XXXVIII (July 28, 1962), pp. 31-32, 34, 36, 38, 43-44, 46-47, 49-50, 52, 54, 56-69.
Troy, William, Review of *TITN, The Nation,* CXXXVIII (May 9, 1934), pp. 539-540.
Turnbull, Andrew. *Scott Fitzgerald.* New York, 1962.
Untermeyer, Louis, *Makers of the Modern World.* New York, 1955.
Wagenknecht, Edward. *Cavalcade of the American Novel.* New York, 1952.
Walton, Edith H. Review of *TITN, Forum & Century,* XCI (June 1934), p. iv.
Wheelock, John Hall, ed. *Editor to Author, the Letters of Maxwell E. Perkins.* New York, 1950.
Wilson, Edmund, ed. *The Last Tycoon.* See under Fitzgerald.
——. "A Weekend at Ellerslie," *The Shores of Light.* New York, 1952.

Index of Names and Titles

This index does not include F. Scott Fitzgerald, *Tender is the Night*, or characters in that novel. Unless otherwise indicated all titles refer to works by Fitzgerald.

"Absolution," 28
Adams, J. Donald, 6
American Mercury (periodical), 70
American Tragedy, An, by Theodore Dreiser, 18, 27
Arlen, Michael, 66
L'Assommoir, by Émile Zola, 86, 87
"At Your Age," 84
"Author's Mother, An," 22

"Babylon Revisited," 72, 73
Bantam Books, 218
Barry, Philip, 19
Basil Duke Lee stories, 65, 68
Beautiful and Damned, The, 78, 82, 122, 192
Being Geniuses Together, by Robert McAlmon, 241
Ben-Hur, the film, 22
Bishop, John Peale, 202
Booth, Wayne C., 238
Boy Who Killed His Mother, The, xxii, 23
Boyd, Thomas, 66
Brady, Cecilia, 40, 201
Brickell, Herschel, 3, 4
Bromfield, Louis, 66

Canby, Henry Seidel, 6
Callaghan, Morley, 240
Carraway, Nick, 15, 39, 40
Cerf, Bennett, 199, 215
Chamberlain, John, 4, 5, 6
Chanler, Theodore, 21, 22, 30
Charles Scribner's Sons, xx, 10, 18, 58, 196, 218
Conrad, Joseph, 15, 25, 39, 40, 130

Cowley, Malcolm, xiv, xv, xx, xxi, xxii, 2, 3, 5, 10, 12, 140, 199, 206, 209, 210, 213, 214, 215, 218, 237, 244
Cozzens, James Gould, 84
Crack-Up, The, 9, 20, 71, 72
"Crazy Sunday," 84
Curtiss, Thomas Quinn, 241

"Death of My Father, The," 123, 125
Dedalus, Stephen, 83
"Dialogue and Theme in *Tender is the Night,*" by W. F. Hall, 243
Doctor Diver's Holiday, xxiii, 164, 165
Doctor Martino, by William Faulkner, 6
Dos Passos, John, 19, 55
Dreiser, Theodore, 18, 27
Drunkard's Holiday, The, xxiii, 37, 52, 54, 78, 86, 101, 128, 132, 164

Eliot, T. S., 198
Ellingson, Dorothy, 18, 22
Ellis, Walker, 21, 22
"Emotional Bankruptcy," 72
"End of Another Chapter in Film-Making," by Thomas Quinn Curtiss, 241
"Eve of St. Agnes, The," by John Keats, 166

Fadiman, Clifton, 4, 6
Faulkner, William, 6, 81, 88
Fay, Monsignor Cyril, 124
Fictional Technique of F. Scott Fitz-

gerald, The, by James E. Miller, Jr., 39
Fie! Fie! Fi-Fi!, 21
Fiedler, Leslie, 12, 95, 96, 201
Finney, Benjamin, 78
"First Blood," 69
Fitzgerald, Edward, 123-125
Fitzgerald, Mrs. Edward, 22, 23
Fitzgerald, Frances Scott (Mrs. Samuel J. Lanahan), 80, 166
Fitzgerald, Mrs. F. Scott, 18, 27, 60, 69, 72, 73, 80, 81, 82, 123
Flaubert, Gustave, 196
Ford, Ford Madox, 15
Friedrich, Otto, 11, 12
Fussell, Edwin S., 11

Gannett, Lewis, 5
Gatsby, Jay, 23, 96
Gauss, Dean Christian, 29, 198
Geismar, Maxwell, 12
Graham, Sheilah, 75
Grattan, C. Hartley, 4, 239
Great Gatsby, The, xx, 1, 2, 4, 8, 9, 11, 15, 18, 19, 25, 28, 33, 39, 40, 47, 55, 64, 75, 82, 123, 237
Gregory, Horace, 4

Hall, W. F., 243
"Handle With Care," 19, 120
Harding, D. W., 7
Hawthorne, Nathaniel, 165
"Heart of Darkness, The," by Joseph Conrad, 40
Hemingway, Ernest, 9, 18, 20, 57, 75, 78, 119, 120, 129, 130, 198
Hergesheimer, Joseph, 8
"High Cost of Macaroni, The," 28
Hoffman, Frederick J., 1
"Hotel Child," 72
Hotel Universe, by Philip Barry, 19
House of the Seven Gables, The, "Preface," by Nathaniel Hawthorne, 165

"Indecision," 72, 84
Ingram, Rex, 60, 61
Italy, Fitzgerald's dislike of, 22, 28, 29

Jack, Peter Monro, 9
"Jacob's Ladder," 50, 66, 84, 97, 127

James, Henry, 15
Josanne, Edouard, 243
Josephine stories, 69
Josephson, Matthew, 86
Joyce, James, 25

Kazin, Alfred, 9
Keats, John, 166, 174
Kelly, Nicole and Nelson, 71
Kipling, Rudyard, 71
Krafft-Ebing, von, Richard, Baron, 81
Kuehl, John, 239

Lardner, Ring, 30
Last Tycoon, The, 40
Lee, Basil Duke, 55
Leopold-Loeb case, 18
Liberty (periodical), 33, 50
"Living Well is the Best Revenge," by Calvin Tompkins, 239
"Love Boat, The," 84
"Love in the Night," 18
Lubell, Albert, 12

Madame Bovary, by Gustave Flaubert, 197, 243
MacLeish, Archibald, 19, 20, 21, 78
"Majesty," 84
Matthews, T. S., 70
McAlmon, Robert, 97, 241
McArthur, Charles, 78
Melarky Case, The, xxii, 23
"Mencken, Fitzgerald and *Tender is the Night*," by Joseph V. Ridgely, 243
Mencken, H. L., 7, 129, 243
Metropolitan Magazine, The (periodical), 192
Meyers, Carmel, 239
Miller, James E., Jr., 39
Modern Fiction Studies (periodical), xvi
Modern Library, 8, 199, 215
Modern Monthly (periodical), 7
Moran, Lois, 39, 81
Murphy, Gerald, 19, 20, 21, 31, 34, 76, 78, 182
Murphy, Sara, 19, 20, 21, 76

"New Leaf, A," 84
New Republic (periodical), 5
News-Week (periodical), 5
New York Times, The (newspaper), 5
New York Times Book Review, The (periodical), 6
"Nice Quiet Place, A," 69
Nigger of the Narcissus, The, by Joseph Conrad, 130, 243
"A Night at the Fair," 84
North American Review (periodical), 3

Ober, Harold, 18, 33, 56, 58, 60, 65, 68, 69
"Ode to a Nightingale," by John Keats, 174
Of Time and the River, by Thomas Wolfe, 196
"One Trip Abroad," 66, 69, 71, 72, 84
Our Type, xxii, 23, 27

Patch, Anthony, 23, 122
"A Penny Spent," 84
Perkins, Maxwell, xi, 8, 9, 27, 50, 56, 57, 58, 59, 60, 67, 68, 75, 128, 174, 180, 206
Piper, Henry Dan, 123, 208, 243
Poe, Edgar Allan, 12
Post, Emily, 124
Princeton University, 21, 198
Princeton University Library, xiv, xvii, xviii, 17, 215

Quennell, Peter, 5

Reynolds, Paul, 56, 60
Rhetoric of Fiction, The, by Wayne C. Booth, 238
Richard Diver, 180
Ridgely, Joseph V., 243
"Ring," 240
"Rough Crossing," 59, 66, 84
Rougon-Macquart, Les, by Émile Zola, 86

Saturday Evening Post, The (periodical), 68, 70
Savage, D. S., 12
Sayre, Judge Anthony, 74

"Scott and Zelda," by Carmel Meyers, 239
Scott Fitzgerald, by Andrew Turnbull, 239, 241, 242, 243
"Scott Fitzgerald's Reading," by John Kuehl, 239
Scribners. *See* Charles Scribner's Sons
Scribner's Magazine (periodical), xxiii, 4, 70, 140, 167, 181, 182, 187, 190, 192, 198
Seldes, Gilbert, 55
"Short Trip Home, A," 70, 241
Smart Set (periodical), 70
"Snobbish Story, A," 69
Sound and the Fury, The, by William Faulkner, 2
Stahr, Monroe, 23
Stanton, Robert, 11
Stein, Gertrude, 25, 64
Steinberg, Abraham H., 96
That Summer in Paris, by Morley Callaghan, 240
"Swimmers, The," 84
Symbols, meaning of symbols used in manuscript catalogues, xx

Tales of the Jazz Age, 22
Taps at Reveille, 71, 241
"That Kind of Party," 55
This Side of Paradise, 4, 39, 82
Times Literary Supplement (periodical), 4
Tompkins, Calvin, 239
Troy, William, 5, 6, 7
Turnbull, Andrew, 239, 241, 242, 243

Ulysses, by James Joyce, 83
Untermeyer, Louis, 1, 2

Vanity Fair, by William Makepeace Thackeray, xxi
Vegetable, The, xiii
Viking Portable Fitzgerald, The, 218

Wagenknecht, Edward, 1
Warren, Charles Marquis, 244
"Weekend at Ellerslie, A," by Edmund Wilson, 54
Wheelock, John Hall, 196
Wilson, Edmund, 1, 27, 54, 55, 83, 196, 199, 200

Wolfe, Thomas, 39, 196, 243
"Woman with a Past, A," 69
World's Fair, The, xxii, 23, 27, 47, 50, 86, 96

Yale University, 76

Zola and His Time, by Matthew Josephson, 86
Zola, Émile, 86, 87, 88, 196

DATE DUE

APR 2 0 1977			
APR 1 8 1980			

810.92
F576b

39892